Moral Re-Armament

D1665449

Moral Re-Armament

The Reinventions of an American Religious Movement

Daniel Sack

MORAL RE-ARMAMENT
Copyright © Daniel Sack, 2009.

Cover image: A billboard from Moral Re-Armament's advertising campaign, summer 1939. From the Records of Moral Re-Armament, Prints and Photographs Division, Library of Congress.

First published in 2009 by
PALGRAVE MACMILLAN®
in the United States—a division of St. Martin's Press LLC,
175 Fifth Avenue, New York, NY 10010.

Where this book is distributed in the UK, Europe and the rest of the world, this is by Palgrave Macmillan, a division of Macmillan Publishers Limited, registered in England, company number 785998, of Houndmills, Basingstoke, Hampshire RG21 6XS.

Palgrave Macmillan is the global academic imprint of the above companies and has companies and representatives throughout the world.

Palgrave® and Macmillan® are registered trademarks in the United States, the United Kingdom, Europe and other countries.

ISBN 978–0–312-29328-4   ISBN 978-0-230-10188-3 (eBook)
DOI 10.1057/9780230101883

Library of Congress Cataloging-in-Publication Data

Sack, Daniel.
    Moral re-armament : the reinventions of an American religious
    movement / Daniel Sack.
        p. cm.
    Includes bibliographical references and index.

    1. Moral re-armament. 2. United States—Church history—20th century.
    I. Title.

BJ10.M6S23 2009   2009023736
267'.16—dc22

A catalogue record of the book is available from the British Library.

Design by Newgen Imaging Systems (P) Ltd., Chennai, India.

First edition: December 2009

For Ann and Robert Sack
In honor of my father
and in memory of my mother

CONTENTS

CONTENTS

ACKNOWLEDGMENTS

Frank Buchman, the founder of Moral Re-Armament, believed that evangelists should not work alone. He worked to build "an intelligent, workable team" for his movement.[1] Scholars don't work alone, either. In writing this book, I have been supported by an intelligent, workable team, and I am very grateful.

Almost eighteen years ago, John Wilson suggested over dinner that the story of Moral Re-Armament would be worth looking into; he helped me turn that story into a dissertation at Princeton University. During and after my Princeton years, many people have read and given me feedback on large or small pieces of the manuscript, including Albert Raboteau, Brad Verter, Peter Thuesen, Tyler Flynn, Hannah Schell, and the members of the Religion and Culture Workshop at Princeton University and the American Religious History Workshop at the University of Chicago Divinity School. Paul Kemeny has been a particularly dedicated reader.

This project relies heavily on primary sources, and, consequently, on the librarians who helped me get them: Ben Primer, Nanci Young, Dan Linke, and the rest of the staff at the Princeton University Archives; Mary George and Margaret Sherry at Princeton's Firestone Library; the staff of the Archives of the Episcopal Church; Edna Madden and Carolyn Spiel at the Hartford Seminary Foundation Library; Barbara Natanson of the Prints & Photographs Division of the Library of Congress; and the staff of the Penn State Room at Pattee Library at Penn State University. Special thanks go to the men and women of the Manuscript Division of the Library of Congress, who helped me work through the large Moral Re-Armament collection during many visits over more than a decade.

Because these sources are all over the country, my thanks go also to the folks who put me up on my research travels: John Evans in Austin;

Heather Janules in Washington; Carl and Shirley Dudley in Hartford; and Ann and Bob Graves in State College. My most frequent host was Margie Jones in Washington, who during numerous visits housed me, fed me, and asked good questions. Some of this travel was supported by grants from the Center for the Study of Religion at Princeton.

Many of the best primary sources were not documents, but people. I am grateful to the people who told me stories and shared materials, including Sally Shoemaker Robinson, John Grier Hibben Scoon, Kenaston Twitchell Junior, and alumni of Princeton University and Mackinac College.

Since one cannot live by scholarship alone, thanks are also due to the people who employed me while I worked on the book: James Hudnut-Beumler of the Material History of American Religion Project, Elizabeth Hayford at the Associated Colleges of the Midwest, and Richard Rosengarten and Cynthia Lindner of the University of Chicago Divinity School.

A corps of editors helped me keep the project coherent and under control. Nancy Carnes proofread the dissertation, evidently quite voluntarily. Lauren Bryant reviewed the first half of the project and suggested useful midcourse corrections. Most importantly, Spencer Dew read the whole thing and helped me tighten and focus the final product. Completing the book would have been impossible without his help. As always, of course, any errors or infelicities remain my responsibility.

The ladies and gentlemen of Palgrave have been patient, encouraging, and directive in appropriate amounts: Michael Flamini, Gayatri Patnaik, Amanda Johnson, Christopher Chappell, and Samantha Hasey.

Parts of chapter two initially appeared in " 'Men Want Something Real': Frank Buchman and Anglo-American College Religion in the 1920s" in the *Journal of Religious History*, reprinted with permission.

I am grateful to the friends and family who have supported me and distracted me in turns through the life of this project. My father has been more supportive than he'll ever know. I am sorry that my mother will not see the final book, but I remain grateful for her life and love. Jannene Shannon is a newer but welcome part of our family's life. Princeton friends egged me on at the beginning of the project, and Oak Park friends at the end. I send a special shout-out to the men and women of FUSH (First United Senior High) who have welcomed me in their fellowship.

I got to know Frank Buchman before I met William Tweedley. Fortunately, however, William has not been jealous of the time I have spent with Buchman and his devotees. He read many of the chapters, offered good advice, and asked good questions. We built a life together while I wrote this book; I pray we will remain an intelligent, workable team for many years to come.

Introduction

On a summer night in 1939, four searchlights stabbed the sky over the Hollywood Bowl. After a trumpet blast, an unseen voice proclaimed a new hope sent by God in the hour of crisis—Moral Re-Armament: "It spread like wildfire across the world. Today on every continent, in over 60 nations, men and women of every race, color, and point of view are finding in Moral Re-Armament the common sense way to a better world. As civilization plunges from crisis to crisis, a prophetic voice rings out again with a Call to the Nations for Moral and Spiritual Re-Armament."[1] A lengthy procession filled the stage, with hundreds of people from around the world carrying their nations' flags. The audience of thirty thousand sang patriotic songs. Prominent citizens of Los Angeles, including famed dancer Ruth St. Denis and the former president of the Chamber of Commerce, gave inspiring speeches.[2]

The four searchlights symbolized Moral Re-Armament's four absolutes—absolute honesty, absolute unselfishness, absolute purity, and absolute love. A sign on the rim of the bowl proclaimed, "New Men—New Nations—a New World!" Japanese and Chinese people greeted each other, finding peace while their nations were at war. Labor and industrial leaders put aside their strife to shake hands. British tennis star Bunny Austin challenged the audience "to give our lives to change conditions by changing human nature which created them." Printed greetings from political and business leaders welcomed the meeting, including statements from President Roosevelt and Henry Ford.

The Hollywood Bowl meeting on July 19, 1939, was a complex mixture of evangelical revival meeting, show business revue, and world-saving earnestness. The gathering introduced many Americans to Moral Re-Armament, a rapidly growing transnational religious and social movement dedicated to changing the world through changing people.

Figure 1 Spotlights above the Hollywood Bowl, July 19, 1939, symbolizing Moral Re-Armament's Four Absolutes. From the Records of Moral Re-Armament, Prints and Photographs Division, Library of Congress.

Moral Re-Armament (MRA) was the latest incarnation of a movement established twenty years earlier. It had been known as the First Century Christian Fellowship, the Oxford Groups, and—by its critics—Buchmanism, after its founder Frank Buchman. It changed names as it changed its work—with a different audience, or a different public image, or a different social agenda. The fundamental message remained the same, but over more than 50 years, MRA's leaders regularly reshaped its work as it adapted to new circumstances.

This book traces that process of reinvention, from ministry among elite college students to the earnest showmanship of "Up With People." Members drew on a wide variety of theological ideas and religious practices, mixing them with psychological theories and a hefty dollop of popular culture. Scholars call this process bricolage—combining elements at hand to address a particular need. American religion is a rich field of bricolage, as religious practitioners mix sometimes conflicting beliefs and practices in their spiritual lives. In our time, the results include megachurches with food courts and synagogues with jazz bands. In the middle of the twentieth century it produced Moral Re-Armament, with its small group meetings, celebrity-focused rallies, and uplifting musicals.

The possibility of bricolage and reinvention are an important characteristic of evangelical Christianity, a lively tradition in American religion. Unlike Calvinism or Catholicism, evangelicalism believes that human nature can be changed through a personal experience of God. This experience is more important than adherence to particular doctrines or practices. Evangelicals have religious experiences, and convert others by sharing those experiences. This understanding of Christianity lends itself to bricolage and reinvention, as churches and believers adopt and adapt practices and beliefs so they can more effectively bring people to an experience of God and a changed life.

MRA was rooted in this evangelical tradition. It began as an attempt to convert American college students before World War I, to bring them to a vital religious experience. Its evangelical approach continued, however, long after it moved away from its revivalist roots. Moral Re-Armament sought to change the world by changing human nature, even in political and economic arenas, not through rational persuasion or logical argument but through storytelling. Members told stories of how their lives had been changed in order to change the lives of others. Movement publications were compilations of stories—of people having their lives changed by meeting a member, or finding faith in a cell group, or a nation becoming more unified through its witness. Its plays and movies were stories of lives changed for the better. The message was not always explicitly Christian, but it was still evangelism—"come and see what God has done."

The movement believed that changed human beings would lead to a changed world, a world without war, poverty, hatred, or fear. Theologians call this millennialism, the belief that God can and will create a perfected world, possibly through human actions. MRA members believed that God was working through them to bring about a better world, in families, workplaces, and nations, and around the globe. In an increasingly complex and impersonal world, they felt that the actions of just one person could change the world.

This millennial mission shaped the movement's world view. Their belief gave cosmic implications to small actions, which shaded into arrogance or self-aggrandizement. Devotees praised Moral Re-Armament as the only real solution to the world's problems and its founder as a veritable saint. Critics, on the other hand, questioned MRA's claims and sometimes its integrity, calling it fascist, pacifist, heretical, or sexually perverse. In MRA eyes, such critics were in league with the evil forces out to block its work.

Most accounts of the movement reflect this controversy, with a strongly polemical tone on one side or the other. Contemporary journalists tried to plumb the mystery of Moral Re-Armament, while supporters recruited other journalists to defend it. Sociologists and psychologists interpreted it as a cult.[3] Like many new religious movements people either loved it or hated it, and worked to condemn it or sanctify it.

Behind the conflict, however, an untold number of Americans— and others around the world—found God and community in Moral Re-Armament. The movement's message and small groups helped them deal with uncertainty in their lives and with a very complex world of hot and cold wars. The movement may have failed in its attempts to change the world, but its impact remains in the lives of many followers.

Moral Re-Armament had its greatest impact through two organizations that grew out of the parent movement. Up With People began as MRA's youth outreach in the 1960s, trying to spread the movement's message to the baby boom generation through popular music. It soon outgrew MRA and spun itself off, but it retained its goal of connecting youth to the world. The more important offshoot was Alcoholics Anonymous, founded in the 1930s by men influenced by the Oxford Groups. The Oxford Groups gave Alcoholics Anonymous and other twelve-step groups their focus on personal change, story-telling, and making amends.

Although little known today, at its peak Moral Re-Armament was a wide-spread organization, with headquarters on three continents, over a thousand full-time volunteers, and countless adherents. As a result, it could be the subject of lots of books. One would evaluate the movement's claims of impact on a variety of national and international issues, ranging from stopping cheating in a school to preventing war between nations. Another could focus on its work with individuals, churches, and communities. A third would concentrate on its activities in any one of dozens of countries around the world. Another book could tell the stories of the men and women involved in the movement, including how they joined and why they left. Yet another history could look at the movement's distinctive perspective on gender and sexuality.

This particular book about MRA describes the American roots and American trajectory of this international movement. It charts the transformations and reinventions of Moral Re-Armament over fifty years, changes brought about through either new circumstances or new leadership. It shows the ongoing importance of MRA's evangelical tradition—experience, life-changing, and story-telling—even in its political work. And it highlights the movement's millennial self-understanding, as it sought to change the world through changing people.

These three themes, I believe, faithfully summarize Moral Re-Armament's mission through its history. They also tell us something about American religion. While MRA had cells around the globe, and its members saw themselves as citizens of the world, at its heart it was an American religious movement. Evangelicalism's commitment to religious experience and the sharing of witness runs through American religion, from the Puritans to Oprah. The tradition of utopian communities and social reform organizations reflects America's fundamental millennialism. And MRA's pattern of reinvention reflects the American habit of reshaping identities and institutions to fit the times.

Each of this book's seven chapters reveals a reinvention of Moral Re-Armament. The first describes the early ministry of movement founder Frank Buchman, who brought together a variety of influences to create a unique evangelical style. In the years after World War I, Buchman repackaged his evangelical work to appeal to the men on elite college campuses in the United States and Britain, the focus of the second chapter. That movement matured in the 1930s, the third chapter shows, as Buchman and his followers take his message to new audiences. The fourth chapter describes the birth of Moral Re-Armament, as the movement used spectacle and adopted antipolitical politics, trying to make political change from outside the political system. After the outbreak of World War II, movement members shaped its message to create harmony in labor relations, the topic of the fifth chapter. As the cold war took hold, MRA developed a range of ideological weapons—plays, books, and movies, effectively propaganda—to fight the ideological war, the focus of chapter six. The last chapter describes the movement's focus on young people in the 1960s, as it worked to catch the attention of the baby boom generation. The time periods for these chapters overlap, reflecting the sometimes slow process of change within MRA.

I have been reading the letters and diaries of MRA leaders for over a decade, and feel that I have gotten to know them pretty well. Since the movement encouraged confession, I must confess that at times I have found them prickly and self-righteous. But as an observer of American religion, I am amazed by the vibrancy and creativity of this movement and its people. More personally, I am moved by their commitment to their movement, and to each other.

In the summer of 1940, a year after the big rally at the Hollywood Bowl, Buchman summoned his closest followers to the shores of Lake Tahoe. He felt they needed to rethink their work and rebuild their relationships. Years later, one man remembered that summer as "a time of complete spiritual overhauling. We took time to look at ourselves and our motives, to examine the places where we had sinned and apparently gotten away with it. There were lots of old hurts and wounds that for the first time were really brought to light and cured."[4] Their work together, another wrote, revealed "the personal experience of Christ" as "every human alternative has slowly disappeared in the light of a working, sharing, constant fellowship."[5]

Moral Re-Armament was a movement of intimacy as well as spectacle. Members dedicated their lives to changing the world, in many cases sacrificing their careers and families for the movement. All through its many reinventions, they stayed true to its message and to their fellowship. It may not have changed the world, but it did change lives.

CHAPTER ONE

The Soul Surgeon

In 1921, at the age of 44, after two decades of practicing and teaching evangelism in the United States and Asia, Frank Buchman decided to strike off on his own. During those 20 years, Buchman had built the foundation for a remarkable and controversial religious movement. He developed a style of work, based on nineteenth century Anglo-American evangelicalism, that appealed to an elite audience. He built a network of followers and supporters around the world. Now he was unemployed and relying on the guidance of God.

Although Moral Re-Armament was bigger than Buchman, understanding the movement requires understanding his early years. In his roots and in his early career, from his parents' home in eastern Pennsylvania to the mission fields of China, Buchman found elements and influences that he combined to develop a unique evangelical style. He met people who would become long-time colleagues and supporters. His experiences during these years became stories that he told through the rest of his ministry.

An Apostle in Training

Frank Buchman was an outsider, a handicap for someone who wanted to be part of the American establishment. Born on June 4, 1878 in Pennsburg, Pennsylvania, he grew up in eastern Pennsylvania's German subculture; like most of his neighbors, Buchman's father, a shopkeeper and innkeeper, spoke more German than English. Buchman was baptized in a small ethnically German Lutheran church rather than one of the better-known American denominations. He wanted to attend

Princeton University, an establishment citadel, but instead his father sent him to Muhlenberg College, a less prestigious institution associated with his church.[1]

Buchman's ethnic sub-culture was nevertheless a mixture of religious traditions. His home church was a union congregation of two denominations, Reformed and Lutheran, that were competitors in Europe but partners in Pennsylvania. Both observed a creedal orthodoxy and followed a rigid liturgy. In the nineteenth century, however, these traditions were influenced by the evangelicalism that was spreading through American Protestantism. Evangelicalism downplayed creeds and liturgy, focusing instead on the importance of a life-changing experience of Christ and sharing that experience with others. Despite the denominations' wishes, these ideas percolated into churches like Buchman's. He also briefly attended a high school run by the Schwenkfelders, a German pietist sect. They were more mystical and less orthodox than their Lutheran neighbors, believing that Christians should be in daily intimate contact with God. This mixture of religious traditions, common in American religion, shaped Buchman's ministry and movement. Although he was a life-long Lutheran, he easily crossed denominational and confessional boundaries. He was dedicated to bringing others to Christian experience, and taught the importance of intimacy with God.

Buchman showed an early interest in ministry. In a high school essay called "The College Hero," he argued that the true hero is not the football star, but the man who "saved a fellow student from the snares of hell." When the hero of his story "saw that his classmate was leading a dissipated life bravely went to that student's room locked the door taking the key and then opened his Bible prayed with the man and then asked him to lead a different kind of life. The student was thankful and appreciated the interest he had taken and promised to reform." Anticipating his future work, Buchman felt that such a Christian life took "courage and only brave students will fight such battles."[2] This language of battle repeated throughout Buchman's life.

The young man also demonstrated social ambition. While in college he visited a young woman of means and reported to his mother, "I am perfectly lionized here."[3] After graduation from Muhlenberg, Buchman thanked his father for supporting his education. "My advantages have been exceptional. More will be expected of me. If I did not possess the culture and refinement that I do, I would not be entertained and have the friends which I have on all sides."[4]

In the fall of 1899 he began his studies at the Lutheran Theological Seminary at Philadelphia,. He took to his calling enthusiastically.

His first sermon was "a splendid experience for me," he told his parents. "My life work has begun."[5] While in seminary he discovered the American evangelical world and spent several summers at Dwight Moody's conferences in Northfield, Massachusetts, connecting him to the network of student Christian associations.[6] The budding evangelist graduated from seminary and was ordained in 1902.

A Strong Current of Life

Although Buchman's first job was in a suburban Philadelphia parish, he soon became interested in ministry with young men in the city. His church's City Mission Society shared his interest, and in September 1905, they opened the first American hospice, with Buchman as housefather. The hospice provided a home for single men who had come to the city seeking employment, who might otherwise "fall prey to the temptations and vices found in every large city."[7] The hospice thrived, and taught Buchman a great deal about ministry. Years later he still told stories of the young men, struggling with various sins, who found a home at the hospice, such as one lad he led to sobriety and Christianity.[8]

Buchman's stories also had a villain—the Mission Society. In its annual report the Society praised the hospice's "Christian atmosphere [where] young men are influenced only for good," but worried that, unless the house were kept full, the board "will continue to have financial difficulties of greater or lesser magnitude to deal with."[9] The directors criticized Buchman's expenditures, but he argued that the hospice's work was too important to economize on staff or food. He told stories of young men helped by the hospice, including one who went into the ministry and another he convinced to stop visiting prostitutes. In a 17-page report in the summer of 1907 he declared that "the results of this work are not to be weighed in the scales of mammon." He insisted on a free hand to run the hospice—and a raise.[10]

The board refused to meet his demands, and Buchman resigned. The event entered the Buchman legend, interpreted to fit the storyteller's perspective. A supporter wrote that he "had come up against the power of bureaucracy coupled with the power of money. He was never to forget the lesson, though in this case he took it personally. He was so bitter that it made him physically ill."[11] A critic, on the other hand, suggests that after the dispute Buchman "fumed, collapsed, quit, and threw what seems to have been a prolonged fit of hysterical sulks."[12]

Buchman's time at the hospice taught him some important lessons. He learned that people—especially young men—benefit from one-on-one attention, that it can truly change lives. He developed his belief in the importance of changing individual lives rather than more comprehensive social programs. And he learned to distrust bureaucrats and committees.

Buchman's bitterness consumed him, leading his doctor to prescribe a trip to Europe. Wallowing in misery through the Greek islands, he told a fellow traveler that he would never forgive the hospice board. Despite his bitterness he showed an early glimpse of his lifelong talent for cultivating relationships with the rich and powerful when he met Princess Sophie of Greece on board the ship. The Princess, his biographer reports grandly, "hoped that he might help Greece and Turkey live at peace together."[13]

More important, Buchman attended the annual convention of the Keswick movement in England. The annual meetings at Keswick, in the Lake Country, brought together English and American Christians who sought to lead a more holy life. They were part of the Holiness movement, which grew rapidly in the late nineteenth century. Many Protestant theologians like Calvin and Luther taught that Christians remained sinners but were forgiven of their sins through the death of Jesus. Holiness thinkers, on the other hand, preached that Christians could be freed from sin through the blessing of the Holy Spirit. Keswick participants believed that "when we renounced the sins...we mean that we have broken with them forever." The key to avoiding sin, they held, was unbroken union with Christ; it was not a one-and-for-all experience, but an ongoing need.[14] Because of their conviction that Christians could be perfected through the work of the Holy Spirit in their lives, Holiness belief was also known as Perfectionism.

In June 1908 Buchman attended the Keswick convention, but its preaching offered him no rest from his despair. One Sunday afternoon, wandering in the countryside, he found a service in a small Methodist church, led by a woman who spoke about the Atonement.[15] Buchman recalled later that although he had often studied the Atonement—the belief that Christ's death paid for human sins—he actually experienced it for the first time that day. He saw the Crucified; "I knew that I had wounded Him, that there was great distance between myself and Him, and I knew that it was my sin of nursing ill-will." He acknowledged that he "did not have victory because I was not in touch with God." This mystical experience changed Buchman's life. He came away from the chapel with "a vibrant feeling, as though a strong current of life had suddenly been poured into me."[16]

The Keswick convention taught that "if the soul is to be completely restored, and made right with God, it will be necessary for an act of restitution to be made to the injured party."[17] Feeling truly converted, Buchman wrote to all the members of the hospice board, asking their forgiveness for his ill-will. More importantly, that afternoon he told the story to an acquaintance, who committed his life to Christ and became Buchman's first convert.

That afternoon in Keswick transformed Buchman's work. At the convention he encountered Holiness doctrines that would shape his evangelical style for the next fifty years. Thanks to Keswick, Buchman's teaching focused on the necessity of surrender and closeness to Christ and the importance of personal devotions and restitution for sin. It taught him to think about the full Christian life as "victory." Buchman did not attend a Keswick meeting again, but these themes influenced him deeply. It also gave him an experience. Buchman's native Lutheranism had stressed the importance of correct belief—of orthodoxy—as the mark of true Christianity. In that world he had studied and preached about the Atonement dozens of times. But at Keswick he *experienced* the Atonement. That experience strengthened his embrace of evangelicalism, where true Christianity is marked by a personal encounter with Christ. For the rest of his career, Buchman encouraged experiences of faith rather than orthodox teaching. This mixture of evangelical experience and Keswick perfectionism became keys to Buchman's work.

The Penn State Laboratory

Buchman left Keswick with a renewed sense of vocation and a strong commitment to evangelism. When he returned to America in the fall of 1908, however, he was unemployed. Through connections he had made at Northfield, Buchman got a position with one of the country's leading evangelical groups, the Intercollegiate Young Men's Christian Association, leading the student Christian association at the Pennsylvania State College (now Pennsylvania State University). Over the next several years Penn State became a laboratory where Buchman developed his evangelical style.

The YMCA was founded in London in 1844 to provide young men with Christian fellowship and a refuge from the city's immorality.

Established in the United States in 1855, it was international and inter-denominational; the only criterion for membership was membership in an evangelical (i.e., Protestant) denomination. To keep peace in this ecumenical mix, the YMCA downplayed theological distinctions, focusing instead on the importance of religious experience and united mission.[18]

While the early YMCAs were mainly for young business men, in the 1870s the national YMCA leadership also built a network of Christian associations for college and university students across the country. These campus groups were governed by elected students—often athletes or other prominent men on campus—but usually led by professional staff who organized the work and did personal ministry. Traveling secretaries, employed by the Intercollegiate Movement, visited campuses to lead revival rallies and connected college groups to each other. Association staff also did mission work in the nation's cities and overseas. The Student Volunteer Movement, a YMCA affiliate, recruited American college students to commit their lives to world mission.

While local campus associations were autonomous, they shared some distinctive marks, what might be called the "YMCA style" of evangelical work. For evangelicals, American religion in the early twentieth century had become too conventional, dry, and book-focused, particularly in the growing universities. While denominational churches were obsessed with institutions and doctrines, YMCA leaders wanted students to have an experience of God that would give them a vital and exciting faith, aimed at bringing young men to Christ. They organized Bible studies and other courses for members, and sent deputations of students out to preach the gospel. Members participated in small prayer groups and individual silent prayer.[19] This style set the pattern for Buchman's work at Penn State.

While evangelicalism is perhaps best known for large revival meetings, YMCA secretaries like Buchman also did a great deal of intense personal work with individuals. While at Penn State, he organized "confessional groups" in the fraternity houses, where men could confess their sins or describe their religious experiences. At a retreat house in the country, a Penn State historian remembers, "the students would all gather together on the floor before the blazing fire and the session would develop into an experience meeting. Confessions came out in the form of a problem and solutions would be offered."[20] These groups set the model for the house parties that were the core of Buchman's work in the following decades.

The YMCA was also known for appealing to "key men," athletes and other prominent students, as a means of attracting other members of the community. Scottish evangelist Henry Drummond told his followers that "if you fish for eels, you get eels; if you fish for salmon, you get salmon."[21] Drummond used athletes to lead his work, relying on their prominence and popularity to get the attention of other students.[22] In State College Buchman followed this model, reaching out to student leaders in athletics and student government.[23] The phrase "key men" is not unintentional, for Buchman clearly directed his early ministry to men. At Penn State he approached a Bible study for women with "fear and trembling," preferring to focus on prayer meetings in the fraternity houses.[24]

Buchman also learned from the YMCA the practice of the "morning watch," a private devotional first thing in the morning, and gave it an added twist. Adapting techniques he may have picked up at Keswick or from the Schwenkfelders, Buchman instructed his followers to take time in the morning to listen for what God might be telling them. "Any man can pick up divine messages if he will put his receiving set in order," he told them. "Definite, accurate, adequate information can come from the Mind of God to the mind of men. This is normal prayer."[25] Buchman believed that God would tell the listening Christian His will for the day—trips to take, people to convert. He urged followers to listen and write down these leadings in a notebook, a practice that came to be known as guidance. It was not Buchman's invention; Christian mystics have long listened for God's word, and the quiet time was a part of YMCA spirituality.[26] Buchman, however, gave guidance a central place in his evangelical work.

Using these evangelical tools, Buchman developed a successful program at Penn State. The college alumni magazine reported on a 1911 evangelistic campaign that "lasted over a period of six days, consisted of a series of large and small meetings, exceeding 50 in number." The report continued, in telegraphic fashion, "Meetings in the fraternity houses, boarding houses, dorms, and classrooms, together with intimate addresses to the men and women, influential. The effects far reaching. The town and college are both cleaner for it."[27] College leaders were pleased with the Y's growth, from 166 students in 1906 to 1,200 in 1911, on a campus of 1,620 people. The chair of the Y's advisory committee reported that "we have grown from a small organization numerically to the largest student organization in the world—one whose influence was circumscribed; now it is a dominating factor in the life of the College as well as a pacemaker for other colleges and universities."[28]

Buchman left no doubt who deserved the credit for the success. "Your Secretary has doubled the effective membership of the Association," he wrote the alumni in a 1909 fund-raising letter, "although he did not arrive til [sic] after the opening of the year. For years a resident Secretary was a need daily felt. He has made himself a necessity."[29] In a report to the YMCA board, he noted the national—and even international—acclaim; in the grandiose language that became familiar in his later work, Buchman stated that "Penn State…has become a world factor, and is making her influence felt in many centers."[30]

Years later Buchman called his work "the making of a miracle." "After three years' work," he told his followers in a 1948 speech, "it was no longer good form to hold drinking parties. The College began to win their games, and scholarship improved."[31] He told one supporter that at Penn State he had changed "the entire moral and spiritual life of the faculty and the student body, and [gained] the full support of the Board of Trustees."[32] In the 1950s, two followers wrote that "in almost every fraternity house at least once a week the Bible was studied as a handbook of how to live a life and how to help other men do the same." They concluded that what Buchman did at Penn State "is a picture of what education could have become in America and must become."[33]

Not all sources support this legend. A faculty member who helped to hire Buchman acknowledged that he was "the most efficient secretary the college ever had." Nevertheless, "Buchman was no saint and no super-man and no messiah." Just because Buchman "got nearly the entire student body to sign the Y.M.C.A. rolls does not say he converted them."[34] Some students found him excessively moralistic; one YMCA observer wrote that "he was so absolutely uncompromising in his convictions and so lofty in his moral standards that they dubbed him 'Pure John.'"[35] Another believed that he was obsessed with sexuality, remembering that Buchman's "most frequent topic of conversation was some story or another about homosexuals and how he cured them of their sin."[36] Other people just found Buchman's personality annoying. A faculty member wrote that Buchman "oozed the oil of unctuous piety from every pore."[37]

Buchman, meanwhile, felt that the local YMCA board did not adequately reward his work. After requesting a bigger salary when he first came, he renegotiated his contract every year. In his 1914 report to the committee, Buchman asked for a raise, from $3,000 to $3,250. "The reason for this is, that I need it." He had much contact with wealthy supporters of the YMCA and of the college, and he needed to "live on a plane such as is not required of men who are not in a similar position."[38] A letter to the board's chair objected to its oversight of his financial management. "I have been a jealous watch-dog for that treasury and have had constant criticism, and those things hurt." Nevertheless, Buchman added, "I have no feeling of bitterness or rancor towards any man."[39] This exchange echoes the conflict at the hospice six years before.

In 1915 Buchman took a leave of absence from the YMCA to do missionary work in Asia. Although he never returned to Penn State, he gained a lot from his seven years there. It was his longest ministry in one place, and there he developed many of his techniques. Most importantly, he developed stories that he told for the rest of his career, shaping those stories to serve the needs of his audience. In his 1948 speech, for instance, he told the story of a graduate student, converted from atheism by Buchman's winning ways, and the conversion of the college's dean, convinced by miracles of Buchman's work. He used these stories to illustrate both the power of God and the dangers of a secular education.

This speech also included features typical of Buchman's storytelling. The graduate student was no typical student, but American nobility, "who possessed every physical grace and charm. He was one of the most attractive personalities I ever met. He was the son of a Supreme Court judge and the grandson of the Governor of a State." The conversion of this key man, Buchman declared, caused the conversion of 80 more. He mentioned other nobility, including a French family who had somehow found their way to central Pennsylvania, and a Chinese diplomat. There is also some embroidery of the truth, as when Buchman supposedly told the graduate student that he had visited the grave of Confucius—several years before his first trip to Asia.[40]

The best-known stories from Penn State concerned a campus character and local bootlegger known as Bill Pickle. After much talk and a little bribery from Buchman, Bill became a Christian. He participated in Buchman's meetings for over twenty years and served as an object lesson for much longer. The crusty old character, almost legendary himself, made for a lively story that caught the attention of Buchman's audience. When Buchman was criticized for paying too much attention to the wealthy and influential, he could use Pickle as an example of his appeal to the poor as well.

The rural bootlegger, the agnostic dean, the noble graduate student— these were what Buchman called "interesting sinners," vibrant characters who, through his ministry, gave their lives to Christ. He enjoyed telling stories that served a variety of purposes. They showed that

Buchman could overcome challenges to win over recalcitrant potential Christians. These people also served as examples; if they could be
converted, the message seemed to be, anyone could. Buchman believed
that interesting sinners made interesting Christians.

On the Road: India, Hartford, and China

Buchman learned a great deal during his seven years at Penn State, but
he hungered for a mission field larger than State College. In the fall of
1915 he received a wire from Sherwood Eddy, a traveling evangelist
for the International YMCA. Eddy was planning a campaign through
India, and needed someone who could travel ahead of him, training
personal workers to follow up on his large rallies.[41] Buchman, who
had wanted to be a missionary when he was a child, jumped at the
chance. Over the next four years he traveled through Asia on behalf
of the YMCA.

   While in India, Buchman met another American who shared his
convictions about personal evangelism. Howard Walter, a graduate of
Princeton University and Hartford Seminary, was literary secretary at
the local YMCA, mainly researching and writing about Islam and its
relation to Christianity. He was also interested in evangelical methods;
when Buchman visited his station, Walter found a fellow believer in the
principles of personal evangelism. They worked together on the Eddy
campaign and shared ideas about evangelical work. Out of their collaboration Walter wrote *Soul-Surgery: Some Thoughts on Incisive Personal
Work*.[42] Although Walter was the main author, he credited many of the
ideas in the book to Buchman, who used it as a textbook of evangelism for the rest of his career. It is the most systematic presentation of
Buchman's evangelical method.

   Walter and Buchman shared evangelicalism's focus on a personal
experience of God, in contrast to churches that focus on the necessity
of creeds or rote participation in a sacrament. "God outside of us is a
theory; God inside of us becomes a fact," Walter wrote. "God outside
of us is an hypothesis; God inside of us is an experience." Unlike many
nineteenth century evangelicals, however, they scorned big revival
meetings; Buchman said they were like "hunting rabbits with a brass
band."[43] Instead, they focused on personal work—concentrating on
individuals or small groups instead of large audiences. Such one-on-
one outreach, they felt, was the task of every Christian. According
to Walter, "the terms 'Christian' and 'Personal Worker' ought to be

interchangeable. A professed Christian who is not busy to some extent in the work of witness-bearing to individuals, can be no true follower of Christ."

Personal work was not new—evangelicals had been doing such work for decades—but Walter and Buchman urged a more scientific approach. They called it "soul surgery," echoing the era's confidence in science; if medicine could be systematic, efficient, and scientific, they reasoned, so should conversion. Walter called the evangelist a "soul-physician" and urged readers to look at personal work "viewed from a physician's standpoint." In soul surgery, Buchman and Walter stated, the evangelist examined the potential convert as a patient, seeking to excise the sin that blocked a fulfilling relationship with God. They adopted this medical model from Scottish evangelist Henry Drummond, whose *Spiritual Diagnosis* (1873) marked "the beginning of the modern move-ment of scientific personal evangelism." Soul surgery used the same tools as medicine—examination, diagnosis, and treatment—and was taught in the same way—through case study and clinical observation. Instead of the priest's confessional, the soul surgeon used a clinic.

For Walter and Buchman, the conversion process followed the "Five Cs": Confidence, Confession, Conviction, Conversion, and Conservation. The evangelist—the soul surgeon—should begin by getting close to the potential convert and gaining the patient's trust, "coming so wholly into the confidence of the one we seek to help along the avenue of personal friendship that we know his verdict on his own case, see him through his own eyes. The physician of souls must know his patients intimately, or he cannot diagnose their troubles accurately." This required not just "an abstract 'love of the crowd' but a warm, sympathetic, enduring interest in individuals around them."

To truly help individuals, Buchman and Walter believed, soul sur-geons had to "be as ready to give as we are to receive, realizing the need of reciprocal confidence." They encouraged the evangelist to open up his own life, describing his own sins and conversion to the patient, confessing his "own shortcomings honestly and humbly." Such shar-ing would gain the other person's confidence, enabling him to confess more freely. This was why Buchman told stories—it encouraged the listener to tell his or her own storiy in response. After his own conver-sion at Keswick, for instance, Buchman described his experience to a friend and won his conversion.

Once he had the patient's confidence, the soul surgeon moved to diagnosis, identifying his or her sin. While some Christians might define sin as disbelief or wrong belief, Walter believed that men lived

their lives on four levels—"spiritual, intellectual, social, and physical—
and that the diseased spot, the center of infection that is spreading in all
directions, may be in any of the four." He mentioned such sins as pride,
dishonesty, selfishness, and impurity, but sensed that the heart of most
sins was physical. "Those who best know the facts declare that ninety
percent of the ultimate sin around us is on the lowest physical level, to
which we penetrate most rarely and with the greatest maladaptation
in our personal work." Man after man, Walter wrote, had been felled
by impurity, sins which Buchman was particularly good at identifying. Walter told the story of a Yale student who, during an evangelistic campaign, looked for help in resolving his doubt of the existence
of God. Sherwood Eddy, the lead evangelist, "gave him all the proofs
he could think of and the man went away unconvinced." Buchman,
however, "came in touch with the same man, found that he was living in gross sin, and was able to bring about his genuine conversion."
Such moral problems, Walter concluded, blocked complete surrender
to God. This focus on impurity—sexual sin—runs throughout the history of Buchman's movement.

Because it pursued these often-shameful sins, soul surgery was
painful for the patient, but Walter urged his readers to leave no stone
unturned. True evangelism should "not leave to the sinner a vestige
of the old prideful pose behind which he had shielded iniquity. The
secret thing must be exposed before it can be dealt with effectually,
permitting the repentant sinner to go forward on a new basis of utter
honesty, looking the whole world in the face." No one—not even
clergy—was immune to moral problems, Walter believed, and they
should not be spared soul surgery. "Take nothing for granted. A man
may be president of a Christian Endeavor Society, superintendent of a
Sunday School, an elder or vestryman in a church... [and] still stand in
need of moral surgery."[44] For the soul-surgeon, evangelism sometimes
required confrontation.

While most confession took place in the privacy of the "clinic,"
Walter wrote, public confession was sometimes necessary. He told the
stories of Chinese ministers who confessed their failures to their congregations and offered restitution, and of an American student who
revealed his secret sin to an entire YMCA conference. Such revelations,
Walter concluded, had two benefits—helping the one who confessed
and giving his audience a powerful witness.

Once the patient had confessed his sins, the next step was conviction.
The goal, wrote Walter, was to "help the man to see himself as God
sees him, to view his own life, as we would have him view sin...from

the standpoint of eternity." At that point, he was ready for conversion, or, as Buchman described it, surrendering his will to God. The rhetoric of surrender became a core part of Buchman's work. He often quoted American evangelist Dwight Moody, who declared that "the world has yet to see what God can do in, for, by and through a man whose will is wholly given up to Him."[45] One Buchman supporter regularly cited the authority of "William James [who] says that the *crisis of self-surrender* has always been, and must always be, regarded as the vital turning point of the religious life."[46] The goal, Walter stated, was to help "the repentant sinner to go forward on a new basis of utter honesty, looking the whole world in the face." Buchman wanted converts to experience what he had experienced at Keswick.

The final step in the treatment was "conservation," strengthening the faith of the new Christian. Many evangelists, Walter wrote, missed this step. "The trouble with the revival is that it too often stops at [conversion]. Every psychologist understands the danger of an emotional arousal which finds no expression in practical activity." Like all evangelicals, Walter and Buchman recommended prayer and Bible study to prevent backsliding. They also prescribed three other practices for the new Christian. First, he should offer restitution to anyone he may have injured through his sin. Second, Buchman required new Christians to go out and make other new Christians. "Following conversion the new convert must be ready to win others." Walter also encouraged converts to have a morning quiet time. "At that hour there come to us the mysterious 'leadings' of God's spirit which, when tested and proved and followed, bring to pass moral miracles in individual lives." Such listening—what Buchman called guidance—would help conserve the faith of the new convert.

Buchman's work with Walter strengthened his convictions about evangelism, especially the importance of personal work. Meeting other missionaries in India, however, dismayed him. They were obsessed with building institutions, he felt, instead of converting individuals one at a time. As he told YMCA leader John Mott, "there are agencies abundant and many Christian workers, but they do not seem to get into close, vital touch with the people. There is an utter lack of consciousness everywhere of the need of individually dealing with men."[47] Walter agreed, telling a former professor at Hartford Seminary that there are "many missionaries who have no real passion for souls but are half-heartedly engaged in dreary routine duties."

Walter believed that the solution was personal work in the seminaries so that new missionaries "should not leave the school without a vital

experience of the living Christ and a passion to make Him known." He
suggested that Hartford should "set the pace" not only for scholarship
"but also in the quality and degree of sympathetic helpful approach
to individual students by faculty members and in the scientific training that is given to make them successful and enthusiastic personal
evangelists."

Perhaps on Walter's suggestion, Hartford hired Buchman as a part-
time lecturer in personal evangelism, making it "the only theological
school we know of where an actual clinic in personal evangelism is
conducted and where there is continual emphasis laid on the need and
importance of personal evangelism."[48] The position gave Buchman a
salary, an expense account, and the freedom to travel. He did mission
work overseas and visited American colleges to recruit students for the
seminary.[49]

On fire for personal evangelism, Buchman saw his job, actually
the job of the entire seminary, as evangelizing the students as well
as teaching them evangelism. Worried that the seminary's curriculum had become too dry and academic, he wanted the curriculum to
bring students to a personal experience of God. Years later a student in
one of Buchman's courses recalled little of its content but remembered
that the teacher was anxious to convert each member of the class.[50]
Buchman's classes were not traditional lectures, but rather "a 'spiritual
clinic,'" Walter wrote, "in which personal evangelism is studied, as law
is studied, by the case method, instead of through vague generalization
and exhortations."[51] Essentially, Buchman's teaching was storytelling;
another student remembered that his lectures "consisted of stories of
people whose lives had been changed by God's power working through
him."[52]

Buchman put his teaching into practice. He did the personal work for
Billy Sunday's revival meetings in New York in 1917.[53] Buchman and
Sunday remained friends; Sunday invited Buchman to join his work,
while Buchman tried to persuade Sunday to join him in the foreign mission field.[54] Buchman's successful evangelical work impressed Hartford
administrators. "His record is that of one of the greatest workers among
college men in this and other lands," President Douglas Mackenzie told
a correspondent. "I do not think he is anything of a public speaker, but
if you want someone to inspire and organize and direct personal work
of a quiet and vital type, here is your man."[55]

Buchman's most important evangelical adventure during his Hartford
years, however, was his 1917–1919 tour of China, where he believed he
was a major player. In a report to Hartford dean Melancthon Jacobus he

listed the members of the "Buchman Team," which included H.W. Luce (father of journalist Henry Luce) and Roscoe Hersey (father of novelist John Hersey). Buchman wished that he could give the dean "some adequate conception of the wonder-working power of God through the lives of those who are associated with me." He believed that "God has been literally following our work with signs and wonders that no man can gainsay." Billy Sunday had asked Buchman to return and join him in America, but he sensed "a very strong feeling in China that it would be ruinous to the work and might hinder Evangelism for years in China if I were to pull out of the Movement right now and return home."[56] China was a far bigger stage than State College, and Buchman claimed a prominent role.

Buchman saw the China mission as an opportunity to demonstrate the impact of "soul surgery." According to a Methodist missionary connected with the campaign, 8,000 people had attended a series of meetings, with more than half expressing interest in being Christians and hundreds joining the church on one Sunday. "Every non-Christian who attended was personally invited by a Christian, who accompanied him, sat with him, and followed him up," another missionary reported. "Each man had been prepared for several months: otherwise he was not eligible to obtain a ticket." This was what Buchman called a personalized meeting. He traveled from city to city, teaching Christian workers the fine points of personal work.[57] He also taught Chinese converts about personal work, believing that the best way to "conserve" a convert was to have him make more converts.

In addition, the evangelist planned a series of retreats for missionaries and converts, similar to the house parties he led at Penn State. In 1917 he told some supporters in New York about a meeting in Canton, "one of those hallowed days when Christian workers bared their own souls in confession of sins that were keeping them from power." During the gathering missionaries recommitted themselves to individual work. It was a "personalized meeting," with the 150 personal workers and 150 nominal Christians carefully selected. "The result is beyond telling. There have been miracles after miracles. The thought was wonderfully carried out that 'Not one of those which Thou gavest me shall be lost.'" Buchman claimed epochal impact for the retreat. "The old missionaries say that the meeting on Sunday will make history in the South China Missions. They realise how truly they failed in just planning big meetings without the thought of undergirding them with individual work." Unlike other events, he declared, the emphasis was on "the propagation of life rather than the propagation of a plan"—that is, spreading faith rather than building institutions. His own contribution, Buchman added, was significant. "I have been working sixteen to eighteen hours a day."[58]

In these meetings Buchman was highly critical of many Western missionaries in China. They were being too nice to potential converts. "Jesus Christ certainly had complete victory," he told them, "but he had no hesitancy in cleaning out people when they desecrated the temple. Think of the things He said to the scribes and Pharisees!" He encouraged them to show converts "that fine fire which was in the life of Jesus Christ, the fine equivalent of war. It's the kind of courage that makes a man go to another and say to him, 'I'm disappointed in you.'"[59] As Walter showed in *Soul-Surgery*, evangelism required confrontation.

Buchman believed that missionaries avoided such confrontation because they were covering up sins of their own. The Canton meetings, he noted, "have been marked by confession of sin on the part of Christian workers. Some of them have been costly, but they are releasing lives that were under the domination of sin."[60] He talked in particular about "absorbing friendships," most likely coded language for some sort of sexual impropriety, such as same-sex relationships or relationships with native women.[61] The hidden sins of Western missionaries, Buchman concluded, were the greatest obstacle to the success of the China mission.

During his time in China Buchman did find some Western missionaries he could work with, and built them into a team of colleagues and disciples. He and Howard Walter were joined by Sherwood Day, the first of his longtime traveling companions. Day, a 1911 graduate of Yale, worked with the university's YMCA before working three years for the YMCA in India, where he might have met Buchman. In 1915 he enrolled at Hartford Seminary, where he became committed to Buchman's model of individual evangelism.[62] Buchman and Day worked together in China and in the United States.

While in China, Buchman attracted the attention of another follower, who would be closer and more valuable than Day. Samuel Shoemaker was the son of a wealthy Maryland family; after graduating from Princeton he joined the staff of the Philadelphian Society, the university's Christian association.[63] In the spring of 1917, as the United States was preparing for war, Sherwood Eddy visited Princeton and called for volunteers to run YMCA huts for soldiers in England. Shoemaker resigned from the Society and answered Eddy's call. He wanted to do personal ministry among the soldiers, he wrote a friend, but "the thing is to feed the hungry crowd. They think we're killing

time the worst way when you go out of the counter to talk with the
men—so that it is almost impossible to do any religious work at all."
He felt that personal work was "the only kind that counts much when
the score is all added up."[64] When Eddy asked Shoemaker to go to
China he seized the opportunity.[65] Shoemaker spent two years at the
Philadelphian Society's settlement house in Peking (Beijing), teaching
English, Bible, and insurance, and doing evangelical work.[66]

He made no headway with his ministry in Peking, drawing fewer
men every week. Looking for a new approach, Shoemaker invited
Buchman to speak to his class. Buchman refused, suggesting instead
that the problem was with Shoemaker himself, that sin might be getting in the way of his witness to his Chinese students. Shoemaker was
furious, refusing to participate in such "morbid introspection."[67] But
Buchman's words haunted Shoemaker, who alone in the middle of
the night confessed his sin and dedicated himself to God's work. The
next morning, his biographer records, Shoemaker hurried back and
reported to Buchman. "Frank! You were right. Without realizing it,
I have been a pious fraud, pretending to serve God but actually keeping all the trump cards in my own hands. Now I've told the Lord how
sorry I am; and I trust that you will forgive me for harboring ill will
against you. This sprang up the moment you used that word *sin!*"[68]
That night, he wrote in his journal, "I *did* put away every sin in my
life to which I willfully clung. . . . As I look back upon that day, it was
as near a conversion as I ever had. Before I was not really devoted to
Christ wholly. Now I believe I am."[69] Following Buchman's suggestion
of restitution, Shoemaker wrote a letter to his father, "a very hard one
to write—saying I was sorry for anything hard I had said or thought of
him, and hope never to do so again."[70] His conversion narrative echoes
Buchman's own experience at Keswick.

Right after seeing Buchman, Shoemaker talked with one of his
Chinese students. The story illustrates Buchman's method so well that
it is worth repeating in full.

Crossing his threshold, I prayed God to tell me what to say. And
it seemed to come to me, "Tell him what happened to you last
night." My Chinese friend asked me to sit down, and in a pair of
creaky wicker chairs we began to talk. "I believe you have been
interested in my class," I began, "but not satisfied with it. The
fault has been mine. May I tell you something that happened to
me last night?" He listened to my story intently and when I had
finished surprised me with, "I wish that could happen to me." "It

can," I replied, "if you will let God in completely." And that day he made his decision and found Christ.[71]

The student was Shoemaker's first convert. His meeting with Shoemaker reflected the evangelistic style—personal work, sharing, confession—that Shoemaker learned from Buchman. He continued this work, and made ten converts within three months. "To be used of God is the joy of all joys," he wrote in his journal.[72]

Buchman and Shoemaker quickly developed a close, almost father-son relationship. Soon after his conversion, Shoemaker sent his thanks to Buchman, writing that "never before was I wholly given over to Him. Never before had anyone held out to me so unselfish a *reason* for letting go of sin as yours—that one must be sinless to be used."[73] Buchman replied, "I have often thought of you. Do not judge me too harshly, remember a physician, who has discovered a new disease, in his first flush is apt to think that any rash he sees is scarlet fever."[74] He clearly took great pride in having changed Shoemaker. Some months after Shoemaker's conversion, Buchman wrote that he was "profoundly grateful that you feel that I have gone deeper than any other man."[75] Buchman and Shoemaker maintained this close relationship for more than twenty years.

In his own eyes, Buchman's time in China was a triumph. He had built a team of effective personal workers and led a series of meetings that that reached missionaries and Chinese converts alike. In the spring of 1919, however, Buchman left China under a cloud. MRA's legend suggests it was because he had challenged sin among the missionary establishment. Buchman believed that "the people at headquarters have never been won, and the opposition was evident in most subtle forms." That opposition increased, he felt, as he "got deeper into the personal lives of men."[76]

Some of the sin involved, according to rumors, was sexual. One of Buchman's later disciples charged that the missionary most responsible for Buchman's ouster was being blackmailed because of sexual indiscretions.[77] There were also rumors about Buchman and his colleagues. Years later Sherwood Day suggested that Shoemaker confessed to Buchman in Peking his temptations to homosexuality. Day denied rumors about Buchman's own homosexuality, although they have persisted in succeeding years.[78] A subterranean current of sexuality runs through Buchman's time in China—and through the rest of his movement.

Whatever the cause, Buchman's later devotees found world-shattering implications in his departure from China. Reflecting the movement's later obsession with communism, one follower argued that if the missionaries in China had listened to Buchman, Sun Yat-Sen would have prevailed and Mao's revolution never would have succeeded.[79]

Buchman returned to Hartford frustrated by religious institutions. He believed that the seminary's task was converting the students to evangelical Christianity, but he saw the Hartford faculty as too focused on academic work and not interested in conversion. A student in Buchman's personal evangelism course complained that no other teachers "showed any interest in my Christian life unless I went to them with some question that touched on it in some way, and then their interest wasn't lasting."[80] When Buchman complained that the rest of the faculty wasn't interested in personal work, Mackenzie replied that Buchman evidently "wanted to do all the personal work himself, and for this reason they readily left it all to him."[81]

Buchman tried to change the curriculum to increase the focus on personal evangelism. He demanded permission to offer another course, "a sort of clearing house where we can bring reports of the work that is done at the different house parties and parishes." In an obvious criticism of his colleagues, he told the president that "there is a feeling among the students that they do not have an opportunity to select the most vital courses."[82] Supportive of Buchman though he was, the president was unwilling to narrow the seminary's "efficiency to one aspect or method of the church's life and work."[83]

As at Penn State, he rubbed some faculty the wrong way and caused discord in the dormitory.[84] Buchman campaigned for a more prestigious academic title, a larger salary, and a personal secretary, noting to the dean, "We are losing men from Hartford because there [sic] personal needs are not met and they are not living lives of personal victory." Only his own work, Buchman suggested, was making the students into Christian ministers.[85] In the midst of all this conflict, one faculty member felt that Buchman had been lacking in charity, and told the president that "compatibility is essential in all relations involving Faculty membership in an educational institution."[86]

Sherwood Day, a Hartford alumnus, saw a darker motive behind the faculty's resistance. He believed that they objected to Buchman's work because they could not abide his rigor and evangelical commitment. "Mr. Buchman's message cuts deep and wide and makes uncomfortable those who do not measure up to the standards he sets. When men are uncomfortable they oppose or vitiate."[87] He told Buchman that the seminary administration was "just plain afraid. It is too bold a programme for them—they are afraid of their relationships with other seminaries and perhaps afraid of what may be started in the staff of Hartford. They may be afraid of a revival among themselves." He concluded that "it is easy to give chapel talks but it's lots harder to break out and let God take complete command."[88]

By 1922 Buchman felt constrained by Hartford and disillusioned with religious institutions. The seminary had rejected his vision for its future. On February 1 he resigned, feeling that his future was elsewhere. Buchman's later followers blamed the faculty for the break. One described them as "justifiable spiritual eunuchs."[89] Mackenzie, according to another, said that "the greatest mistake Hartford ever made was to let that man go."[90] On the other hand, a Hartford faculty member wrote in 1943 that Buchman "left bitterness and divisions on the campus long after he was gone. Even today one can sense their traces."[91]

★   ★   ★

In two decades of ministry Frank Buchman sketched the outlines of his movement. Based on his experiences at State College and in Asia, he developed a set of evangelical tools and a strong commitment to personal work, especially among young men. He became convinced of the importance of God's guidance. He learned the importance of "key men." He also developed a strong distrust of church institutions. His evangelical style brought together Lutheran theology, Schwenkfelder mysticism, Keswick perfectionism, and YMCA personal work.

In these years he also began to accumulate a stock of stories that he would tell the rest of his life. There were the "interesting sinners"— like Bill Pickle, the Penn State bootlegger, and Sam Shoemaker, the patrician Princetonian—who found new and more victorious lives through telling their sins to Buchman. There were Chinese ministers led to confess their sins to their congregations.

Most importantly, there was Buchman himself: his selfless work among the poor in Philadelphia, and the perfidy of the hospice board; the princess he met in the Mediterranean, and how she asked him to bring peace to Turkey and Greece; the success at Penn State, where the preaching of the Gospel improved the football team; the immoral missionaries who invited communism into China by chasing Buchman out; and the faculty who kept Hartford Seminary from being a center of world-changing power. Buchman and his followers told these stories to invite confession and conversion, attract support, rally the troops, and justify their actions.

Finally, during these years Buchman built a small network of supporters and contacts. Some were dedicated followers, like Shoemaker and Day, while others simply admired his work from a distance, like Sherwood Eddy. During the coming years Buchman would use these connections to build a network on the elite college campuses of America and England.

CHAPTER TWO

Men Want Something Real

Frank Buchman found a new society when he returned to the United States in the spring of 1919. The social upheavals of the Great War had changed the country's economy, politics, religion, and social relations. The Victorian culture he left behind had become modern America. Flappers and philosophers had replaced the temperance advocates and evangelical preachers he knew in 1914.

In the evangelist's eyes, this social change created a spiritual crisis. One follower wrote that Buchman was overwhelmed by "all the irreligion, sensualism and reckless abandon of the post-war years." He saw the worst results of this crisis on the college campuses of American and Britain. Students were "for the most part bewildered and nauseated with things as they were, tumbling over one another to get a new sensation, tolerating conventional religion or despising it outright."[1] Samuel Shoemaker, Buchman's right hand, said his generation was "feverishly trying to find its way to fullness of life," and concluded that "we have found ourselves pretty dishonest, pretty raw, pretty animal about a good many things."[2]

Buchman and his colleagues believed that they had the answer to this social disorder and spiritual upheaval. Drawing on his experiences in Asia and State College, they built a network of cells on college campuses on both sides of the Atlantic. They attracted and converted students using creative methods of personal evangelism, such as the house party. Buchman helped these young men deal with their shame and find spiritual excitement through a more intense and rigorous Christian faith. The groups created a welcoming and friendly community for students, but challenged modern education with a sectarian style that often led to conflict.

It was an American movement, attracting students from colleges along the Eastern seaboard and from British universities. Buchman targeted the brightest and most popular men on those campuses, men who would be society's future leaders. With those men, he could build an army to change the world.

Fun and Faith after the Great War

Religious life on America's campuses reflected the postwar social upheaval. While most students identified themselves as Christian, few were active in the faith. After the rigors of the Progressive Era and the crusade—and carnage—of the Great War, American college students instead wanted to have fun. The postwar years saw the birth of a rich and vibrant youth culture; in the 1920s, writes historian Helen Lefkowitz Horowitz, "the deeds of flaming college youth, seemingly squandering their opportunities, alternately frightened and titillated an older generation and led to a minor genre of college fiction."[3]

For many Americans the best expression of this youth culture was F. Scott Fitzgerald's *This Side of Paradise* (1920). The story was set at Princeton University, where the young men were more concerned with parties and poetry than with class work. The students are charming and clever, the dances are exciting, the campus is lush and romantic, and the faculty is almost invisible. Although it was set in prewar Princeton, *Paradise* nonetheless became the definitive image of Jazz Age campus life, defining the decade and making Fitzgerald's reputation.

Fitzgerald's Princeton was far different from the evangelical college established by Presbyterians in 1746. Like most American universities, it had been influenced by the German university model of the late nineteenth century, becoming more focused on research and science and less on Christian character formation.[4] This shift had an impact on American students. One survey of undergraduates in the 1920s found that university life had led some students to be indifferent or hostile to religion. The researchers wrote that many students "made a definite statement that their study of science had caused them to revise their ideas as to the literal truth of the Bible." Almost a third of the surveyed students said that they had moved from a literal to an allegorical or ethical view of the Bible.[5]

But many more students were indifferent to religion simply because it was not socially acceptable, especially at elite institutions like Princeton. The complaints of one Princeton student—an outsider because of his allegiance to a strongly orthodox faith—offer an example. Looking on his more social classmates with puzzlement and pity, Nelson Burr told his father in 1924 that his classmates talked and laughed before chapel services, and "do not regard prayer and the sacrament very much— they think going to church to pray is platitudinous and '*pious.*' "[6] These students considered themselves Christians, but felt that an active faith would mark them as strange.

With Christianity both intellectually suspect and socially unaccept- able, college campus in the 1920s was unlikely territory for a religious revival. Students still wanted meaning in their lives, however. Just a few years after Burr's letter home, a young undergraduate at Columbia argued that many members of his generation were sincerely looking for religious faith, but found the church "a non-essential." While there were atheists in American colleges, A.D. Britton wrote, "there are hosts of young men and women who are religious and who would like to have the church mean something to them, but to whom so far the church has been able to make no effective and lasting appeal." These young people were disillusioned by the Great War, but they found the church's tra- ditional mores no longer suited to modern society. "What the church now teaches morally, many of this generation feel is interesting as his- tory but not essential to living." The church's task, he concluded was to "build a new code, a new moral system for our present society, but not in the manner of the careless advanced thinkers of the hour."[7]

Listening to Witness

In 1923, in the midst of all this upheaval, a British writer observed "a new seriousness among undergraduates, an increasing sense of respon- sibility, a visible movement towards spiritual life." He believed that this growth "has received no impetus from official quarters. Swiftly, as if some mysterious power were at work, the spirit spreads from University to University."[8]

There was no mystery involved; this movement towards spiritual life was directed by Frank Buchman. In the decade after World War I he and his colleagues carefully developed a network of cell groups in America and Britain, designed to address the needs of the decade's youth culture. It offered the fun and excitement sought by the postwar generation. It gave them a new structure of meaning. In an increas- ingly mass culture—with burgeoning universities and ubiquitous mass media—Buchman's personal work built an intimate community.

Buchman spread his message through a variety of networks. He used connections within the Intercollegiate YMCA movement to secure invitations to visit colleges in the early 1920s. Students, meanwhile, used the collegiate social world—dances, athletic contests, and prep school friends—to spread the word about religious experiences on their campuses. The Protestant Establishment—an informal web of relationships among people with influence in church, government, and society—also provided a way for people to learn about Buchman's work, through church, social, and business connections.[9]

The heart of this cell movement was Princeton, a school that had long fascinated and perhaps even obsessed Buchman. He believed that Princeton—a capital of the Protestant Establishment—would give him intellectual, religious, and social prestige. Buchman had wanted to attend Princeton as an undergraduate before his father sent him to Muhlenberg, and he had visited the campus several times in the 1910s as part of his YMCA work.[10] In the summer of 1919, Samuel Shoemaker—his most important Peking convert—was appointed the secretary of the Philadelphian Society, Princeton's student Christian association. He hired Henry Pitney Van Dusen, another recent alumnus and Buchman supporter, as his assistant. This gave Buchman his long-sought Princeton connection.

The second cell was at Yale, another important Establishment institution; as at Princeton, the cell's nucleus was the student Christian association, there called Dwight Hall. Sherwood Day, a Yale alumnus and Buchman's China companion, joined the Dwight Hall staff in the fall of 1920. The next year Day proclaimed that "our Revival is on! Things happening here that make me cry for joy! [The] Wednesday night group converted 5 men."[11] In private meetings, he told Buchman, several students had "come clean—impurity—pride—dishonesty—all the regular sins."[12] As in China, sexual sins loomed at Yale; one student "came in the other night and opened up his absorbing friendship and crushes. . . . So all the subtler forms of sin are here as well as the more gross."[13] Eventually Day's evangelical style clashed with others on the Dwight Hall staff, and he resigned to work full time with Buchman.[14]

In 1921 Buchman told Shoemaker that he had been invited "to begin at any time a program of Personal Evangelism on the Harvard Campus."[15] While in Cambridge he met Frederic Lawrence, the son of the Episcopal Bishop of Massachusetts and a student at the Episcopal Divinity School. Lawrence and several colleagues spent several years working with students at the Harvard and Episcopal Divinity Schools, using Buchman's methods. The diocese supported this work, but by

1927 some of the local clergy and members of the university administration became uncomfortable with Lawrence's aggressive evangelical style. He and his colleagues moved their base of operations to a local parish, continuing the work with students and other young adults.[16]

Buchman's evangelists reached beyond the "Big Three" of Harvard, Princeton, and Yale to other elite institutions, including Lafayette, Williams, Amherst, Ursinus, and the University of Virginia.[17] In 1923 Buchman and a team led a campaign at Colgate for undergraduates and seminary students, at the president's invitation. He invited a friend to meet a fraternity group, "a smooth crowd, top notchers, excellent politicians, and you know the rest." He told the friend to "have a wad for them, and let them have it in nice chunks. It is one of the best houses here, and you will have every physical comfort. Give them a simple, direct, personal, concrete message that has a razor edge in it."[18] Sensing "a real victory" on the Colgate campus, Buchman marveled at "how men respond to the vital truth."[19]

Unlike traditional evangelism, Buchman's work appealed to students because of his individual approach. One of his frequently repeated truisms noted that "you can't drop eye medicine out a third story window"—meaning that any Christian approach must be precise and direct. The evangelist and his colleagues spent hours talking personally with students, identifying and addressing their spiritual needs—practicing soul surgery. After speaking at Princeton Theological Seminary, he wrote, he "was busy in interviews until Friday morning, seeing a different man every half hour. I saw my last man on Thursday's schedule on Friday morning at twenty minutes to three, and my first man on Friday's schedule came at half past six."[20] He followed up these interviews with personal letters. Evangelizing other students was "a great game," he told a Princeton student. "The fun of it comes when you get your first man, and you are getting good practice by letting down the bars between your room-mate and yourself. I am keen to know every development, and it is mighty decent of you to say that our little talk helped you. Let's come across all the time, all the way—and it's fun."[21] One young man wrote about his success with personal evangelism, stating that Buchman's "letter certainly came right in the nick of time to give me new strength to do the work that we have been talking about."[22] Another student confessed his lack of evangelical success, admitting to "Mr. Bookman" that "I am still the coward thru and thru [sic] and have not been able to approach anyone to make of him a Christian."[23] This intimate pastoral attention was a real rarity in society increasingly dominated by large institutions and mass media.

Inspired by Buchman, Princeton's Philadelphian Society made this kind of personal evangelism the foundation of its work. Shoemaker told the Society's board in 1920 that "individual evangelism has been given a place on the programme every year, and little or nothing has been done. This year it has *been* the programme." Everything the Society did centered on personal work. They asked preachers to talk about individual evangelism. "The Sunday evening meeting has been turned over entirely to discussion of personal religious questions, and the sharing of spiritual experience, and the method of reaching other men."[24] Shoemaker told the board that the students themselves had done the best personal work. "We have tried to bring men to fundamental decisions, through vital religious experiences, and to get them to share these with their friends." While college men enjoyed arguing over philosophical niceties, Shoemaker concluded that this focus on individual evangelism "differs radically from trying to get men to share a certain set of intellectual views, or to cooperate in a piece of work."[25] The key was religious experience, not theology or ethics.

In Buchman's eyes, he had an incredible impact on these college campuses. He reported to Day that "things are certainly happening" at an unnamed college. "Two souls have been born today." Not only was he winning converts, he was also changing behavior. After a "luminous thought"—another term for direct guidance from God—he organized "a marvelous skating party last night…which has set everyone buzzing in that particular circle and it may mean that the entire crowd will give up dancing."[26] After a visit to the University of South Carolina, Buchman told Shoemaker, "There has been a mighty movement begun here. The Y.M.C.A. Secretary says that nothing has come into the Christian life of the University—Eddy's campaign, and the other things—that has so vitally stirred the men to definite action for Christ."[27] Similarly, Shoemaker reported significant success at Princeton. As he told the board of the Philadelphian Society in 1920, the work resulted in "unlikely men brought into the Kingdom by their friends; men living defeated Christian lives awakened to new power; men on the outside roused to an unprecedented interest in religion; and the group at the centre bound together in a bond of common experience and a joy of conquest that has not been known here in years."[28] Wherever they went, Buchman and his followers claimed a substantial impact on the religious lives of students and the moral character of the school.

These statements have to be taken with a grain of salt, however. The work was narrow as well as deep; it affected a small group of students profoundly, but appears to have made little impact on most. The Princeton cell—the strongest in the network—gained the fervent dedication of a group of men, but one Buchman follower suggests the group was small.[29] This reflects a pattern that runs throughout the history of the Buchman movement, of grand but unsubstantiated claims for its own importance.

Buchman and his followers realized that they could expand their reach on college campuses by starting with students at prep schools, mainly in the Northeast. The potential benefits once the boys got to college, they felt, were large. Before he left Hartford, Buchman told President Mackenzie that the prep school students are "the finest and the best. They, for the great part, go on to one of the four great schools, Harvard, Yale, Princeton and M.I.T.—there invariably becoming the leading factors on the college campus. Here is your point of contact— which will give you an intimacy when the fellows go on to college."[30] At a prep school in Chattanooga, Day took a "picked group of boys (some interested in religion and some not, but all leaders)" off by themselves for the weekend. "Here we were able to meet their real needs under conditions that make it all very normal and natural." The boys then shared their experiences with the entire school. "They were able to do what no outside speaker could possibly do and the life of boy after boy was changed. I was kept busy from eight a.m. till one and two a.m. the next day seeing boys every half hour and then they came in groups at the end."[31]

Buchman and the rest sensed that seminary students needed even more spiritual help than did those in college or prep school. Day told a reporter that men preparing for ministry were caught in "mental misery." Despite the church's expectations, "they are assailed by temptations which make them ashamed. They do things which choke them with a sense of self-contempt, a sense of hypocrisy. . . . One feels that these places are full of repression, full of unuttered sin." He believed that seminary faculty, more concerned with theological minutiae than with the religious experiences of their students, were no help. "Their only experience of religion is a memory. They tell the students what happened years ago, not what happened coming down in the tram, or in the home last night. They have no reality for these desperate students, who spend half their time studying the soul-killing controversies of long-ago theologies, and the other half in fighting temptations sharp as steel."[32] Day told Buchman that "our whole method in the training of our ministers is wrong. We need men on our faculties who are living in the glow of first hand experience in winning men to Christ. With most of our professors these experiences have become a memory and they have no fresh food to give their men."[33] This critique of seminary education echoed Buchman's experience at Hartford, where he felt that the faith of the faculty was too dry and intellectual.

To meet these needs, Buchman proposed furthering "the vitalisation [sic] of our theological seminaries by having the little groups of two's and three's entering and getting thereby an opportunity to change the life."[34] After a visit to Virginia Theological Seminary, Shoemaker reported that "there is something close to a revival going on. Those men are thinking in terms of each other and of really winning people. . . . I talked with men in interview from nine in the morning to twelve at night two whole days and I never saw greater hunger or greater sincerity. One or two real conversions."[35] Buchman and his colleagues believed that all ministers should be personal evangelists, and they aimed to turn all seminaries into training schools for that work.

To strengthen these various cells and to build connections between them, Buchman and his colleagues developed the hallmark of his movement—the house party. After his days with the YMCA and in China, Buchman sensed that revival rallies were not effective, especially for the elite audiences he was hoping to reach. Pastorally, he preferred personal evangelism to big meetings. Culturally, rallies smacked of sweaty preachers on the sawdust trail. In place of sermons and speeches, Buchman believed that young people wanted to hear people like themselves talk about their religious experiences. As one follower put it, "they wanted neither creed nor argument but they would listen to witness."[36] This story telling—which included both confessions of sin and experiences of salvation—came to be known as "sharing."

Buchman found that house parties—weekend gatherings at a private home or a country inn—provided settings conducive for sharing. Young people from prominent families were used to spending the weekend at country homes, playing tennis, dancing, and mingling with others from their set. Buchman used this model for his meetings. In intimate and comfortable surroundings, house party participants could tell others about their sin and salvation. Over the course of the weekend, individual and group sharing was interspersed with good meals, athletics, and casual conversation. Buchman invited Melancthon Jacobus, dean at Hartford, to a party, noting that "these houseparties [sic] are very informal, and proceed on a program of life. We never make any arrangements for formal addresses, but there are abundant opportunities for personal interviews." There was nothing ascetic involved; he assured

Jacobus that the location "has the atmosphere of a large country house, with excellent table."[37] The house party was a creative adaptation of an elite social practice for religious purposes.

The first American house party was at Yale in the fall of 1921, with students from Princeton and elsewhere also in attendance. Instead of a large crowd, Buchman invited a select group. He chose the group leaders carefully, too, observing that "some men can land one man while others can land another."[38] This "personalized" model worked so well that they organized house parties for prep school students as well as students at women's colleges, including Vassar and Wellesley. As Buchman told a Princeton colleague, "We had our first women's House Party last weekend and it was a corker."[39] Most of the parties were gender-segregated, although men led most of the parties for women. Buchman hoped that Shoemaker could help with one women's meeting, because the woman organizing it "has not yet had enough background to adequately guage [sic] the weight of different opinions and diagnose people and situations. We do not want these house parties to deteriorate into conferences talking pious platitudes."[40] By the spring of 1924 Buchman could report that "house parties are in rare power.... Harvard will have had her fourth house party for this year by the time this reaches you, and you simply can not stop the movement. Williams, Vassar, and Juniata will have had their second."[41]

The house parties were extraordinary experiences for the participants. "Everybody was impressed with the spiritual power of most of these meetings," one group report declared, "the utter frankness of the speakers, and the perfect peace, abandon and unconventionality which characterized them."[42] The meetings usually opened with the participants getting to know each other on a deep level. As they talked, an observer noted, Buchman pointed out "that the walls dividing us are already crumbling and that from now on, we completely drop our masks of self-consciousness or anything akin to that; that sincere, natural attitudes one toward another are one of the big objectives of House Parties, and it certainly gives an air of wholesomeness to the whole gathering." Once the barriers were down, participants began to tell stories "of their false hypocritical standing, living the conventional life among their associates" while hiding their "jealousy, pride, [and] prevarication.... Gossip and criticism behind one's back, is [sic] frankly confessed to." This observer hastened to point out, however, that it all felt natural; "Buchman has come along and put a sugar coating on the pill by keeping the emotional reaction one of joy and happiness in new-found friends."[43] Buchman and his colleagues knew that their target population looked down on the emotionalism of traditional revivalism, and so tried to keep the house parties "natural."

Nevertheless, the house parties often provoked deeply emotional responses. One woman realized "that I have never been happy before Sunday. Since then my whole life has changed, and I am just so wonderfully happy that I can't help wanting to share it."[44] Another told Sherwood Day that a house party "was the entrance to a new life, a real 're-birth' as you call it. The wonderful frankness, the disappearance of all superficialities were a revelation." Since the party "people are so much more interesting; everything has added zest. It is really like taking a dose of moral and spiritual cod liver oil. (Please excuse the analogy.) And then the sheer good fellowship and fun of it."[45] But the parties were not always happy affairs. In trying to convert another, one participant noted, "Confession from ourselves doesn't count—unless it be confession *that hurts*. People know when you're really telling something that counts for you to tell, and when you're only telling an experience that, though sacred, may not hurt you to tell."[46] After struggling for two weeks after a house party, one woman wrote Day, "I've decided I might as well go to it and get it done. I *have* cheated at school, and I've always been so desperately ashamed of it that when you shot this question at me at Havre de Grace I denied it."[47]

Building on connections he had developed in China, Buchman also planted cells in England. Ever since his first visit in 1908, Buchman had a pronounced case of Anglophilia; he particularly seemed to enjoy dropping the names and titles of the aristocrats he met. In Britain in 1920 to look up the sons of a China acquaintance, he met several students at Cambridge, many of whom had fought in the war. He told Dean Jacobus at Hartford that "a movement akin to that at Princeton has developed at Cambridge," adding somewhat immodestly, "those closest to the work feel that it is vital that I stay for most of the first term."[48]

Buchman reported to Hartford president Douglas Mackenzie that his work in Britain was a great success. One person told him "that this message is the only constructive solution he has yet found for England." Anticipating his later work in international affairs, he noted guidance "on the part of one of the young men who has changed, in a very wonderful way, a country's policy." Unfortunately, Buchman did not name the country or the policy changed. He breathlessly described an upcoming meeting in England, to be attended by several important athletes and organized by "the fourth most influential undergraduate at Cambridge."[49] Buchman's reference to the elite athletes reflects his

concern for the "key men," his fascination with influential people, and
his self-importance.

The center of Buchman's work in Britain soon shifted to Oxford.
His colleagues often compared his work with that of John Wesley's
Oxford evangelists of the eighteenth century and John Henry
Newman's "Oxford Movement" of the nineteenth. As one supporter
stated, "Oxford would contribute the dignity so essential to a revival of
religion." He concluded that "Cambridge [is] the sports University, and
Oxford the home of new religions."[50] Some Oxonians, however, did
not like Buchman's movement. The Buchman movement, one stated,
only sought "the reflected glory and reflected publicity of the true
Oxford Movement."[51] A somewhat critical Catholic priest described the
work as "simple" and "primitive," reflecting the movement's American
roots. "The appeal to a crowd instinct is more successful over there;
people are less afraid of looking ridiculous."[52]

Stories of the Twice-Born Men

In the early 1920s British writer Harold Begbie had heard rumors of
"a new knowledge of religion [that] is spreading among men who may
exercise a strong influence on English-speaking civilisation during the
next fifty years."[53] The author of several books about religious leaders
and their conversions, he wanted to know more. He attended one of
Buchman's English house parties and he met several of the evangelist's closest followers, who told him their stories, which he assembled
into a 1923 book called *More Twice-Born Men*. The stories reveal how
Buchman understood the spiritual maladies of postwar college men.

Begbie noted that Buchman considered "privacy essential to his
method," because of his "intense preoccupation of individual persons." To protect this privacy, the author gave each of the young men
nicknames, and referred to Buchman with only the initials "F.B." His
description of Buchman, however, is unmistakable, and worth quoting
in full.

> In appearance he is a young-looking man of middle life, tall,
> upright, stoutish, clean-shaven, spectacled, with that mien of scru-
> pulous, shampooed, and almost medical cleanness, or freshness,
> which is so characteristic of the hygienic American. His carriage
> and his gestures are distinguished by an invariable alertness. He
> never droops, he never slouches. You find him in the small hours

of the morning with the same quickness of eye and the same athletic erectness of body, which seem to bring a breeze into the
breakfast-room. Few men so quiet and restrained exhale a spirit of
such contagious well-being. A slight American accent marks his
speech, and is perhaps richly noticeable only when he makes use
of American colloquialisms. The voice is low but vigorous, with
a sincere ring of friendliness and good humour—the same friendliness and good-humour which are characteristic of his manners.
He strikes one on a first meeting as a warm-hearted and very
happy man, who can never know what it is to be either physically
tired or mentally bored.

This was the Buchman—kindly, energetic, fresh and respectable—that
attracted the devotion of young men on both sides of the Atlantic.

Over the course of a weekend, Begbie talked with several men in
Buchman's circle, three Americans and three Britons. Some, he noted,
criticized Buchman's theology or his style, but they were all fiercely
loyal to "the man who had worked a great miracles in their lives, and
who was by far the most remarkable man of their experience in spite of
everything that troubled either their taste or their judgment."

The men and their stories had much in common. They were all
attractive, intelligent, and talented, from socially prominent families.
They impressed Begbie deeply, "some of them so brilliant in scholarship, others so splendid in athletics, and all of them, without one exception, so modest and so gloriously honest." He noted that "they were
men of the first class, men whom one may fairly call not only the fine
flower of our English-speaking civilisation, but representative of the
best hope we possess of weathering the storms of materialism which
so palpably threaten to overwhelm the ship which carries the spiritual
fortunes of humanity." One was an athletic star—Begbie named him
"Rugger Blue"—at Cambridge. Another, Begbie wrote, "was 'an absolute topper.' I was told that everybody loved him. Again and again he
figured as the hero of a tale or the author of a good saying." Another
Englishman, "Beau Ideal," "conspicuous in the house-party for his
good looks...was a man well known at Eton and Oxford." Begbie
summarized him as "the perfectly healthy, sport-loving, and well-bred
young Briton at his topmost best." Without exception, these men were
those Buchman tagged as "key men," influential leaders who could be
useful if converted.

Buchman's movement was unique, Begbie felt, because it appealed
to such men. He found that Buchman "was able to do, quite quietly,

rationally, and unconventionally, a work among the educated and the refined which hitherto I had chiefly associated with a more exciting propaganda directed to the broken earthenware of our discordant civilisations." Begbie seemed almost surprised that evangelical Christianity could appeal to men of their class. "I discovered that he could change the very life of students and scholars in the course of conversation, change that life as profoundly and persuasively as ever I have known it changed by emotional missionaries among the ignorant and base."

These men had all grown up in conventionally religious homes, but they felt spiritually inadequate. One young philosopher was the son of an English vicar; in his youth religion meant "wearing black clothes, playing no games, and reading only 'Sunday' books on Sunday." Another reported that his father had never spoken to him "with the least intimacy about religion. His exhortations consisted of a friendly smack on the back, accompanied by the admonition, 'Keep straight, old man,' as if that could do any good to a fellow up against it." One student, Begbie reported, "spent his boyhood in a small American country town, characterised by all the respectabilities and pruderies of a thoroughly compromising civilisation, entirely without the inspiration of the great realities." If these men did encounter warm faith in their childhood, it came from their mothers, not their distant and cool fathers. Almost all of them grew up in the church, but their Christian commitment was intellectual, not personal.

They found this same conventional religiosity once they went to school. An American remembered that the religion taught in his prep school was lifeless. A Briton observed that at Oxford he avoided anything "so contrary to the established customs of good breeding as personal discussions concerning the hypothetical relations of an unproved soul with a theoretical God." Even their ministry was formal. Shoemaker, named "The Virginian" by Begbie, went into missionary service during World War I, but confessed "that if he had touched one man that summer it was all he did, and that man not vitally." Henry Pitney Van Dusen of the Philadelphian Society, nicknamed "Princeton," told of talking with a young man with a personal problem—most likely a physical, even sexual one. Van Dusen recommended "cold baths, no lounging about, brisk habits of mind and body." When this did not work, the young man asked if there were other options. Limited by his conventional faith, Begbie reported, "Princeton" could suggest nothing else.

Despite—or perhaps because of—their conventionally Christian homes, each of these young men struggled with sin. Their sin, and their shame about their sin, was an obstacle to living a truly Christian life. In Begbie's eyes, the distinguishing mark of Buchman's work was "the exclusive and pathological emphasis he lays on the power of sin to rob a man's soul of its natural health—sin being understood, not merely as great vices, but as any motion in the will contrary to such excellence as that soul might reach by a genuine desire for spiritual evolution."

In some cases the sin was fairly explicit. For instance, one young man, the athletic star, found himself caught up in an unnamed "moral struggle," most likely sexual. "It was something of which the mere disposition made him ashamed." He "was more than disheartened—I was pretty sick of myself." Among his fellow students, "there were discussions on the subject. Some were for cold baths, others for physical exercises, and a few were advocates of developing will-power." Another alludes to bad habits inspired by a schoolmaster "who was tormented by a devil of lust." The church with its conventional faith was no help in resisting these carnal temptations.

More often, however, sin was a mental or spiritual block that kept the believer from God. Buchman told Begbie that a healthy will could choose God, but sin divided the will and blocked out God. Rather than just a bad act, Begbie wrote, "sin is that which hinders the evolution of the human race and the growth of the individual man. . . . It may be murder or pride; it may be dishonesty or intolerance. It is anything which impoverishes spiritual power, and deflects the personality from fulfilling its highest purposes." For instance, the "Virginian" had "a certain sense of lordship in his mind" when he was a child. "He liked his own way, felt himself irritated by check, stung by correction, and incapable of seeing life from any point of view but his own." Another man remembered having spent his youth under the cloud of resenting his parents, which led to a picture of God as distant and uncaring. This led him into atheism.

For these men Buchman connected sin and shame—one theological and one psychological, but both reflecting a self that is tormented by repression, self-will, or doubt. His converts were most often burdened not by sin itself, but by guilt for what they might have done. Although Begbie did not use the term, Buchman and his followers came to call this living in sin or shame "the defeated life," language borrowed from the Keswick movement.

Unlike many Christians, Buchman adopted a subjective definition of sin, focused on feelings instead of a detailed code of behavior. Sin was whatever made one feel sinful. His yardstick for these feelings was what Presbyterian mission executive Robert Speer called the Four Absolutes.

"Jesus was the teacher of absolute principles," Speer wrote. "Perfection was His standard. Right is to be right. To know whether it is right or wrong, drag it into Jesus' presence, and see how He looks at it and how it looks before Him." Jesus' absolutes, Speer wrote, were honesty, purity, unselfishness, and love.[54] Throughout his work Buchman used these absolutes as the guideline for judging all actions, and suggested that his followers use them to critique their own behavior.

Buchman's favorite absolute seemed to be absolute purity, reflected in the emphasis on sex in much of his work. As noted in the previous chapter, Buchman got a reputation at Penn State for his great interest in sexual sinners. Day told another evangelist that sex problems were "almost universal—9 out of 10 was underestimate [*sic*]."[55] This interest in sexuality may have had its origin in either theological or practical reasons. Buchman's biographer Lean argues that he saw "sexual indulgence as one of the most common barriers to a full experience of Christ," while another historian suggests that Buchman used sexual sin as an evangelical tool, an easy way to convict young men.[56]

The men featured in Begbie's book came to see their sin at some time of crisis. For Shoemaker, it was a crisis of confidence, when his missionary work in China felt unproductive. Other crises were more immediate. The rugby hero fought his moral battle in a "pitiful condition of mind." Another athlete found himself in the hospital after a "Rugger smash," leaving him to wrestle with sexual temptations.

Almost miraculously, Buchman appeared at each moment of crisis. He visited the bedside of the injured rugby player. He came to Peking as Shoemaker struggled with his ineffective missionary work. In other cases, a friend introduced Buchman to a man in need. In each case, the evangelist went to the heart of the matter—he confronted the young man's sin. Buchman told one Oxford student, "You are disorganized, without a centre—without Christ." As another undergraduate talked about the social issues of the time, Buchman cut in, "Those things aren't disturbing you. You know what's robbing you of peace, don't you?" Then and there, the student said, Buchman "began stirring up the mud." Buchman brooked no nonsense, and cut directly to the hidden sin, the shame that was keeping the man from victory.

Buchman was skillful in eliciting confessions. One British student remembered that "for the first time in my life I had deliberately and gladly made a fool of myself before a perfect stranger. I had told him things I had never breathed to another; I had told him of all my laughable vanities and dishonesties that make the stuff of a man's most intimate life." For the first time in his life, the rugby star tore up his moral life by the roots "and held it out to another man. The feeling of this was not, as I should have thought, one of shame and disgrace, the bitterest humiliation a decent fellow can experience; on the contrary, it was one of tremendous relief." In Peking, Shoemaker told Buchman "my temptations and my sins. They came out almost before I knew it. For the first time they were outside myself, in words, words that startled and shamed. He understood. We got it all into the open."

This was "soul surgery" in action. When men came to him talking of their theological difficulties or intellectual objections to Christianity, Begbie wrote, Buchman listened and said, "It isn't any intellectual difficulty which is keeping you from God. It is sin." In nine cases out of ten, Begbie noted, "the diagnosis is true, for he is now so great a master in what he calls soul-surgery that he knows the facial indication of almost every sin which men think they can keep to themselves." One of Buchman's American followers saw the work in scientific terms, rather than religious ones. "He deals with the secret sinner not emotionally, not creedally." The evangelist challenged the "patient's" rationalizations. "If the man again protests that he has asked God again and again to come to him, F. asks, 'With your whole will?' Then he explains that the sufferer is attempting to lie to himself, as well as to God, and that it is only disease, this secret sin, which could make him so foolish." The convert continued the medical metaphor, describing Buchman as focused on

> getting the sin into the open, and showing it to its victim in all its horror and loathsomeness. He uses the knife, for he is a surgeon and no dispenser of drugs. He doesn't believe in narcotics; he believes in eradicating the disease, cutting it clean out by the roots. He is terribly incisive, in love. He makes you hate your sin, almost yourself, but he makes you feel he cares for you all the time. It is F.'s ruthless insistence on sin as an act of the will, a deliberate act, an act of the affections, which rouses men in this case to confront the truth of their condition.

This is deeply physical language about shame.

As Walter and Buchman wrote in *Soul-Surgery*, the cure for sin and shame was surrender to God. Since, for Buchman, sin was a matter of a divided will, turning from sin required healing that divide. Begbie reported that Buchman told men "that if they would be happy and undistracted they must be *whole-hearted*"—they had to surrender their entire lives to God. One English convert declared that change was surrendering "the sins of our choosing, the fear and shame, with which we tie ourselves about, which prevent us from living always thus simply and nobly." Conversion also required surrendering control over one's life, putting one's fate in the hands of God. He stated "that only this faith in the tireless working of God in our lives could let loose our buried energies, could bring us to take risks with our wealth and reputation." At his time of crisis in Peking, Samuel Shoemaker "knew that he was at a turning-point in his vocation." He could either surrender to the world, or surrender to God. As he lay in bed, he remembered, "there came to me a distinct Voice, and that Voice said, *'There is no work of Mine to do for him who is not wholly Mine.'*" Surrender meant giving up sin and ambition, and being totally open to God.

Buchman believed, however, that surrender wasn't enough. A convert could remain converted only by converting others. As he told one man, "if you sit still, it's hopeless; help other men." Each of Begbie's stories concludes with the subject's work among fellow students. They organized groups in their universities "with the object of keeping that spirit alive by maintaining touch with each other." They encouraged other men to meditate in the morning, so that "evil thoughts drained clean out of [them], and [they] really did become vitally conscious of invisible power." One spoke to a gathering at an English college, Begbie reports; "all this he did in so masculine and sincere a fashion that a group soon formed in his room of men who really longed for spiritual life—a life which they could not find in the formal ritual, however beautiful, of churches and chapels."

In small groups or in one-on-one talks, Buchman encouraged his followers to confess their sins to each other. He told Sherwood Day that if he really cared about men he "should be willing to share my temptations with them, to confess to them my secret thoughts." Day told of talking with a fellow seminarian "who seemed to me to be troubled...and confessed to him my own secret sin—impurity." After hearing Day's confession, "the student came to life, confessed his secret sin to me, and ended our talk by saying, 'Prayer is going to mean something now; the Bible is going to mean something now.' To both of us it seemed that religion had never been real to us before, never been alive, and that now it was the very biggest thing alive." Day concluded, "Until a man confesses his sin to another man he can never really be spiritually vital."

The result of this personal evangelism, Buchman's followers believed, was a new and full life for believers. If living in sin was defeat, conversion was victory. Such victory often had physical as well as spiritual signs. Shoemaker reported seeing Buchman's converts in Peking, previously suffering men "with shining eyes, glad voices, happy as the day is long.... Changed men! A wonderful thought; changed from darkness to light, from blindness to vision, from misery to happiness, from death to life, laughing in the joy of that change." Key to that change, Shoemaker believed, was "an experience of the *hilarity* of Christianity really lived." For Buchman's followers, Christian life was a challenging yet joyous experience, liberation from shame into a vital faith.

A key part of this vital faith was community. The university of the 1920s, with growing enrollments and specialized classes, could feel impersonal to students. Buchman's network helped to fill that need. "They are fellows who have found something worth finding," Shoemaker said. "We never meet but what we have a good time. This is far from the professional mirth of certain sorts of religious people. It is the laughter of men who really know there is a way out in this world, and who are doing their best to make it known to others."

Garrett Stearly, the son of an Episcopal bishop and a long-time Buchman supporter, remembered meeting the evangelist and a dozen other students in Princeton in the spring of 1924.

> The men struck me as modern, capable, out-going, happy and friendly. I felt I was with people who really enjoyed life and had a refreshing and neverending sense of humor. Yet all of them gave the impression, in an indefinable way, that they knew where they were going and genuinely relished it. Buchman was obviously the center of their interest. They enjoyed his company and were quite clearly looking to him for stimulus and creative direction. They were at ease with him; not at all dominated, as is so often the case with a "religious leader." We were all "at home" with each other.

Stearly noted that this group was "quite different from what I had been used to at Yale."[57] It gave meaning and structure to the lives of these young men.

This cell group community became the heart of Buchman's movement. Most worked with the movement for their entire lives, dedicated to bringing others the same vital Christian experience they found. With Buchman they found an answer to the spiritual crises of elite college men in the 1920s—a compelling faith, a way to deal with guilt or shame, and a tight community. They told their stories in Begbie's book and elsewhere, to change others and change the world. The movement did not have a systematic theology or dense theoretical works—it had these stories of changed lives. They were the core of Buchman's gospel.

The Furnace that Forges the Prophets

This evangelical work among college students built Buchman's movement, attracting his first and most dedicated supporters. Despite his efforts at confidentiality, it also led to the movement's first controversy when conflict at Princeton University drew the attention of national media. The controversy reshaped Buchman's evangelical work.

Buchman and his colleagues had a confrontational evangelical style, committed to challenging men's sins and tearing them out by the roots. The result, they believed, would be a vital Christian faith. That approach, however, clashed with the culture at schools like Princeton, where Christianity was socially acceptable but fervent Christianity was not. A secretary of the Philadelphian Society, Princeton's student Christian association, argued that few students made a commitment to Christ because they thought it was socially risky. "To be a good, all-round, Brooks-suited Princetonian is the ambition of most. And that ideal is way below the Christian one."[58] While many students may have claimed to be Christians, one evangelist wrote, they only mouthed "religion on this basis of a play-it-safe conservatism [which] becomes part of the *code of a gentleman,* instead of that impassioned power that finds itself at the heart of every true believer."[59] Their Christianity was cultural rather than committed.

Buchman's evangelists believed, however, that students wanted something exciting in their lives, and that a vital and exciting Christianity could supply it. Postwar young people were looking for intense experiences of reality, associate secretary Ray Purdy declared, wherever they could find them. "They drink. They are immoral. They do the things in the whole gamut of flagrant commandment breaking, and exult in it," he told the Society board. "Men want something real," he concluded, "and if they can get it in the realm of supernatural Christianity they are going to take it. It means that religious revival, if revival there is, is going to be tremendous, sincere and vital. It means that Christianity is going to possess the whole man, or none of him at all."

To bring about such a revival, Purdy believed, required challenging Princeton, its students, and their cultural Christianity. He told the Philadelphian Society's board that its first purpose was "to confront men, individually and collectively, with the whole Gospel of Christ and its implications for them, and to guide men in Christian decisions."[60] Purdy wrote in the campus paper that "Christianity is nothing more nor less than a passionate devotion to Jesus Christ, and a desire to follow Him in all things, even unto death." He regretted that few Princeton students felt such a passion or were willing to live a God-guided life. In their fear of "being thought queer," men consigned themselves to mediocrity and "unconstructive" religion.[61] Privately, Purdy told a university administrator that "the day in which we live demands a far greater absolutism, both in moral life and in economic life, and I am convinced that the real key to solving these lies in a complete acceptance of Christ."[62] This was a challenging, demanding Christianity, sectarian instead of cultural. Purdy and his colleagues expected a lot of themselves, and of students.

This challenging attitude often rubbed people the wrong way. A Princeton alumnus recalled seventy years later that Buchman and his followers "wanted people to be better than people could possibly be, setting high standards that people couldn't live up to." This moralism was not popular with many on campus, he concluded. "If you were following Buchman, you were a goody-goody."[63] Shoemaker's wife recalled that a group of undergraduates thought one of his sermons "far too judging, exaggerating both the sins and needs of the undergraduate body, and they found him demagogic."[64]

Buchman and his colleagues welcomed this controversy as proof of their impact; in their eyes, Christianity was difficult and martyrdom was a sign of fidelity. In the midst of one crisis, Buchman told Shoemaker that "persecution is the furnace that forges the prophets."[65] In 1921 Van Dusen noted that "no Christian Association which is worth the name can fail to arouse some hostility." The Philadelphian Society's vigorous work "raised issues, drove wedges, brought men face to face with the futility and inadequacy of their own lives and drove home with power and persistence the full implications of Christian life and Christian service."[66] At times the opposition at Princeton was so strong that Buchman and his followers sensed that they were caught up in a supernatural struggle between good and evil. Buchman wrote Shoemaker "we must be on our guard that we are not deflected from the pathway by the Evil One who oftentimes poses as an angel of light."[67]

Buchman's critics at Princeton had a variety of reasons for their opposition. Some objected to being treated as pagans ripe for conversion. Others found evangelical Christianity vulgar. Several objected to Buchman's focus on sin, specifically on sins of the flesh. According to one student, the Philadelphian Society "seems to think that Sin equals sex." He heard stories of how visiting evangelists attempted to convert men, entering "a student's room and gradually accusing him of 'Sin,' and thus taking him off his guard, to lead up to a possible confession of sometimes imagined 'sins,' and thence to the general subject of religion."[68]

These rumors about sex and confessions of sex at Princeton echo others throughout the Buchman movement's history, particularly concerning homosexuality. According to his biographer, "Buchman's supporters believed that a number of their most active opponents were practicing homosexuals who felt that Buchman's message posed a threat to their life style."[69] Meanwhile, as at Penn State and in China, critics suggested that Buchman and his colleagues were obsessed with homosexuality and might themselves be gay.

These rumors led Princeton president John Grier Hibben to worry about Buchman's influence on students. In 1922 he told Shoemaker that the evangelist was not welcome at the university. "He really feels you have been unwise in handling certain men," Shoemaker told Buchman, suggesting that these misunderstandings were due to "hearsay" or "because you had put to [men] a proposition too great for them to face honestly and they took it out criticizing you."[70] Less than two years later, Shoemaker himself was forced out by the student leaders of the Philadelphian Society. He was succeeded by Purdy, however, so Buchman remained influential at Princeton.

While Buchman's work among college students was controversial at Princeton, it had a low profile nationally until the fall of 1926. That September a group of Buchman-influenced students, led by Shoemaker and several others, organized a revival in Waterbury, Connecticut. A reporter for an Episcopal magazine was alarmed by the students' confrontational style and focus on public confession. In the first printed use of the word, the reporter concluded that "Buchmanism is becoming a very powerful cult in the Episcopal Church."[71] *Time* magazine, founded by Henry Luce, the son of a China missionary who had worked with Buchman, picked up on the story. It described Buchman as "smooth, with a long, intelligent nose, a hungry eye. He is to be seen from time to time traveling first class on the principal transatlantic liners." The evangelist was "*persona grata* among a group of serious-minded young men distinguished by their piety and their wealth" on campuses in the United States and Britain. Buchmanism, the article argued, was preoccupied with "the strain of auto-eroticism,...one 'sin' which, it is remarked, The Founder never mentioned."[72]

The *Time* article hit Princeton like a storm, with students demanding an investigation of the Philadelphian Society and the possible presence of Buchmanism on campus. The editors of the campus paper demanded that it be driven out.[73] Hibben declared that "there is no place for Buchmanism in Princeton."[74] These Princeton voices used the term "Buchmanism," but none of them ever defined the word or stated why they opposed it.

Fascinated by news of a new "ism" and captivated by religious controversy at a prominent university, reporters from New York papers rushed to cover the story. An article in the *New York Sun* repeated opponents' charges that Buchmanism "is an emotional rather than intellectual process and that it places a hysterical and psychologically damaging emphasis on sex, which is particularly undesirable on account of its public confession."[75] Buchman told the *New York Times* that he was not irritated by the Princeton fracas. "One must expect that, in my work. It's the sort of attitude they had in the New Testament, isn't it?" Echoing a familiar Buchman theme, Shoemaker stated that the movement simply offered "evangelism, and evangelists have always aroused opposition. Buchmanism does for educated people what the Salvation Army does for down and outs."[76] Used to using stories in their evangelical work, Buchman's colleagues scrambled to respond to stories used against them.

After investigating the Philadelphian Society, a university committee supported its work without commenting on Buchman or Buchmanism. Under pressure from both Hibben and Buchman, however, in the spring of 1927 Purdy and the other Buchman supporters resigned from the Philadelphian Society and headed to England.[77]

★   ★   ★

During the decade of work among American and British college students, Buchman and his colleagues had created the core of a religious movement, with a network of supporters in America and Britain and connections around the world. They had developed a cohort of leaders, mainly men, who dedicated the rest of their lives to the movement. Even those who left the movement remained active in the church; some years later Van Dusen wrote that "of the fifty ablest younger ministers on the Atlantic seaboard today, somewhere near half were directed into their vocation through [Buchman's] influence."[78] The Princeton group alone included several future giants of the Protestant establishment—such as Eugene Carson Blake and Van Dusen himself, early adherents who fell away—as well as prominent lay leaders, including John D. Rockefeller III.

During the 1920s the movement continued its creative religious practices. At its house parties, it adapted a familiar social event for evangelical purposes, creating a comfortable setting to convert elite college students. It offered young people seeking excitement vital Christian experiences in place of fast cars or bootleg booze. Members wrestled with questions and rumors of sexuality, adopting psychological definitions of sin and shame. And they created a tight-knit community as a refuge in an increasingly impersonal culture.

The movement changed after the conflict at Princeton, however. Perhaps in reaction to the controversy, it became less confrontational, giving the work a more welcoming face. As the group of leaders—most of whom had been college-aged in the 1910s and early 1920s—grew up, they shifted their work to focus more on issues concerning adults. Leaving behind their previously sought anonymity, Buchman and his followers cultivated their movement's image, using the media and public meetings to present their message.

CHAPTER THREE

Possessing and Reproducing a Quality of Life

On a warm spring evening in 1931, 1,000 New Yorkers filled a ballroom at the city's plush Plaza Hotel to hear about a rapidly growing Christian movement. After prayers by an Episcopal bishop and the pastor of one of the city's leading Presbyterian churches, the gathering heard Samuel Shoemaker—now rector of New York's Calvary Episcopal Church—praise Frank Buchman and his "First Century Christian Fellowship." Twelve people testified to their personal religious experiences in the fellowship, the *New York Times* reported, "with emphasis on their intimate difficulties before they 'surrendered themselves to Christ.'"[1]

Four years after sailing for England, Buchman and his colleagues had established their movement at the heart of the American establishment. They had spent the late 1920s working in the United States and overseas, attracting ever-increasing crowds and favorable publicity. At the movement's house parties Americans, Britons, South Africans, and others found an important community and a more vital relationship with God.

Moral Re-Armament regularly recreated itself to adapt to changed circumstances. In the late 1920s and early 1930s, movement leaders expanded the focus beyond college students, reaching out to adults and families. While professing to be anti-institutional, they developed institutions to sustain their work. After more than a decade of anonymity, they embraced publicity. They reshaped their methods, pursuing personal work while organizing large evangelical campaigns for cities and countries. Buchman and his colleagues maintained their fundamental concepts and methods, but by 1932 their movement had a new public face.

An Intelligent, Workable Team

By the early 1930s, Buchman's most dedicated followers, converted as students, had become young adults. Many took outside work and attended group meetings in their free time, while a few dedicated their lives to the movement, working full-time to spread Buchman's message around the world. The group coalesced into cells, local clusters where believers could strengthen their faith and talk about the intimate matters of their lives.

Members saw the group as a surrogate family. After the death of Buchman's mother, for example, Purdy offered "our love and fellowship and eternal brotherhood[.] There is always a place for you in our little house, Frank. It may be a haven for short or long. And what we have is eternally sharable as deeply as our fellowship."[2] This family was particularly important for those whose families of origin did not understand or support their involvement with Buchman's work.

Correspondence within the group reflected the intimacy of their relationships, as members regularly reported on their activities, plans, and physical and spiritual health. In a typical letter from late 1927, Day reported to Buchman that "Phil has gone on to Montreal. Will return in a few days. God is using him. I do not yet see clearly how to help him most. He needs care and discipline and his physical weakness makes it hard often to discipline him." He also noted "Han and Virginia are always a joy. Their baby should be along any day now. They are marvelous about it. Ray is at Sam's resting."[3] No detail was too small to share.

Some of the reports were less positive. There was a lengthy correspondence about one member's spiritual status, and whether she should go to Europe with another member. "There has been too much gabbing, interfering, etc., in the matter by people more or less out of real touch with the situation," one man observed, and then proceeded to gab: "Harry Jacobsen for instance rather upset the applecart by going to Gene first, and telling her what he thought, and then by sharing it all around." Meanwhile, he reported, "Han rather jumped on Eleanor Forde for lack of fire, and a feeling of insincerity he felt in her Monday afternoon."[4] The letter continues like that for four pages. While almost unintelligible out of context, the intensity of this spiritual gossip suggests the movement's intimacy. It also shows how their commitment to absolute honesty sometimes made for confrontational friendships.

Movement members shared God's guidance for each other and the movement. Each morning, individually or in groups, members listened for God's voice, hoping to receive direction for their lives. Sometimes this guidance was momentous—one man felt lead to go to China. Other times it was trivial, like the choice of a particular train to New York. To make sure they had heard God correctly, they "checked" their guidance with each other. Some recorded their guidance in special books, while others scribbled it on random pieces of paper.

Whatever the form, the raw guidance was often vague. In 1929 Purdy listed one day's guidance on the back of a telegram. "Reveal an open door saviour to me. When is Virgil's vacation? Ted stay till train? We'll touch somewhere no rigidity with Virgil. Virgil in power. John is going to right. Virgil and Paul stay to fill envelopes. Help in the work. Marge help with the large packages."[5] Shoemaker's notes in the back of a datebook are a similar mixture of spirit and routine. "The spirit of deep peace shall be upon you. Drink deeply of me. Without me ye can do nothing. Fear not. Go and be my witnesses. Fearlessness. Go to bed—you're tired. Give Al Campbell 50 dollars."[6] These few phrases, ranging from theological insight to practical concerns, served to direct the movement and the lives of its members.

Living under guidance required significant flexibility and faith. Shoemaker told a high school classmate that "the first suffering I had to do was change my plans. I still hate it. I like grooves and routines. That is why God puts me in suitcases and tells me at seven o'clock to take a nine o'clock boat when they say there isn't any berth."[7] During their engagement, Ray Purdy's wife recalled, he "knew it was God's will that we should marry." Even though "humanly" he wanted the engagement, he would have broken it off if the guidance came to do so. "Deeper than that," she concluded, "his wish was that I should find God and live the highest, fullest life possible for me—and if that were to be married to someone else or not married at all, he was ready for it."[8] The opposite of guided living was living "humanly," selfishly relying on personal wisdom rather than surrendering to God's.

Conflict often arose when members received and shared guidance for each other. In the late 1920s, for example, several members of the group were planning an evangelical expedition to South Africa; they hoped that others, including Shoemaker, might join them. One wrote Buchman, "In the same quiet time it had come to me 'Sam go South Africa' although, as I said, it had not been mentioned before."[9] A few days later he wrote again, reporting that everyone else had the same guidance—"Never did I know of anything to so check all the way round as Sam's call to join you."[10] Purdy had gone so far as to make reservations for Shoemaker, adding to Buchman, "This is under guidance—no one has definitely made up their minds as yet. I feel that perhaps Sam may go with you."[11] Meanwhile Shoemaker's own guidance clashed strongly with this message, and—after some struggle—he did not go. After several such conflicts, the movement discouraged receiving guidance for others.

While everyone listened for God's guidance, the guidance that came to Buchman was the most important. He laid out the strategy for evangelical campaigns and freely advised his followers on matters professional and personal. One observer declared that "Frank's guidance is always right."[12] A member reported his guidance to Buchman, but added, "We want always to be available for you in anything you want us to do, and I know you will not hesitate to share whatever guidance comes to you about us."[13]

Buchman was not only the authority on guidance, but also the father of this extended family. Shoemaker's fiancé enthused to him, "Your children owe a good deal to you, you know, and nothing we can do can really repay you!"[14] Purdy and his wife wrote "of our love and prayers and of the profound impression that your life under God has made in our lives. Nothing that we possess is adequate to reflect our understanding and appreciation of your gift."[15]

An important part of Buchman's paternal role was disciplining members. In 1930 he rebuked a young devotee for selfishness and disloyalty. "I could not even for a moment nurse any feeling of ill will, just sorrow, that you have so completely missed the way," he wrote. "I think it's been my sad duty just to show you their utter fallacy so you will have a clear vision of the cross." The man's defection, Buchman warned, wounded not only him but also the entire movement. "You have done it at costly expense to another which unless you make prompt and complete restoration will do far-reaching harm." The news had already spread through the network, and had international implications. "I have already had evidence of this from Oxford and its reverberations in America."[16]

Any betrayal was a calamity because loyalty was the glue that held the movement together. Members regularly signed their letters to Buchman "loyally."[17] Buchman thanked a prominent supporter because his "loyalty to us has been of the highest order."[18] Disloyalty, on the other hand, arose out of sin. "This loyalty business, Frank, is a great thing," Purdy wrote Buchman, "because when people are in sin, justification almost always comes out in criticism of the person who incarnates that issue. You incarnate it for many people, therefore they criticize you."[19]

Loyalty was important because teamwork was the heart of Buchman's work. Unlike many evangelists who worked alone, he created groups who brought together different skills and approaches for shared evangelical work. Such teams were a particular asset for personal work, he felt. They made it possible to reach more people, and made sure that each potential convert would meet a life-changer appropriate for their need.

The importance of teamwork is reflected in Buchman's world tour of 1924. Guidance told him to "go round the world. Take an apostolic group with you. A one-man endeavor is a false principle."[20] He felt that the trip would be an important experience for Shoemaker. "You have been riding rough shod over experiences which have forged Sherry [Day] and I into an intelligent, workable team which any number of forces have constantly been trying to deflect and absorb." The trip would give Shoemaker needed discipline.[21] Buchman recruited another Princeton alumnus, "heartily and cordially" welcoming him to join the trip. This young man, however, was to have a special role. "It would be splendid if you could gain a good knowledge of stenography. This would be a great help to you and us in the trip."[22]

With six young men—American and British students and recent graduates—Buchman visited universities and mission centers in Europe, Turkey, Egypt, and India. They organized house parties in Australia, he reported to stateside supporters, and "the changed lives set conservative Melbourne agog." As they did in American and British universities, they sought out the leading men—the headmaster at "one of the fine public schools in Australia," an Oxford rugby player, the son of a general, a prominent farmer, the prime minister—and dropped their names.[23] In a newsletter Shoemaker reported that they had done personal work everywhere they went. "This work is not spectacular, but it moves men's hearts.... We have talked with Kings and with bell-boys, with students and with theological professors."

The trip was an intense experience for the young men. It built a strong fellowship, Shoemaker wrote in a public letter; "there is no organization of our group, no president, no members, no dues, no charter. The cement between us is a common experience, a common purpose and a common faith."[24] In a personal letter to Purdy, however, Shoemaker observed that there was conflict, in part because Buchman did not accept criticism very readily. "He has been at times vindictive, and his self-justification has been most difficult, making it impossible to say *anything* to him which he does not resent or excuse—usually by claiming you are off the track." Despite this, Shoemaker acknowledged that Buchman's "willingness to discipline us and be honest with us is unique and uniquely valuable. I hope we're going to grow some by it.

It is not easy for anyone graciously to accept it, and actually to live up to it. But we want to."[25]

This epic trip helped to shape Buchman's movement. It sowed seeds for what became a world-wide organization. But it also strengthened the leadership of the American cells. Like guidance, sharing, and Buchman's discipline, it turned a group of young adults into a tightly connected movement.

A Feeling of Permanence

Shoemaker left the group halfway into the trip, returning to New York to take a call in an Episcopal parish in New York—a move that did not sit well with his mentor. While he may have been upset about Shoemaker's abandoning him halfway around the world, Buchman's deeper concern was Shoemaker's embrace of the institutional church. After his time in China, where he felt snubbed by the missionary establishment, and the conflicts at Hartford and Princeton, Buchman increasingly rejected institutions. Many of his colleagues shared his anti-institutionalism. As Sherwood Day told one supporter, "I believe God's will for me at present is for me to have no official connection with any organization. The Fellowship holds my loyaltity [sic] just because it is no organization but a very real fellowship."[26]

Despite these words, however, the fellowship did become an organization. While Buchman, Day, and the rest may have wanted to rely on faith, prayer, and individual commitment, their movement also needed money, meeting space, and legitimacy. Starting in the early 1920s, Buchman and his followers developed their own institutions as well as allying themselves with others, generally motivated by financial need. Outsiders wondered where Buchman's money came from. Some, their eye jaundiced by the fictional Elmer Gantry and the actual Aimee Semple McPherson, suspected fraud. Others, wary of the movement's politics, believed that it was bankrolled by—depending on their perspective—either wealthy industrialists or the Moscow Bolsheviks. The reality was less sinister.

After he resigned from Hartford, Buchman's followers often said, he never again held a paying job. He lived as an itinerant evangelist, with no fixed abode or institutional restrictions. But as the movement grew, so did its expenses. In 1929 its budget was more than $12,000—over $140,000 today.[27] Members stayed in big hotels and traveled on transatlantic liners. If nothing else, the group had an image to keep up.

When Buchman sent Day a check, he noted that "you need money for expenses and clothes. I feel that the Fellowship cannot afford to appear dowdy."[28] He publicly defended his lifestyle. "Why shouldn't we stay in 'posh' hotels?," he asked a reporter for *Time*. "Isn't God a millionaire?"[29]

Buchman claimed that the fellowship lived on faith. In 1934 he told a *Time* reporter that "not one of us is employed. Yet we have managed to come across. I have not received a salary since 1922, but I manage somehow to live out of my seven suitcases." He breezily concluded, "I haven't any idea of where all the money comes from."[30] Elsewhere he stated that the ministry was supported by people who were "guided" to contribute. In a handwritten note headlined "Where Does the Money Come From?", Buchman observed that "where God guides, He provides." While "oftentimes I've been down to quarter," Buchman observed, "I've never lacked food, clothes, or shelter." "Sharing," he concluded, "is the answer."[31] In 1921 he thanked a supporter, whose check "came at an opportune time. The Lord certainly does provide for me. There are times I do not know just where the next cent is coming from."[32]

But Buchman and his colleagues did know where the money was coming from. Even as they scorned institutions, they developed a network of people they could call on for money—building, in effect, a parachurch institution. Buchman himself was the chief fund-raiser. Even before he left Hartford he told an Allentown acquaintance that his seminary salary was "limited" and that "my expenses for my trips abroad must be met by contributions from friends." Buchman pointed out that his work was "meeting men's real needs. It's a work that requires money and I am having constant demands made upon me." He asked for whatever funds his friend could provide.[33] Buchman directed Shoemaker to make appeals on his behalf. In 1921 the evangelist asked his colleague to write fund-raising letters to a Greek princess and to the widow of reaper magnate Cyrus McCormick; he included advice on how to target the letter.[34] Shoemaker also developed his own leads; in one note to Buchman he reported on the potential for a legacy, which would provide "finances enough to handle this movement three times over, and to spare." He asked Buchman "to be much in prayer for an elderly English gentleman, near the end of life, with a large fortune."[35]

In his appeals Buchman urged supporters to consider the spiritual benefits of their giving. He thanked one supporter for a donation that supported the American visit of two British college students. "You have this certain satisfaction that many a parent, aunt, and sister will have much more of enjoyment this Easter in a fuller life in the younger generation as a result of their visit to this country."[36] Buchman also suggested the spiritual dangers of property—and how donating to the movement could help avoid them. Buchman told one Princeton supporter that he was "tied up now and what you want is abandon and spiritual release. I believe you want to know first-hand the power of the Holy Spirit—that your pocketbook, as well as anything else, needs to be put under that domination."[37]

Although this fund-raising was effective, Buchman and his colleagues wanted a more stable system of support. Soon after the evangelist left Hartford, they recruited a committee, called "A First Century Christian Fellowship," to support his work. The name "was chosen by a group of lawyers, businessmen and ministers in 1921," Shoemaker wrote, "because it most nearly described the purposes of the movement."[38] In 1928 they incorporated the fellowship, "so that money can be given to our work, and also be left for our work," Buchman told Purdy. He suggested a slate of board members, including himself, Shoemaker, and Day; "this organization is simply necessary from a business standpoint, so that [supporters] can give money to the work, and one of the practical things is that it is deducted from their Income Tax."[39] This committee became the institution at the center of Buchman's anti-institutional movement.

Buchman's strongest support throughout his career came from a group of wealthy New York women. In 1922 seven women made donations totaling $4,250.[40] Margaret Tjader was Buchman's most consistent supporter. From a wealthy New York family, she founded a mission organization in 1900.[41] She met Buchman through a mutual friend in New York before he went to China in 1917.[42] They quickly became close. "What a wonderful Fellowship," Buchman wrote Tjader. "We are proud to have you as the first honorary woman member of the Fellowship."[43] Tjader paid for much of the round-the-world trip in 1924, paying at least $4,000 each for the six participants.[44] She provided Buchman with a personal allowance for years; in 1929 it was $365 a month—almost $4,400 today.[45]

Tjader gave Buchman more than traveling money and friendship. The mission organization that she founded and funded gave Buchman an institutional base, providing both legitimacy and financial support. In the summer of 1925 she reported to Buchman that the mission's board had "voted to have the First Century Christian Fellowship a department of the work of the International Union Mission." She thought "if you are favorable we could so arrange that you and Sherry [Day] could eventually have salaries from the money that will be taken in for the International Union Mission as we grow and the public becomes acquainted with what we are trying to do."[46] Buchman used the mission's New York headquarters as his office.

While they welcomed Tjader into their fellowship, Buchman and his colleagues criticized her behind her back. As he prepared for the round-the-world trip that she funded, Day told Buchman that he was relieved that Tjader would not be coming along.[47] Several years later he wrote the evangelist that "we can not have compromise in any way." Tjader, he said, could only be part of the fellowship if she surrendered her self-will. "We want her to have the very best—we know what that best *is* and so we must hold her to it," Day concluded.[48] Movement members believed that only they were right, criticizing anyone who wasn't with them 100 percent.

While Tjader and her mission provided Buchman's movement office space, financial support, and legitimacy, Calvary Episcopal Church in New York was a far more important institutional base. The parish, where Shoemaker became rector in 1925, served as a headquarters and a laboratory. As one follower told Buchman, having Calvary as a center gave the movement "a feeling of permanence and a sense that the work is always going on to those of us who are away."[49]

Calvary had been one of the city's leading parishes, set on Gramercy Park on once-fashionable lower Park Avenue. By 1925, however, the neighborhood had changed, and the parish was struggling with its mission. The bishop convinced the church that Shoemaker, then traveling with Buchman, could help. Shoemaker found the idea attractive, he wrote Ray Purdy; it offered the "chance to touch many in the city in certain groups we could form; no organization which wd. [*sic*] crush life out; chance to preach."[50] He hesitated briefly—largely because Buchman had doubts—but finally accepted the call.

Calvary served Shoemaker, the movement's leading spokesman and theorist, as a laboratory, a place to refine the movement's work. He focused his ministry at Calvary on changing lives, just as Buchman had since his days in India. In one of several books from the period Shoemaker mourned that "we ministers are not putting within reach of our people the dynamic, transforming experience of conversion: we help many people, but we change few."[51] Individual change had to be the centerpiece of the entire evangelical task, his widow remembered years later; "the natural order was: change lives first; then provide groups for their fellowship and training so that the message could be

spread."[52] While the Sunday morning service at Calvary hewed closely
to the Anglican tradition, Sunday evening featured a series of speakers,
each witnessing to their faith. Shoemaker wrote that "the Sunday evening services have a place that is central in bringing new people into
touch with vivid Christian experience told in terms they can readily
understand, by people like themselves."[53]

Even more important was the regular Thursday night meeting, a
weekly three-hour house party and training session. "We asked those
persons to come who wanted to learn how to win others, one by one,
to the living Christ," Shoemaker wrote, but it also attracted others who
were new to Christianity or religion. The group used "simple terms,
to keep our words definite and elemental, to think of the very A B Cs
of religion." It became a place "for the discussion of all the varieties of
personal religious experience. Some of the personal stories which are
told of transformed lives, and the new and radiant power of Christ, are
filled with spiritual power and human interest." After two years, the
Thursday night meeting was attracting over 150 people every week,
not limited to members of the parish.[54]

A New York columnist, visiting a Thursday night meeting, described
Shoemaker as "the unmistakable American....Gaiety rested lightly
upon him, and the stamp of race. Just the magnet for a crowd of young
people." The audience was generally younger than 25, "types duplicated
at debutante parties, seen in the private offices of Big Business, at the
desk and adding machines of banks and insurance houses, in tea rooms
and automats. Evidently there was a representative there from nearly
every walk in life, and they were all at home together." Shoemaker
started the evening with a brief prayer and the biblical account of the
conversion of Paul. "It was the come-and-deliver attitude of the athletic coach to the crew; it had the thrust yet the informality of the up to
date college professor who is top-hole with the class." He called upon
one woman to tell her story, which started a flood of stories. "The idea
seems to be that the mere telling of the surrender to Christ, no matter
how simply or informally, is the act that puts a seal upon it," the journalist concluded.[55]

Shoemaker collected these stories into a series of books, each a compilation of religious experiences. "There is something perhaps which
is finally and innately dogmatic about all actual experience," he wrote
in the introduction to *Children of the Second Birth* (1930); "it happens,
and what happens is a fact, and you can't budge facts."[56] In *Twice-Born
Ministers* (1929), Shoemaker contrasted these vital experiences with
most of mainstream American Christianity, with its "singularly tame

kind of religious experience that is comforting and peace-giving but anemic, sub-normal, and very different from its prototype of apostolic days." He also criticized fundamentalists, on the other hand, who argued dogmatic points instead of changing individuals.[57]

Most contemporary Christians shied away from religious experience, Shoemaker believed, because of their "characteristically modern self-consciousness about emotion."[58] People hesitated to get emotional about religion, he believed, because they were concerned they might appear unintelligent or old-fashioned; he noted the "common opinion that an evangelical movement, which wears an emotional aspect to the average man, may succeed in picking up the lame ducks, the maladjusted, the emotionally suggestible, the gullibles generally, but that it cannot command the attention of the competent, the thoughtful, the sufficient, especially of the intellectually brilliant."[59] For example, "some old-fashioned evangelists" once visited a group meeting at Calvary. They worked "in a manner quite unlike our own, but who try, none the less, to win lives to Christ. It was an offensive method for most of us," he confessed, "and we were rather hard on those who used it."[60]

Shoemaker's books, on the other hand, contain stories about "normal" people—intelligent, socially prominent—who had had vital religious experiences. *Children of the Second Birth* contains 17 narratives of personal spiritual experience. One of the subjects was a newspaper boy, but the rest were educated, well-employed, and well-connected. Each, however, was held down by some spiritual weight. One young woman was the shyest person Shoemaker had ever seen. "There was in her beauty of spirit, and eagerness of mind, and unselfishness enough to change the world. But she was thwarted and repressed." After her change, however, "she has been used of God, and most marvelously used" in all sorts of evangelical work. An older woman came to find "an entirely new relationship of understanding" with her family; "she now often waits sensitively for the approval of a daughter she has lorded it over for years, and whom she now feels spiritually to have gone beyond her."[61]

Shoemaker shaped his ministry at Calvary to reach such people. He was "after the outsider." Reaching the "up-and-outers" required strategy and creativity, he told a colleague. "You don't approach trout with a hammer or try to grab any kind of fish by the lapel. Jesus once said be 'as wise as serpents.' There's strategy, there's humor, and there's love. When the right bait is offered with patience, the fish will take it."[62] Even in large groups, a friend recalled, Shoemaker paid attention to outsiders; he "lingered afterwards, making himself available to

strangers; speaking to anyone who might have been moved by what
had been said and wanted to talk."[63] Sensing that traditional evangelical
appeals would turn the outsiders away, he told his readers that the witness at group meetings "is all so natural, in such good taste, seasoned
with the salt of laughter, and unspoiled by threadbare phraseology."
In contrast to traditional appeals, the meetings "are kept vital by the
continual fresh experiences of those who have found the living present
power of Jesus Christ: we do not trade in stale stories, but in things that
are happening to us every week."[64]

Calvary Church served Buchman's movement as a laboratory for
evangelical techniques and as a base for its work—providing meeting space, community networks, visibility, and legitimacy. Although
Buchman shunned institutions, proclaiming his reliance on faith, he
and his colleagues used a variety of institutions, including the First
Century Christian Fellowship, Tjader's mission, and Calvary to sustain
the movement's work.

A Nationwide Revival of Personal and Realistic Religion

Several of Buchman's American colleagues became leaders in the
movement's British cells after leaving Princeton in 1927. Soon after
he arrived at Oxford, Kenaston Twitchell, one of the Princeton men,
warned Buchman that "there is need for much work and workers are
scarce."[65] There was great potential in England, he observed in another
letter. "The past weeks have enlarged our scope." But still "we have no
adequate leadership to cope with it. There are only six or seven who
can see leadership or can carry people clear through. These are rushed
to death. We need to concentrate on Oxford."[66]

As in the United States, the movement focused its attention on house
parties for students and, increasingly, adults. The printed invitation to
a house party at St. Andrews in the spring of 1928 gives an impression
of what they were like.[67] "The keynote is simple frankness and honesty
with oneself and with other people. We learn to drop the masks which
most of us assiduously keep up in our usual living. We learn not to be
afraid of each other. We make friends." Typical of the movement, the
text included testimonies. " 'It is far more interesting than any play,'
one business man said, 'the wholesomeness of it all was refreshing.' "
One woman reported that she came "a question mark and left an excla-
mation mark!"

Hastening to allay suspicions, the invitation noted that the atmosphere was "neither formal nor dogmatic; people can do and say what they like. Nothing more free from emotionalism, sentimentality, or any false pressure, could possibly be imagined." The movement was nothing new, the invitation promises; "it simply seeks to realise in practical life, the principles of the New Testament.... The naturalness of it all becomes contagious." Such parties, the invitation said, provide "lots of real laughter but also will have enduring results in individual lives, in families, and in daily life generally." They offer "another way of living that means power, peace, and right relationships with other people."

Thanks to the house parties, the movement expanded its outreach to adults. In 1929 Twitchell reported that a London man wanted to get the work going on a larger scale, particularly among business men. Twitchell was excited because the man was "on many important committees and his backing of such a venture alone would lead us into touch with most of the important people of the City."[68] Another house party— featuring "a great new advance coming and a subsequent testing by the evil one"—attracted over 140 people. "There are now about twelve centers in England and Scotland," he concluded.[69] They were also invited to work in English parishes. A vicar in Watford, a town north of London, had heard of the movement's work and asked Twitchell "to bring over a team of undergraduates to work his parish."[70]

As the movement spread, Buchman continued his fascination with nobility. Twitchell reported that the meetings in London regularly attracted "Sir Arthur and Lady Windham, very much interested." They also allowed for a "lovely time with the Queen [of Greece]."[71] Buchman enjoyed royalty—particularly Greek royalty, some of whom he met on his first European trip in 1908. He reported to his American followers from London that "the King and Queen of Greece have come in constantly to lunch and tea."[72] In 1928 he told Purdy that "King George of Greece arrived yesterday [in London]; Sam and I met him at the station, and he came and spent the evening with us. He was full of beans."[73]

Buchman's noble friends in Europe helped to build the movement. By 1928 Buchman planned a series of continental house parties, including "a house-party this weekend at Baron Wassenaar's at Cambridge; a fortnight later we go to the Dutch house-party, then probably a house-party in Germany under Countess Plessen's direction."[74] A woman in the group told Buchman that she had become "great friends" with the Greek Princess Irene. The Princess, she reported, "has the real thing now and she's simply on fire with it and says she has never been so *'internally'* happy in her life. As soon as Prince Paul arrived from England she pitched into him—and she has written to her sister in Roumania [*sic*] who is apparently very unhappy and in need of help, and told her all about it."[75]

The movement also extended beyond Europe, often into current and former British colonies; in those places Buchman's connections in Oxford, a nerve center of the British Empire, were an asset. An early success story was South Africa, where the fellowship found a pattern for its future work. In 1926 Loudon Hamilton, an early British convert, told Buchman that a group of South African students at Oxford had proposed an evangelical trip to the universities of their homeland. "Such a trip would be of enormous value to the work of the team in Oxford afterwards. It seems as if God has especially raised up this group of South Africans, who have responded marvelously."[76] Seven English- and Dutch-speaking students went to South Africa in 1928, followed by much larger parties in 1929 and 1930, including British and American leaders.[77]

Initially fellowship members visited universities and secondary schools in South Africa, doing the same work they had done in America and Britain. The headmaster of a secondary school in Rondebosch reported that thanks to the visitors some boys were "influenced directly, others indirectly, and the life of the whole school is the better for their work and what the Chapel stands for is a more real centre of our lives."[78] Another group led a ten-day meeting in Martizberg for "Varsity" students, concluding with a weekend camp. "Most of the leading spirits in the Varsity came out," an American reported home. "We had the usual happy laughter, the periods of silence, at first awkward, but soon living. Then the periods of deep and spontaneous sharing." The problems facing South African students, he noted, were just like those of students in Oxford, America, or India—"not, curiously enough, those of sport and girls and popularity; but of defeat or victory over temptation." The meeting resulted in forming two groups at the university "centering round two of the 'interesting sinners.'"[79]

As in Britain and America, the South African work was very personal; an excerpt from a letter from 16-year-old school boy to his rector shows its impact. He had talked with a visiting American and "confessed all my sins" and "felt a better man for it. Soon afterwards I made my surrender and since that moment my life has been all sunshine." A Christian's work, he learned from the visitors, was "to talk of your own sin and how you were cured by surrendering to Christ, where you know it will help others to make their decision." The result was a group "of about 30 chaps of which I am one. How glad I am they came sir! I can't tell you how much light they have enabled me to see." He ended with the conviction that "Christianity as [they] teach it is *the* religion that works."[80]

Group members worked with clergy and other adults as well as students. During a series of meetings in Durban, fellowship leaders met with twenty local clergymen and organized a camp for some younger businessmen. One declared that "he has always been a salesman but now he intends to sell something else—vital Christianity."[81] While the movement had an ambivalent relationship with the organized church in the United States and Britain, South African churches embraced its work. Local Baptists asked group members to address their annual young people's conference. Three of the British and American visitors presented information on the fellowship to the 1928 South African Presbyterian General Assembly, and group leaders met with 150 clergy in Bulawayo, Rhodesia, in 1929.[82]

Unlike their experiences in Britain and America, group members faced little controversy in South Africa. Complete strangers praised Buchman for what the group had done in the country. Churches and schools asked group members to visit, while individuals wrote requesting invitations to house parties. This success was in part due to the leaders' outreach to the local media. In 1928 one of the South Africans from Oxford visited with a newspaper editor in Cape Town, who "was most genial and offered to do anything we liked to help," he reported to Buchman; "copy in the paper, introductions anywhere in the country, etc. We felt at the moment no publicity, but probably later."[83] Later came in 1929, when group members did national radio broadcasts and reached out to other sympathetic journalists. "The publicity here has been absolutely unprecedented," an American reported, "with hardly a negative note anywhere to date." The general impression was that the work was "sane, solid, scientific, spiritual."

While the movement worked with relatively small cells in the United States and Britain, in South Africa its work reached a much broader audience. During the Johannesburg house party in 1929, 800 attended a reception at the City Hall. Clergy members of the group preached at churches all over the city. There were special groups for clergy, nurses, and doctors. The same year, close to 1,000 people attended a meeting in Pretoria where members of the group spoke informally about their personal experiences. While in the capital, group leaders met with the Governor-General, bishops, and Boer hero General Jan Smuts.[84] These large gatherings represented a change in scale for the movement.

Group leaders worked to balance this national reach with the movement's focus on individual work. One reported that the 1929 Johannesburg house party "proved immensely popular—too much so to keep them fully personalized so latterly we held separate meetings for the sermon tasters. As the H.P. [house party] progressed we drew off small groups of people, hand-picked, who were sufficiently far along to form the nucleus of local groups."[85] The group newsletter saw real potential in outreach on the national level. "Indications are that a nationwide revival of personal and realistic religion is in the offing in this country—something that will embrace church, state, professions, schools and universities, and business circles."[86] The success in South Africa, with large meetings attracting media attention, offered a pattern for the movement's future.

As the fellowship's visibility grew, members tentatively began to engage public issues as well as personal ones. At a 1929 national house party in Bloemfontein, a Professor Brooks was asked to speak "more particularly on what the Group has to say on our national problems." He told his audience that they were not "to rest satisfied until we have founded in South Africa that city whose Builder and Maker is God." Brooks identified a number of challenges facing the nation, and argued that the answer to all was "in Church and State Unity in Christ." He learned from the house party that "we have just got to give ourselves personally," surrendering to Christ.

Among the issues Brooks discussed was "racialism...between English and Dutch South Africans." The answer, he said, was individual effort—for instance, having the English-speakers learn Afrikaans. "Christ lives in all peoples and in all languages. It means thoughtfulness and courtesy on both sides." Brooks also talked to his audience about "something even harder than that"—the relation between white and black. His told his all-white audience that God's guidance "need not lead us to any particular line of action," but added that "we can build up nothing great on prejudice, hatred or even fear. There is only one solution and that is the solution of love and obedience to the demands of Christ."[87] The fellowship's answer for these public issues was the same it gave for personal problems—the need for individual change.

As the large meetings and increasing interest in public issues helped make the fellowship a national phenomenon, the time in South Africa also gave the movement a name. Like much in this history, the exact details are lost in the mist of legend, but Buchman's biographer reports that, during the 1928 visit of the Oxford students, a railroad porter chalked their luggage "Oxford Group."[88] The South African press, looking for a convenient name for the new phenomenon, adopted that name for the movement. Buchman's colleagues quickly took to the name and soon made it official when they incorporated the organization in the United States and Britain.

The Oxford Group name wasn't quite accurate—the movement had American roots and few members had an official connection with Oxford—but it was convenient. As one observer noted, "Buchman was not reluctant to let the misnomer spread because of its obvious prestige value."[89] In the British Commonwealth and other Anglophile countries, the name Oxford symbolized social status and academic rectitude— valuable for a Christian group trying to make evangelicalism socially and intellectually acceptable. The name also invited fortuitous if accidental confusion with the group of Oxford students, including John Wesley, who founded Methodism in the eighteenth century, as well as the Oxford Movement of Anglo-Catholics of the nineteenth century. An Oxford graduate pointed out that the Group started using the name during the centenary of the Oxford Movement, which "caused a natural confusion in the mind of the public." She added that "Oxford is proud of such [Anglo-Catholic] men as Newman, Keble, and Pusey, but it repudiates the Buchmanites. In the whole University there are only about two hundred members."[90] Others in Oxford welcomed the movement, while some attributed its defects to its roots across the Atlantic, calling it "an inevitable adjunct of American revivalism." "If the Oxford Groups could forget their place of origin, and become naturalized, it would increase their possibilities of useful work in England to an incalculable extent."[91] To its benefit and to the dismay of some, Buchman's movement was known as the Oxford Group (or Groups) for at least the next decade.

The success in Britain and South Africa prepared Buchman's team for building up the American work. In the fall of 1928 Ray Purdy, who left the United States after the Princeton debacle, told Buchman that "the time is coming when we will need a thorough mobilization for the American work. We shall want a vital advance in the colleges and churches. As never before the need is being cried and from all religious groups—personal evangelism. And there is nowhere else to turn but to the message."[92] From Oxford Twitchell agreed, proposing to "pick up and go home and settle down to work out a new center, probably from a Presbyterian Church." The British work could sustain itself with British leadership, he concluded.[93] A year after the Princeton controversy, movement leaders began returning to America.

The revitalized movement in America learned valuable lessons from its success elsewhere, most particularly an outreach to adults rather than students. The campaigns in Britain and South Africa showed the benefits of working with adults, including greater visibility and more social impact. It also helped that the main leadership group—Purdy, Twitchell, and the rest—were now in their late twenties and early thirties, and interested in reaching their peers. Although they continued working with students, movement members found adult work more productive.

As movement leaders matured, they downplayed some of its more controversial aspects. A psychologist noted that "the influx of the so-called 'respectable' clergyman and older, stable people into the movement" changed the tone of the house parties. "Sexual sins are not confessed in public, although they are still a large factor in private confessions, while the more mentionable sins of 'pride, selfishness, and dishonesty' are more frequently mentioned." The lessened prominence of college students was a blessing, he concluded, since they often exaggerate and embroider their sins.[94] A member of Calvary Church's staff told the New York *Herald Tribune* that the tone of the house party groups were no longer "smut sessions." "It used to be that a guy would tell how he took out a jane," he said. "Now the most you hear is when some one said he has had difficulties with women."[95] The resulting decline in controversy was an unanticipated but welcome consequence of a focus on adults.

The shift of focus to adults required a change in the movement's style. Instead of talking about the issues that trouble students—sexuality, identity, or vocation—group members focused on adult concerns, especially those of businessmen. Meetings at Shoemaker's Calvary Church, one member recalled, looked at "the kind of questions businessmen and wage earners needed to air and discuss: answers to pressure, personal hang-ups, honesty in competitive business dealings, fear, or unemployment."[96] That message was even more important after the onset of the Depression, Shoemaker remembered years later. He visited Detroit and met businessmen who "had been changed during the past year and had a very fresh and vital message for men in business, some of whom were in utter despair and at the point of suicide." He was impressed to hear businessmen facing economic challenges "speak of their condition with calm faith in God, and say that He alone was keeping them from worry and rebellion."[97] These men may have been in college during the 1920s, but they were now older and had different worries. The movement shifted to address the concerns of these adults—concerns like those of the movement's leaders.

A Dynamic Experience of God's Free Spirit

As in Britain and South Africa, the Groups' signature event in America was the house party. Although they were increasingly designed for adults, the parties kept the pattern Buchman developed in his work with students—a group of people invited to a comfortable place for as much as a week of informal and structured sharing, interspersed with socializing and recreation. The goal was cultivating conversion and all manner of Christian experience. As Sam Shoemaker told a colleague, the parties were "a medium for the discussion of all the varieties of personal religious experience... There is about it all a gaiety and gladness, not professional, not put on, but spontaneous and understanding."[98] There were a few house parties in the year after the controversy at Princeton, but by the mid-1930s the Groups organized simultaneous house parties in various cities around the country. In February 1935 alone there was a "school of action" in Cincinnati, a "personalized" group of 1,000 at the Plaza Hotel in New York, a city campaign in Cambridge, Massachusetts, and house parties in Frederick, Maryland, and Oil City and Philadelphia, Pennsylvania.[99]

Some house parties were a response to local needs. A southern cell group member told Purdy, for instance, that "Birmingham, Alabama, ought to be touched soon." There were two small groups meeting in the city, based in Episcopal churches, he wrote, "but they need more boost from the outside."[100] Buchman himself urged Russell Firestone, tire company scion and Akron group leader, to plan house parties in Detroit and in New Jersey, with his friends the Thomas Edisons. "God has used you and will continue to use you."[101]

Many of the gatherings, however, were part of a national strategy, with the goal of changing the country through house parties. In 1933 Buchman reminded Firestone that "your father's original idea in wanting me to go to Detroit was to help there in the severe economic crisis and it may be that Detroit will be the pace-maker for thawing the frozen assets."[102] Shoemaker told members that a party at Briarcliff, New York, would be a "supreme opportunity which God is giving us for fresh vision and united attack." Unified teams from the United States and Britain, as well as "the unmistakable way in which God is guiding, confirms us in the faith that Briarcliff will mark a new day in the spiritual history of our country."[103] He encouraged H. Alexander Smith, his father-in-law and a rising politician, to invite some of his famous friends to another Briarcliff gathering, arguing "we ought to invite those people to come who, as Frank says, if they were changed

America would be different. I feel you certainly ought to deliver a man like [journalist Walter] Lippman."[104]

The planning began with handsomely printed invitations that laid out grand goals for the parties. The invitation to an April 1928 house party declared that it would "teach the 'how' of possessing and reproducing a quality of life which enables the possessor intelligently to change people's lives and in turn make them life changers." Promised topics included spiritual diagnosis, guidance, sharing experience, clinical hours in pastoral work, the place of possessions, and "principles involved in forging a group of disciplined workers."[105] Another party, scheduled for Gainesville, Florida, in February 1932, promised finding "through the sharing of experience in a natural informal atmosphere of honesty the answer men and women are finding together in a fresh discovery of the meaning of Jesus Christ for their own lives. Dogmatism we shun, preaching we may question, but facts of experience we want."

As the Depression wore on, invitations increasingly spoke to public as well as private concerns. Thanks to previous parties, the Gainesville invitation noted, "A dynamic experience of God's free spirit has been found the answer to regional antagonism, economic depression, racial conflict, and international strife."[106] A year later, the invitation to a party in Riverside, California, argued that "the modern world, disillusioned, chaotic, bewildered, demands a solution adequate to its disorder. The problems of to-day are, at bottom, personal problems. Men must be changed, if these problems are to be solved." The party would train leadership for "an army of life-changers speaking the language modern America understands."[107]

Group leaders and members chose the recipients of these invitations very carefully. One leader announced a house party at Swarthmore, Pennsylvania, for June 1929. "This party will be mainly in the nature of a School of Life, in which we will stress Continuance, and the developing of ourselves in Leadership and in handling local situations." He included 25 invitations "to be used as you are guided."[108] Another mailing suggested that members identify possible invitees, "pray for them and get guided diagnosis," so that it can become a personalized gathering. "Who at the houseparty can best meet their needs?" the author asked. "Are you the person? If not, who is?"[109]

As the movement grew, so did the invitation lists—attracting more people, especially more women. While Buchman's earliest gatherings were intimate affairs for small groups of men, the Group issued more than 120 invitations for a party at Minnewaska, New York, in the late 1920s.[110] Another New York-area party over New Year's Eve 1929 attracted well over 200, over half of them women.[111] For the 1931 house party at Montreat, North Carolina, the leaders invited members of the Charlotte ministerial association, people from Asheville, students from Asheville School, and people from elsewhere across the south. More than 100 names were on the invitation list, only 26 of them men.[112] Among 25 converts at a party in Asheville 22 were women.[113]

While the first parties were in private homes, most of these larger gatherings were at resorts and private schools, where participants could find recreation and good food as well as spiritual enrichment. A New York resort offered participants in a 1927 party golf, riding, tennis, swimming, and boating. The invitation said that "those coming to the conference should bring Bibles, note-books, and as simple clothes as possible. No evening clothes." Participants paid a "program fee" of $6 (more than $76 today) in addition to $4–6 per person per day for rooms.[114] Sherwood Day asked the manager of another New York inn, "Could you let me have a few copies of old menus that would be typical of the meals? We do not expect frills, but we do want plenty of good wholesome food, and as one of the group [most likely Buchman] puts it: 'Good food and good Christianity go hand in hand.'"[115] Some of the parties had food prepared by dieticians from John Harvey Kellogg's Battle Creek Sanitarium. "Dr. Kellogg has just promised a cook for our house party so we may have biologic living," Buchman told Day before a 1927 party.[116]

Whatever the setting, house parties kept to a fairly simple outline. The daily schedule for a party at Minnewaska, New York, in the late 1920s, was typical. After breakfast, participants spent a half hour in a group "quiet time"; Bible study occupied the rest of the morning. At noon each day there was a "platform address"—a plenary speech on a particular theme—followed by lunch. The afternoon was free for recreation and one-on-one talk. After dinner were large and small group meetings, where participants shared their Christian experiences.[117]

Group quiet times, a period of silence seeking God's guidance, were a hallmark of the movement's work and a key part of the house party. John Roots, a student at Harvard Divinity School, started the quiet time at one party by suggesting "Let's all get comfortable and focus our minds on God....Let the Holy Spirit really be our guide." After 20 minutes of silence, participants shared their guidance. "Be frank to say that God is all powerful." "Material things are of no account." "The peace which passeth all understanding." "If you give your life to God, there is a general purpose in it and He will make it known." "I must become more humble."[118]

Bible studies at the parties usually stressed the movement's common themes. One lesson asked participants reading Mark's gospel, "Was the interest of Jesus chiefly in crowds or in individuals?"[119] At another house party, the Bible study concentrated on "Christ's dealing with individuals and the training of his disciples."[120] At one party, a participant told Buchman, Purdy kept the discussion flexible, looking to be "adaptable as to what to emphasize and as to what chapters of Mark to pick out to meet the needs of the occasion. All the way through you felt the lessons being pointed right at the needs of the people who were there."

The most doctrinal part of the house party was the "platform meeting," a large-group lecture focused on a particular theme. Most of the parties featured the same set of topics, themes common throughout Buchman's work: Sin, Surrender, Christ, Guidance, Stewardship, and Continuance.[121] More specialized parties included focused lectures; a party focused on developing leaders, for instance, included platform addresses on "How to conduct an interview," "Sharing," "The dynamic Drive of a genuine decision," "How to lead a group," and "Team work and leadership."[122] The lectures were delivered by group leaders, often chosen on the spot through group guidance. Eleanor Forde, one of the few women in the group's inner circle, quipped that she was chosen to lead the session on Sin at one house party because "I know so much about the topic."[123]

Surviving lecture notes reveal both the message of the movement and the tone of the house parties. Ray Purdy's notes for the "Sin" lecture, for instance, start with a distinction between "Bad People's Sins"—obvious ones such as murder, theft, cruelty, and drunkenness—and "Good People's Sins." Assuming that his audience was made up of good people, Purdy concentrated on the latter—mainly minor forms of the more obvious sins, such as selfishness (murdering another's love), gossip (stealing someone's good name), and over-indulgence of any kind. Purdy particularly focused on the sins of pride, fear, and self-indulgence. Self-indulgence, for instance, includes "undisciplined thoughts" and "fussiness," while Purdy lists among the fears "fear of death" and "fear of sentiment and emotion." Among the leading sins of "spiritual people" are "unwillingness to suffer" and "loving people rather than God."[124] These sins reflect the high spiritual expectations—resisting self-indulgence and sentiment—that Group members set for themselves and for potential converts.

Purdy's notes on "The Cross" echo these expectations. Sin—especially unbelief, pride, and self-centeredness—keep us from God, he told a 1930 house party; the only way to overcome it is the cross. But crucifixion is not just for Jesus, Purdy added; "there is only one way to an *experience* of the Cross of Christ and that is over a crucified self." Not only must we accept forgiveness, "we must *let self die*." Christians must be crucified and resurrected. "In the end the Cross cannot be described, explained, only faced. Don't let's face it in terms of our sins, but our sinful selves." Purdy concluded his talk with the hymn Buchman heard at his own 1908 conversion experience:

> When I survey the wondrous Cross
> On which the Prince of Glory died,
> My richest gain I count but loss,
> And pour contempt on all my pride.[125]

Although Bible study and platform talks were invariably part of the program, the heart of every house party was sharing—large and small group sessions where participants told stories of change in their lives. During the day, a house party guest noted, there were small groups—including the girls' group, the young married group and the men's group—where "the intimate questions were discussed." More important were the large group meetings after supper. Everyone was "so sincere and natural," the guest observed. "One evening a young man carried us through the story of his misspend [sic] life and in a tone so heartfelt that the words trembled and his face was wet with perspiration as he asked God to forgive him and said he wished to start anew." Next came "a sweet school-girl of eighteen who wanted to say that she had been selfish and thoughtless many times in her life and wanted to make a definite surrender." The guest contrasted modern days, "when people are very frank with one another," with "the reticence of the victorian [sic] age...when it was a sin to be natural in any way. This is frankness in religion, and it is a most wholesome message."[126]

Members saw these sharing sessions as crucial spiritual experiences. Movement leader Cleveland Hicks reported to Buchman on a 1928 house party, where in the evening "we met to share with one another the good things God had done for us and how sin, self-will and self-importance and self-indulgence had blocked His power in our lives. The meetings were real."[127] In 1927, Logan Roots—the Episcopal Bishop of Hankow in China and father of John Roots—told house party participants that he was "moved tremendously as I have heard the testimonies to the Power of God." Sharing helps the listener as much as the speaker, Roots continued, "Because there isn't anything that is so contagious as a little glimpse into the realities of the growing power of Christ and that is what you get in this kind of sharing." In a small group that morning, he reported, he had confessed his life-long habit of biting his fingernails. It was difficult, he admitted—"It seemed so foolish"—but "the moment I spoke that out, I felt that I was down where I wanted to be, on a level with that group, and a miserable sinner, and I wanted them to know it and I did not want to keep it away from because then I knew we could talk as one person to another in the fellowship of Christ."[128]

Some stories told at house parties were dramatic. At one New Year's Eve house party, early convert Howard Blake reported, a young New York business man "brought a marvelous message of the apostolic trip he had made in his Christmas holiday down south," while a Princeton student "rededicated himself that night and is still in power."[129] Another party, reported a group newsletter, included "a person who had been helped out of a dissolute life to a life in Christ, and, at the other end of the line, the Dean of the Cathedral." The same party heard a "striking" witness from "Edna Walker, a shop girl of seventeen from Wilmington who has been responsible for the change in a drunken father and a dissolute brother."[130] At a New York-area party, a teenager described how the Group message led him and his friends to give up their beer club in favor of group prayer. Buchman suggested that the story offered an "answer to the problem of racketeers and gangsters."[131]

House parties also evoked more personal spiritual experiences. A Moravian seminarian told Sherwood Day that since a house party "it seems like a dream; wherever I go people start talking to me about themselves and their problems and I just let God use me and the results have been marvelous." He had given up smoking and lost his self-consciousness with women. "And the best thing about it all is that lives are really being changed thru [sic] me—and not by me but by God. And my own life has been changed and all that has happened I could never have done of myself. Only the power of God has been able to do it all."[132]

These intimate parties allowed Buchman to do the personal work he saw as his calling, and attracted those turned off by traditional evangelicalism. In the early 1930s, however, Buchman and his colleagues also started conducting city campaigns, an amalgam of house parties and more traditional evangelical rallies. They allowed the work to reach larger groups, and gave the movement increased visibility.

The first city campaigns were in Asheville, North Carolina, and Louisville, Kentucky, in spring 1931. In Asheville between 500 and

600 people attended each meeting, far larger than previous house parties. A local journalist was impressed at how the meetings drew people from all classes and all Protestant churches, "but most of them represent families prominent in the social, business and professional life of the community." He was surprised by "the character of the members of the 'team.' Most of them are young and highly intelligent men and women.... Many have traveled around the world, and are persons of great culture and influence." He wondered how the Group could "appeal to the upper classes who ordinarily would probably be untouched by a fundamentalist's revival." Among other things, he noted, "the speakers do not attempt oratory. They do not try to appeal to the emotions." Perhaps most importantly, "they draw the upper classes because they themselves belong to them."[133]

Some participants in the Asheville house party were also invited to nearby Weaver College, which had a snowballing impact, as one student after another was changed. "On Friday a large part of the student body came clear across," reported an observer. "In the evening, the first group meeting was held by the students themselves; plans were made for quiet time; for separate group divisions; and for the student body, as many as had 'got it'—that's the student phrase coined for this situation."[134] An Asheville resident told Purdy that "the whole town is changed. Personally it's the most wonderful thing that ever happened to me. I always *thought* I was a Christian but now I *know* it and telling it to everyone I know."[135]

The mission in Louisville was larger and had more impact. Before the Group came to Louisville, a group member wrote Buchman, "Depression and a serious bank failure had thrown a pall of pessimism over the city, with all the undercurrent of fear, suspicion, and bitterness bread [sic] of disappointment."[136] The Group's witness, according to the reporter for a local Christian paper, however, "made a tremendous impression upon [Louisville], and many are hoping and believing that this is the beginning of a nation-wide movement that will mean a genuine revival of apostolic religion in all the churches."[137]

A team of 90 led the Louisville work; activities included an opening dinner for 300, addressed by the Episcopal bishop and the president of the Presbyterian and Baptist seminaries, appearances in 58 churches, morning Bible study for 300, and small groups for ministers, business men, young women, girls, and students. The evening meetings attracted between 1,000 and 1,400 people, with two thousand at the closing session.[138] Purdy exulted to Buchman that the campaign would "establish allies for us among the most important people in the South."[139]

A Spiritual Family

These large house parties and city campaigns, echoing the big revival rallies of traditional evangelicalism, were a new method for the Groups, which traditionally had focused on small groups and quiet work. Nevertheless, Buchman's movement continued to develop local cells. Some were bases staffed by full-time volunteers, while others grew around a dedicated local follower. Since the Oxford Group was a network of practitioners rather than an established hierarchy, many of the cells may have gone unnoticed. Several, however, were particularly important.

New York remained the American hub for the movement. Since the 1910s Buchman regularly passed through the city as he traveled between Hartford, Princeton, and other university campuses. It was a gathering spot for college students. The city was the home of many of the movement's financial supporters. It was the major transatlantic port as the movement grew internationally. Most importantly, New York was the home of the American Establishment—financial institutions, church organizations, leading newspapers and magazines, and other opinion leaders. This was the group Buchman wanted to meet and influence, seeing it as the key to reaching the rest of the country.

Group members used a variety of bases in the city. They regularly held meetings at the Waldorf and Plaza Hotels—like the February 1935 dinner for a "selective group" of one thousand at the Plaza. The group, "drawn from the professional, business, and social life of Greater New York," aimed at reaching "those really capable of influencing their respective circles." The group included both President Roosevelt's mother and "Spoons Costello, an ex-highjacker [*sic*] and racketeer from the Bowery." A Group newsletter called it "a pace-making evening in the intellectual life of New York."[140] Buchman continued to use facilities rented by Margaret Tjader for his Bible class, which attracted about 20 people—mainly women.[141]

While the movement held events all over New York, its primary center remained Shoemaker's Calvary Church, including its large new parish house. An eight-story building behind the sanctuary, Calvary House soon became something close to a commune for Buchman's supporters. The building included apartments for the church staff; other rooms were regularly occupied by itinerant members of the group, including Buchman when he was in New York. Various Group members had offices at the church, where they produced publicity materials, kept up with correspondence, and shipped

books. The building's large public rooms hosted meetings of movement participants.[142]

Calvary House residents met together for regular quiet times, where
they shared in prayer and listened for God's guidance. Shoemaker wrote
Purdy in 1934 that the New York group "really is a spiritual family, in
which all matters of personal decision and group policy are checked."
Visitors from all over the world joined the headquarters group, for days
or months. "Whoever else is here, joins us when they are in town,"
Shoemaker added. "We have been meeting about three times a week
and keeping closely shared up to date about all matters."[143] This communal living and decision making reflected their commitment to live
like first-century Christians.

While not as large as the New York base, an important cell developed
in Washington, DC, started by a group of people who had attended a
1929 house party. They organized meetings for clergy and business
men in the city and gave talks at local private schools. After one of
these presentations, Howard Blake reported to Buchman, "other men
in high positions among Christian workers here are ready to cooperate
with us." Blake, a Princeton alumnus and full-time volunteer, and his
wife planned "to settle here for a steady work under God's guidance."[144]
He bought a house and continued to develop connections, including
an informal relationship with a Presbyterian church. Within a year the
Washington cell had 50 people at weekly meetings.[145] Though small,
its connections were important as the movement became more interested in national and international issues.

Cities large and small developed cells. Several members worked
full-time building a network in Philadelphia. Among the leaders was
a society matron of Bryn Mawr—"a niece of Wm. [sic] James and having a large place that has come down in the family direct from Wm.
Penn's charter (that ought to be meat for you—American nobility!),"
an organizer reported to Buchman. The matron offered her house for
meetings of local college students, and "is in touch with wide circles of
interesting and influential people."[146] A small but active cell thrived for
some years in Williamstown, Massachusetts. It included a weekly "big
group," as well as regular meetings for men, women, and high school
students.[147] A Presbyterian pastor in Wilmington, Delaware, started a
Thursday evening group at his church, modeled on the weekly meeting at Calvary.[148] With the help of the visiting Purdy, a Rhode Island
couple prepared for "a 'coming out' party with their speedy coctail [sic]
crowd in Narragansett next week-end. It will be difficult, but it means
for them an open stand in Providence."[149]

Russell Firestone led a sizable group in Akron, Ohio. In the fall of 1932 he planned a small gathering around the time of a Detroit house party. "More and more people are becoming interested and want to know more concerning the group," he told Buchman. Firestone proposed a supper at his home, inviting "certain of our close friends in to meet the group." The rector of his Episcopal parish offered the pulpit to a group member for a Sunday morning, followed by a larger meeting at the Firestone family estate. "It is our thought that we will probably have from 100 to 150 invited guests at this meeting including a selected list of Akron's clergy." Firestone suggested that the visiting team include Shoemaker and Jimmy Watt, a former London communist and labor leader, now a Buchman friend. "Although this is a fairly well regulated industrial town, Jimmy Watt could do a great deal of good.... For your own information, there are rumors about that the groups are only for rich people which, naturally, we want to dispel at these meetings."[150]

Cells in smaller communities faced obstacles to their work. A group had been meeting weekly for vespers in a Presbyterian church in Bloomington, Illinois, until members of the congregation started to criticize the movement; group members shifted their work to "a community approach."[151] The rector of an Episcopal church in North Carolina reported that there were "definitely malevolent influences at work." His bishop had been receiving anonymous letters "which claim that we stir up trouble in local churches where we go."[152] In the summer of 1933 a group member visited cells in small communities across Pennsylvania and Ohio. "There are a lot of little, lonely groups all over the state," he discovered, and they needed help. "They have felt that they should have someone here with them to help shape up further plans and help them to solve various problems which have arisen." They need a house party or a training session, the scout concluded, "because there are so many people scattered over the state who are turning to the Group experience and points of emphasis with hope and with confidence but who are perplexed as to how to proceed. They have seen the promise in the movement and they are very much aware of the problems confronted."[153] Many of these small groups continued for years on their own.

As memories of the Princeton controversy faded, group leaders also tried again to reach American college students. Howard Blake noted in 1932 that several members had been getting guidance "that there was an unparalleled opportunity this year for a new work in the universities in America. There is at least one undergraduate in nearly every major university keen to produce." He had come to believe "that some university will emerge where those in authority will be given vision to see the possibilities of leadership in a new movement for spiritual life in American education through this movement. It is hard to hazard a guess as to which college it will be, but I am confident that we shall be shown clearly in guidance when the time comes." He thought that Duke University and Centre College were particular possibilities. "When this college sees the picture, it may mean the sending of a bullet-proof team for a long enough visit to do a thorough job." Such a mission would require a substantial investment of time, including perhaps a year of preparation.[154]

Alcoholics Anonymous

One of the Oxford Group's biggest legacies—Alcoholics Anonymous—was accidental. The recovery movement's work—particularly the "Twelve Steps" and the group model—has its roots in both the Group's ideas and its people. While AA was never formally linked with the Group and has downplayed the historical connection on occasion, Buchman's influence nonetheless is central to the twelve-step method.

Buchman and his colleagues had occasionally been interested in helping people—usually wealthy young men—with alcohol problems. In the early 1920s he took Margaret Tjader's son Richard to Europe, perhaps to keep him out of trouble.[155] Russell Firestone found sobriety after attending a house party in Denver. This success led to the strong Group cell in Akron, Ohio.[156] Cleveland Hicks told Buchman that another young alcoholic had been changed at a Pennsylvania house party in 1928. "He told me afterwards that when he heard me mention house party to him all he could figure out was a long period of drinking and making merry." At the opening session the young man "blurted out his desire to be free from drink." He and his roommate "talked together about how Christ saves us from sin. That night Jack found the power of Christ which made of him a new creature."[157]

Shoemaker's Calvary Church in New York built another link to alcoholics. A previous rector had established a mission in the nearby skid row area, which Shoemaker revitalized in the late 1920s. "While we worked with people of sufficient privilege to find their way into the rectory and church," he wrote, "what was happening to men in the Gas House district to the east of us?"[158] Soon Group members were leading house parties for the men of the mission, sharing a weekend "packed with the kind of fellowship that flows from a mutual recognition that sin is sin and Christ the only Cure, whether one comes from Park Avenue or a park bench, 'whether he's in jail or in Yale.'"[159]

Among the occasional worshippers at Calvary Mission was an alcoholic stockbroker named Bill Wilson. He had been sent by an old drinking friend named Ebby, who had been changed at the mission. "I learned that I had to admit I was licked," Ebby told Wilson, in a rough approximation of the Oxford Group's language of surrender. "I learned that I ought to take stock of myself and confess my defects to another person." Most importantly, he learned that "I should pray to whatever God I thought there was for the power to carry out these simple precepts." As soon as Ebby had decided to try it, "it seemed to me that my drinking problem was lifted right out of me." Wilson balked at the message and drank some more, ending up in the hospital. As he lay in bed, however, he cried out, "If there is a God, let Him show Himself! I am ready to do anything, anything!" Suddenly, he told an AA convention years later, his room was filled with light.[160] Wilson became a member of the Thursday evening group at Calvary House and began to think how the Groups' message could help his fellow alcoholics.[161]

In May 1935 Wilson was on a business trip in Akron. Finding himself at loose ends and tempted to drink, he instead called every church listed in the phone book. Finally one church directed him to the Oxford Group cell founded by the Firestones, which connected him with Bob Smith—"Dr. Bob"—a local physician and alcoholic. They talked for hours about themselves, sharing their experiences of alcoholism. Wilson also told Smith what he had learned from other doctors—that alcoholism was a disease, a simultaneous allergy to and overwhelming desire for alcohol. The only solution, Wilson and Smith became convinced, was surrendering their will and never drinking again. "Our talk was a completely *mutual* thing," Wilson wrote years later. "I knew that I needed this alcoholic as much as he needed me."[162] They told each other the truth about their addictions and their attempts to fight it. Effectively, they told stories. Together they set off to tell their stories to drunks at the county hospital, and Alcoholics Anonymous was born.

All these stories—Ebby's, Wilson's, and Smith's—show the earmarks of Buchman's evangelical method. At its heart is sharing—the best way to change someone is to tell them your own story. Part of that storytelling is confession, identifying the negative power in your life. For Buchman that negative power was sin, while for Wilson it was alcohol. Another key for both approaches is surrender, admitting that you are powerless over the negative force and giving yourself up to God. For both movements the exact identity of that God is left vague—in both AA and the Oxford Group the confessor relies on personal experience rather than theology to identify the higher power. While the Oxford Group had no doctrine of God, it assumed that people would surrender to the God of the Bible. AA, on the other hand, said that it need not be the God of Christianity, making its message more accessible to people from a variety of backgrounds. Both approaches require that the penitent make amends to anyone they had harmed. Finally, they stress the importance of personal experience and small groups. All of these elements are crucial for Buchman's work and for AA's Twelve Steps, written by Wilson and Smith.

The Group and AA also shared the same target populations, the urban, educated, and well-to-do.[163] Alcoholism had long been thought of as a moral failing to which only Bowery bums were prone. AA redefined it as a disease, making it possible for professionals and other respectable people to admit their alcoholism. Wilson could not identify with the "down and out" alcoholics he found in the Calvary Mission, but he could with the people at Calvary Church.[164] This echoes Buchman's appeal to the "up-and-outers."

Despite these common characteristics, Wilson's movement and Buchman's Oxford Group soon separated, mainly over differences in emphasis. The Group was increasingly seeking publicity, while AA shunned it; Buchman centralized his movement, while AA wanted to decentralize its work.[165] Wilson wanted to concentrate on alcoholics, while the Group wanted him to join in changing the world. They also wanted to impose the Group's stringent absolutes on alcoholics whom Wilson felt weren't ready for such discipline yet.[166] The Oxford Group was simply too religious for Wilson and his alcoholics. Despite the common ground, different emphases divided the movements.

Wilson had separated himself from Shoemaker and the Oxford Group by 1937, and the first edition of *Alcoholics Anonymous* does not mention the Oxford Group connection at all. The second edition does mention the Groups by name, but holds them at arm's length. "Though [Wilson] could never accept all the tenets of the Oxford Groups, he was convinced of the need for moral inventory, confession of personality defects, restitution to those harmed, helpfulness to others, and the necessity of belief in and dependence upon God."[167] Alcoholics Anonymous restored some of its connections to the Oxford Group origins when Wilson asked Shoemaker to speak at its twentieth anniversary convention in 1955.[168] After Shoemaker's speech Wilson concluded

that doctors "gave us the needed knowledge of our illness, but Sam
Shoemaker had given us the concrete knowledge of what we could do
about it."[169] Some AA members are looking again at the Oxford Group
connection, hoping to reclaim what they see as a lost Christian mission for the organization.[170] Alcoholics Anonymous and other recovery
organizations are probably the most vital religious movement of the
late twentieth century, and form the Oxford Group's most long-lasting
legacy.

★   ★   ★

By the mid 1930s, Frank Buchman and his followers had recreated
their movement in response to changing circumstances. They had
shifted their attention from college students to adults as their leadership
aged. They moved from small house parties to city-wide campaigns as
their public image grew. They worked with institutions to pay for their
increasingly international work.

The heart of the movement, however, remained the same. Buchman
sought to change lives by bringing men and women to a vital religious
experience. Once changed, they sought God's guidance and shared
their experiences with others. The delivery may have changed, but the
content remained the same.

The late 1920s and early 1930s laid the groundwork for the movement's future. It became increasingly public—both visible in the media
and concerned with public issues. Its international connections were
important as Buchman became more interested in remaking the world.
As the Oxford Group's agenda broadened, however, it retained the
methods it developed in the house party revival.

CHAPTER FOUR

Rising Tide

In the fall of 1937, Americans started seeing the phrase "Rising Tide" everywhere. It was in newspaper advertisements and bookstore windows, and on postcards appearing mysteriously in the mail. Eventually they learned that "Rising Tide" was a slick one-issue magazine, proclaiming a new hope for America and the world through faith, cooperation, and trust—all being brought about through the work of the Oxford Group.

This publicity campaign, an early example of what is now called buzz marketing, shows how Buchman's movement had once again recreated itself. It started as a quiet network of college students, before becoming a more public but still elite community dedicated to Christian revival. Now, in the late 1930s, Buchman and his lieutenants transformed their work into a mass movement, dedicated to changing the world through changing individuals, using mass media, the young field of public relations, and America's growing celebrity culture to spread its message. They created spectacles, drawing on a wide range of influences, with everything from Christian liturgy to Broadway musicals to fascist rallies. The movement offered an antipolitical politics as the solution to the world's problems.

In the mid- to late 1930s, the Oxford Group also changed religion's place in its work. Explicitly Christian language was less evident in movement speeches and publications, as leaders seemed less intent on bringing Americans to a distinctively Christian experience. The movement's already tenuous links to the church faded, especially as clergymen left its leadership. But the Oxford Group remained fundamentally evangelical, aimed at bringing about changed lives—and thus a changed world—through sharing spiritual experiences. It also preached what theologians call millennialism, promising the possibility of a perfected world through God's intervention. For the Oxford Group, however, the millennium would come about through human rather than divine action. This secularized millennialism became a hallmark of the movement.

This chapter traces how Buchman and other group leaders made the Oxford Group into a mass movement, from a national campaign across Canada to the big rally at the Hollywood Bowl. As the world shuddered through economic collapse and stood at the brink of war, Group leaders worked to create a new and better world through a movement Buchman renamed Moral Re-Armament.

A World-wide Movement of God's Holy Spirit

While Buchman had focused his early work on personal evangelism, the Oxford Group campaigns in South Africa and the United States persuaded him that large meetings could bring about changed lives. Subsequent campaigns in Canada and Scandinavia developed the model—and led group members to believe that their message was the answer for world problems as well as individual ones. They wanted "the dawn of a modern Renaissance for Canada through a quiet revolution under the direction of God's Holy Spirit," reported a Montreal newspaper where the editor had been converted.[1] To bring about this renaissance, group leaders organized larger and larger rallies—a significant shift for a movement initially centered on quiet individual work.

In 1932 a team of Americans, Britons, and Canadians visited cities across Canada. Shoemaker reported that the group's journey made "spiritual history."[2] As in Asheville and Louisville, the team spoke in churches, led small and large group meetings, and talked with individuals. Canadian Prime Minister Richard Bennett told the Group that "as Wesley saved England from revolution, so the forces which you so powerfully represent are the only ones that can save civilization today." Shoemaker noted that the campaign's impact was multiplied by the press. "Judged by sheer depth of influence, there can be no question that the Oxford group [*sic*] is today one of the mightiest movements on earth. Roughly, I suppose, the group touched on this side [of the country] half a million people."

As in South Africa, the Group began applying its message to social issues in Canada. Shoemaker wrote "that personal religion is the great leaven of social regeneration." If you give individuals new values "which center in Christ, you will soon get new relationships with one another and a new view of society." He described how a newspaper changed its editorial policy to favor international cooperation after a reporter was converted, and an employer moved into a cottage so he could keep all his staff on the payroll. The success of the gatherings, according to a movement newsletter, suggested "the possibilities of a nation-wide and world-wide movement of God's Holy Spirit," and offered a model for work elsewhere. "Our vision for the United States can be no less. Under God we must capture business and social leaders, colleges, prisons, city halls, groups of unemployed, merchants, legislatures, everyone for our Lord and Saviour Jesus Christ."[3]

A subsequent cross-Canada campaign culminated with a "North American House Party" at Banff in June 1934. The gathering attracted hundreds of people from Canada, the United States, and Europe for over a week. The proceedings featured a militant rhetoric, reflected in the meeting's daily newspaper. One issue proclaimed "The Challenge of Youth," calling young people to be the vanguard of change in the world. The author noted the importance of youth in other movements that the Group—naively in the early 1930s—saw as peers. "Italy was the first nation to inspire its youth in the great national movement of Fascism.... It was left to Adolph Hitler to recognize in youth the real hope for the regeneration of his country." To bring about this regeneration in North America, youth must "set Christ first in every relationship of life, family, and friends, community and country. Youth must buckle on the full panoply of war, the shield to ward off the onslaughts of a relentless and ever vigilant enemy and the sword of Christ for militant service." Like Fascism and Nazism, the paper reported, the Oxford Group teaches youth the importance of "clean minds and bodies, courage, determination, confidence in victory and an aggressive militancy."[4] The young men's group at the meeting declared themselves "Storm Troops in Action" for God's kingdom. "It was to be 'the fellowship of a Crusade' and not 'the fellowship of a tea party.'"[5] This militant and masculine rhetoric echoed its times.

The Group claimed that its work, however, was more than rhetoric. In the months before the party, the paper reported, Group members, "under God's guidance," played a role in settling a crippling dock workers' strike on the Pacific Coast. "Strikes and lock-outs have no place in a Christian world," the Group proclaimed. "Strikes with their underlying suggestion of force and compulsion are the antithesis of the Sermon on the Mount." Instead, members of the Group brought leaders of the two sides together and "laid the matter before God asking humbly for

His help and guidance." Thanks to the Group, "the strike on the Pacific Coast was the first strike in history in which Christ was called upon to act as arbiter."[6] A Canadian correspondent for the *Christian Century* challenged the Group's claims, pointing out that the strike continued, entering its thirteenth week as labor leaders threatened a general strike. He also questioned the Group's motives in intervening in the strike. The Group's push for arbitration simply continued an unjust situation, the correspondent believed; the Group was "strangely silent regarding the essentially unchristian foundations of the present social order."[7]

Meanwhile, in Europe, Group members laid the foundation for national campaigns that would have—according to Group members— even more importance. Carl Hambro, the president of the Norwegian Parliament, invited the Group to bring its work to Norway for a house party. Twitchell and others had planned for 100 people, but the meeting ended up drawing 1,000 people, including many reporters. Twitchell foretold a broad impact throughout Scandinavia with "important repercussions on the rest of the Europe."[8] There were large and small group meetings all over Norway.[9]

Group members saw the Scandinavian work as epic. A university professor, one newsletter concluded, described the campaign as "the turning point in the history of the country."[10] An American team member told stateside supporters that the work constituted "the most constructive single contribution on the horizon of the nations today. A whole nation has been challenged for Jesus Christ." All citizens were called to commit their lives and the nation to God's guidance.[11] The success of a campaign in Denmark, wrote a British Group member, should cause the Group to prepare itself "to become a national government as soon as the time is ripe."[12]

This revolutionary message, laying the foundation for taking over the government, is far away from Buchman's beginnings doing personal work at Penn State. It reflects the movement's increasing interest in antipolitical politics.

Gabriel over the White House

By the mid 1930s, the Oxford Group was becoming increasingly interested in public affairs. Movement leaders believed that their message of personal change, absolute morality, and listening to God could answer the world's growing problems. The Group was not interested, however, in party politics; it never supported one party's platform or offered its own candidates. It did not offer ethically driven policy prescriptions, beyond adherence to the four absolutes—absolute love, absolute purity, absolute honesty, and absolute unselfishness.

Instead, the Oxford Group advocated an antipolitical politics. In the eyes of Buchman and the rest, traditional politics—the process of deciding policies by choosing between competing interests and ideas— had failed the world in its time of crisis. Politicians and voters were too focused on self or group interest and not enough on what was right. Communism, with its materialism and focus on class conflict, epito- mized what was wrong with the world. Just as the movement hated labor strikes because they were the "antithesis of the Sermon on the Mount," it abhorred the conflict inevitable in electoral politics.

In place of traditional politics, Group members believed the world should be governed by God. People—voters and elected leaders alike— should seek God's guidance daily before making their decisions. As Buchman asked a 1932 house party, "Would not prosperity come to America if the members of the Cabinet, the Senate and Congress only started the day by prayerful communication with the living God?"[13] If people and their leaders would listen to God, the proper course would be obvious. The result would be a perfected social order, free of con- flict and competition. This is politics without politics, a perfected world brought about through God-guided action.

A 1937 manifesto from British Group members, "The God-Controlled Nation," reveals how a guided society would handle employment, health, foreign affairs, and even traffic accidents. "The God-controlled man is disciplined, alert, unselfish, and takes the road free from fears, worries, and inner conflicts. The man at the wheel and the man in the street under God's control will make the nation's roads safe and efficient." Instead of imprisoning criminals, police and lawyers would "admit their responsibility and share with the criminal the places in their own lives where they have proved the efficiency of God-control." Industry would also be God-controlled. "This is the New Industrial Revolution. In the God-controlled business, God is the Managing Director." More specif- ically, God control means "producing what God wants, selling at God's price," and "cooperating not competing with other firms."[14] God con- trol would mean a well-ordered society transcending politics.

Such a world would require God-guided—and thus changed— people. Liberal Christians of the day believed that they were called to change the world's systems, to bring about more justice. The Oxford Group, however, believed in changing individuals. The solution to the unemployment problem, for instance, was changing the unemployed, as individuals, rather than changing the economic system as a whole. A Cambridge student met hunger marchers and "found that their deepest problems were the same as his and that Christ was the answer to both." Another student had flirted with communism but had "found a more gripping and demanding cause in the warfare not of class but Christ."[15] While the economic depression led some to want to overthrow the country's economic system, a Group member stated that "if God thinks we need a new system, he will change the present one."[16]

Changing individuals would lead to national and global spiritual revival, with countries following Oxford Group practices. Entire nations would confess their sins and seek God's guidance. "Think of the nations confessing their sins, instead of the sins of other nations," Shoemaker wrote. "Think of national repentance and restitution, of national conversion and salvation, of the governments of this world deciding the issues of the world on the basis of God's direction."[17] Nations would be unified under God's direction, without conflict over race or class, with the Group at the center of it all. A supportive American journalist predicted "that the Group will become a super-league of Nations at Geneva and will be the Peace- and Pace-Maker of Europe and the World." This vision was inherently pacifist, aiming to bring about a peaceful world through super-national unity, with nations joined "in a God-controlled fellowship— confident of each other's continued honesty, unselfishness, and love."[18]

By the mid-1930s Buchman and his colleagues worked to connect with political circles in Europe and North America, recruiting political leaders and journalists and offering their message as the only answer to civilization's problems. During the 1936 presidential campaign Buchman and others attended both national party conventions, with seats in the hall and rooms where they could meet with party leaders. The evangelist urged both parties to "let God write your platform."[19] During the Democratic convention he told a radio audience that "the country must be governed by men under instructions from God, as definitely given and understood as if they came by wire. This is the true dictatorship of the living God, and the answer to all dictators."[20] When Republican candidate Alfred Landon came through Pittsfield, Massachusetts, during a Group house party, Buchman and Group members gathered around his train car and broke into song.

> Governor Landon, son of the sod,
> Is able to govern when governed by God.
> Listen to God, he'll listen to you
> His plan to see America through.[21]

Group members claimed influence in Europe as well. When the president of Switzerland received the Group in Berne, a Group press release declared, "All of Switzerland took note."[22] After a large rally in Denmark one Group leader anticipated that "we may be called upon either to form, or to be the inspirers of, a government in quite a few years."[23] In the midst of the 1936 crisis over the abdication of Britain's King Edward VIII, several Group members arranged for Buchman to meet prime minister Stanley Baldwin. One member said "that this movement ought to sweep the country and that he was going to put it up to Baldwin to make it his primary concern after the Coronation."[24] The goal of the work in Britain, according to a planning document, was preparing the group "to become a national government as soon as the time is right."[25]

In the United States the Oxford Group diagnosed the national ills in terms that echoed Buchman's description of sin in *Soul Surgery*. "America today is suffering from an inferiority complex proceeding from conviction of sin and resulting in boastfulness among the uneducated and timidity among the educated," proclaimed the anonymous author of "America, Diagnosis and Cure." The memo argued that such sin was manifested in rampant materialism, corruption in business, irresponsibility, immoral art, and the demoralization of the dole.[26] Another document decried America's increased crime and rampant individualism. "From the cradle to the grave we are taught to think of 'I' rather than 'we.'" The author warned of "the menace of an undisciplined democracy—democracy without God control spells chaos." Instead of a well-regulated society, the United States had a "false sense of liberty—the greatest enemies of true liberty are those who insist most vigorously on their personal rights." It decried the "softening of the national fibre—America began as a nation of pioneers, it has become a nation of parasites." Pointing to the popularity of "cosmetics and popular entertainments," as well as the rise of venereal disease, it declared that "as a nation we are sold to pleasure."[27]

The solution to America's social disorder was not only the creation of new people, but the exertion of strong authority. Buchman told a group of women in New York that the world needed "a spiritual dynamic which will change human nature and remake men and nations. There must be a spiritual authority which will be accepted everywhere, by everyone."[28] Elsewhere he argued that social problems "could be solved within a God-controlled democracy, or perhaps I should say theocracy, and they could be solved through a God-controlled fascist dictatorship."[29] The ultimate goal was Christian revolution, putting the nation under God's control.[30]

The Oxford Group, members believed, would be the leaders of the revolution, what an anonymous author called "spiritual storm troops." These "modern minute men" must be "absolutely dependable and instantly available at any time in any place," and "absolutely on fire with determination." They must have "absolute faith in our mission—assuming boldly our God-given leadership of the nation, and carrying the fight fearlessly into the strongholds of the mighty—demanding everything from them and expecting to get it."[31] Garrett Stearly told Ray Purdy that the Group by "its determination to dominate America [would come] to spureme [*sic*] power in the State. It will be Gabriel over the White House indeed." *Gabriel Over the White House* was a 1933 movie produced by William Randolph Hearst, with Walter Huston playing a president who takes on dictatorial powers in the midst of financial crisis, dissolving Congress and declaring martial law, and becomes a national hero.[32]

Some Oxford Group members found inspiration for this national awakening in Germany. In 1933 Buchman and seven other members attended in Berlin "a most interesting and enjoyable dinner given by a club of young Nazis including a grandson of the Kaiser," a friend reported to Shoemaker. "There is no doubt this movement has the loyal support of the elite among the youth. It is essentially a youth movement full of enthusiasm, confidence, and sheer idealism." While acknowledging that "there is always something to criticize in every great social and political revolution—it is essential to recognize that the German people are now committed to a vast program of 'national recovery,'" Shoemaker's correspondent stated. "They must be judged sympathetically, not by excesses in words or acts, but by what catastrophes they may have avoided and by what general good they may accomplish." Buchman heard Nazi propaganda minister Joseph Goebbels speak, and looked forward to meeting him.[33]

Group member and author Hallen Viney was impressed by the Nazi party rally in Nuremberg the next year.[34] He marveled that Hitler was "the first man in history to raise a voluntary army under quiet military discipline for peaceful reconstruction; to use uniforms as a symbol of social equality rather than of military servitude; to mobilize for peace instead of war." Viney saw significant similarities between the Oxford Group and the Nazi party. "Both believe in the primary necessity for individual change, and hence both are criticised for having no social Gospel or for failing to take up their conference with detailed programmes...Both rightly resent armchair criticism." He concluded his report by stating that "the power of self-sacrifice is always eventually greater than the power of the self-indulgent profit-motive, and that a nation which takes to itself such standards as discipline, loyalty and self-sacrifice may well lead the world in spiritual reconstruction." He suggested that Germany might be "the key country, and now may be the time to strike as Jeremiah struck so that the Nazi movement may go on from strength to strength under the dictatorship of the Holy Spirit." He believed that Hitler "would respond at once to anything genuine, and that he would see immediately the principle of disciplined obedience to God."

These accounts raise an inevitable if uncomfortable question: were Buchman and his movement fascists? The accusation was fairly common at the time, and not unknown since. A writer for the *Nation* called Buchman "politically ambitious. He has repeatedly expressed a longing for a dictator and admires Hitler greatly."[35] A Penn State student called the Group "a fascist movement on the religious plane. It makes an appeal to the middle class; it promises economic security; the Dictator is the Holy Spirit represented by the human Buchman and his followers."[36] They weren't alone in leveling these charges; during World War II the FBI kept substantial files, watching the movement and its leader for Nazi leanings.[37] Some of these accusations were rooted in war-related fear or reflexive opposition to the movement's goals.

Fascism is a vague term, associated with a variety of movements and inaccurately used to condemn many others. Fascist movements do, however, tend to have certain markers in common. They arise in response to social decadence and disorder, and work to regenerate their culture and create a well-ordered, organic society. The key to such a society is a "new man," demonstrating courage and daring. Fascist movements favor authoritarian polities and economies that subordinate business issues to the state. They are antiliberal and anticommunist, and militant; they view violence and war positively. Fascism is a mass movement with a rich mythology that exalts youth and the masculine principle; it is nurtured through symbolic activity and liturgical rallies. They often follow authoritarian and charismatic leaders. They tend to be secular, but mirror the messianism and utopianism of millennial religious movements. They are ultranationalist but not necessarily racist or anti-Semitic.[38]

The Oxford Group had some of these markers. It worried about social disorder, called for the creation of a new humanity, and demonstrated intense anticommunism, anti-liberalism, and millennialism. It advocated strong authority and stressed the importance of discipline, spiritual and otherwise. It built a mass movement that employed spectacle and used young men as its icon, as this chapter will show. The Oxford Group rejected violence—in the 1930s it was seen as pacifist—but members certainly employed militaristic language. An anonymous supporter described the Oxford Group as "a far-flung battle-line for Christianity." In order to "save Civilization, every thinking Christian will at once realize that in the inevitable clash with the anti-Christs, which approaches nearer as the world spins towards the end of the present social era, there must be no gaps in that battle-line."[39] At a luncheon meeting for New York women, Buchman called women "Field Marshals in the New World Order."[40]

The Group lacked other crucial marks of fascism, however. Members were not racist—or at least, no more racist than other Americans or Britons of their time. It was internationalist rather than nationalist. And, despite Buchman's centrality, they sought not dictatorship but spiritual oligarchy, leadership by a God-guided, enlightened group. In a 1936 radio address Buchman observed that "many have been waiting for a great leader to emerge. The Oxford Group believes that it must be done not through one person, but through groups of people who have learned to work together under the guidance of God."[41]

In short, Buchman and his colleagues could be called soft fascists—working to build a well-ordered, organic, and united society, but through nonviolent means. Given the upheavals of the 1930s, of course, they weren't alone. Many people across Europe and the United States sought the same goal, from Charles Coughlin, a Catholic priest in recession-wracked Detroit, to Oswald Moseley, leader of the British Union of Fascists. Indeed, for many the Oxford Group provided a safe alternative to more absolutist groups. An American on the staff of World Alliance of YMCAs in Geneva reported that he had seen keen interest in the Groups during a recent visit to Estonia, Latvia, Poland, and Hungary. "The challenge of the absolute which the groups give constituted the only Christian equivalent for the totalitarian demands being made on youth by governments or by political conceptions such as communism, fascism and Hitlerism."[42]

Of course Buchman and his colleagues regularly denied any tendency to fascism. One of Buchman's public statements, however, gave his opponents ammunition. On his return from Europe in 1936, the evangelist gave an interview to the *New York World-Telegram*. What he actually said remains in dispute. The reporter wrote, however, that for Buchman "the Fascist dictatorships of Europe suggest infinite possibilities for remaking the world and putting it under 'God control.'" He then quoted Buchman as saying, "I thank heaven for a man like Adolf Hitler, who built a front line of defense against the anti-Christ of Communism." Buchman criticized Hitler's anti-Semitism, but added,

"Think what it would mean to the world if Hitler surrendered to the control of God. Or Mussolini. Or any dictator. Through such a man God could control a nation overnight and solve every last, bewildering problem." The solution to the world's problems, said Buchman, was "the dictatorship of the living spirit of God."[43] The praise of Hitler quickly became one of Buchman's best-known statements, although it is not certain that he actually said it.

The *World-Telegram* interview dogged Buchman for years, especially after the outbreak of hostilities in Europe. American and British journalists and politicians used the Hitler quotation to question Buchman's patriotism and the movement's loyalty. After the war the movement prepared a lengthy dossier detailing inaccuracies in the initial article and denying any pro-Nazi sentiments on Buchman's part. The Group maintained that the statement about Hitler clashed with Buchman's beliefs. "In fact, the whole tenor of his life and activity points to his rejection in practice of any kind of totalitarianism." The Group's supporters included leaders of the resistance in Germany and France, the dossier noted.[44] The translation of a secret instruction to the Nazi regime's S.S., dated March 1938, called "the struggle against the Group Movement is one of the priority tasks of the Security Police."[45] In December 1945 a letter to *The Times* of London cited a "secret Gestapo report" about the Groups which called the movement " 'the pacemaker of Anglo-American diplomacy' and as a force working 'to bring about new political and ideological conditions in the Reich.' "[46]

These few years—about 1934–1938—were crucial for the Oxford Group, as it evolved from a strictly religious group into a movement with political ideas and ambitions. It moved from creative evangelism to a government-in-waiting. Although dramatic, this evolution was a logical development of ideas that had been developing within the Group's leadership, as they looked beyond changing people to changing the world. While politics became increasingly important, the movement's agenda remained fairly vague, centered on a strong opposition to communism and the need for leaders, voters, and businesses to listen to God. More explicit political beliefs—what they came to call an ideology—developed after the war.

Capture the Newspapers

Changing the world required turning the Oxford Group into a mass movement, reaching beyond the elites who attended their house parties, to catch the attention of the common man. "We must have our finger on the pulse of public opinion," the Public Inspiration team proclaimed.[47] Buchman told a leader of the team that "if we capture the newspapers and the magazine-reading public and without question show them that here is the answer, it will more quickly further the cause than anything else."[48]

Starting in the mid-1930s, Oxford Group leaders developed several techniques to spread their message to a broad audience. Mass media— the newspapers, radio, and movies which were playing larger roles in American and European society—were essential to this work. This outreach—writing press releases, reaching out to reporters, and creating their own materials—could today be called a media strategy. It could also be called, much more negatively, propaganda.

Again, they were inspired by developments in Europe. Mass movements of the 1930s—notably Germany's Nazi Party and its Hitler Youth—showed them how to inspire large groups of people. The Public Inspiration team recommended that Group members read Goebbels' diaries.[49] Team leader Garth Lean urged members to be prepared; when the Group was "called upon either to form, or to be the inspirers of a government," it would be just like "the Nazis were in 1932." On that day the press would have to quickly express an opinion about a Group-led government. If handled well, Lean wrote, "I think we can decide that question for them."[50] Buchman and his colleagues were not Nazis, but the Oxford Group was out to create a mass movement, and they looked to the example of the most successful mass movement of their time.

To this end the Group developed publicity offices at Calvary Church and in London, staffed by teams—generally volunteers—responsible for press releases and working with reporters.[51] "The National Press Team" in New York urged Group members to make friends with reporters, to "help to mold their opinions favorably toward the Group which will be valuable in the future when they begin to write articles or editorials about the 'New American Revolution.'"[52] They also used connections to solicit friendly articles. The editors of *The Churchman* reported receiving a letter from a distinguished minister, relaying the Group's request for supportive coverage.[53] Buchman told Purdy that a British friend, Lady Beecham, was coming to America and could be a useful ally. "She has gone to a number of newspapers here [in London] and simply made them change their tone."[54] He also criticized a New York member who had not been sufficiently active in changing *Time's* treatment. "I feel with your presence there you ought to have insisted on a much more positive statement, deleting certain of the deliberate lies."[55]

To encourage positive press coverage, Group leaders developed what public relations executives now call "Astroturf"—carefully engineered publicity that appears to be spontaneous grass-roots support.[56] After announcing in 1937 that a Hearst magazine would soon be running an article on the Group, for instance, team leaders suggested that "at least ten thousand letters should pour in during the week of March 21st to the American Weekly if each of us fully does his part." They encouraged Group members to give "to this world's largest magazine proof of the fact that America is ready and hungry for positive news. Every time you respond instantly to a suggestion from us asking for a nation-wide backing for an article or a broadcast, etc.,—you are advancing the entire 'Public Inspiration' front."[57] Similarly, Group leaders used "the pressure of some hundreds of wires from all parts of the country" to get newsreel coverage of a meeting at Oxford.[58] This media outreach made the movement look larger—and possibly more newsworthy—than it was.

In addition to changing the movement's image in the press, the Group worked to change members of the press themselves. Group members, some of them journalists, hoped to convert editors and reporters, who would change newspapers and, through them, society at large. At the Banff house party journalists and others pledged "to put Christ in control of the personnel and editorial policy of the Press." In their view, the front pages of most newspapers seemed to consist "of battle, murder, and sudden death while the higher things of Life are relegated to a few pars. [sic] in an obscure corner so that the work of the Groups does not receive the notice to which its human value entitles it."[59] The best index to a changed press, evidently, was good coverage of the Group. British reporter and Group member A.J. Russell looked forward to the day when he could return to London's Fleet Street "to introduce a Life-Changing Department, staffed with surrendered men and women, trained in the highest of all arts—of leading sinners from those dark tunnels of tragedy and misfortune, as portrayed in newspaper columns, into God's sunlight." The department's columns would report of "broken lives mended."[60]

There were already examples of this changed press. In December 1936, while the world's papers were caught up in the impending abdication in Britain, Norway's *Tidens Tegn* devoted its first page to "positive news, a description of Norway of today, its new interests and occupations, new manners of thinking." The Group members argued that such work—creating positive public opinion—was the press's "real function."[61] The editor of a Canadian religious paper, the *Witness*, was changed during one of the first national campaigns; for years afterward the paper included a weekly supplement dedicated to Group news. "I feel that what is displayed in these pages marks the Oxford Group as one of the most hopeful signs on the Canadian and world horizons today," he explained.[62] The editor of the *Berkshire Eagle*, a small paper in western Massachusetts, had become changed and regularly ran Group material on a special page.[63]

Because Oxford Group supporters saw their work as of great importance, they felt that unfair treatment in the press was cataclysmic if not demonic. Buchman worried that a blurb in *Time* would "do untold harm."[64] After a negative story appeared in *American Church Monthly* and was picked up by *Time*, Shoemaker told a friendly bishop that the article, which hurt the movement in Europe, had become "the weapon of forces hostile and critical towards the cause of Christ." Shoemaker said that only a letter to the magazine from the bishop could fix the matter. "Knowing how busy you are, I have taken the liberty to write a possible letter which might answer the purpose."[65] The work of the press team, Buchman said, would "help to overcome the possible attack of the communists at this early stage, and we will have to win them by guile. Though I believe that the two great movements are Christ and anti-Christ, we have to remember that in the American Democracy they are not ready for that truth."[66]

The Oxford Group did not rely only on newspapers to spread its message; members wrote books as well, mainly stories or collections of stories of changed lives. Samuel Shoemaker became one of the Group's leading authors, producing seven books, most of them narrating the spiritual experiences of Group converts. Through the 1930s there were numerous books by or about the Oxford Group, including titles like *For Sinners Only*, *I Was a Pagan*, and *Inspired Children*, many of them autobiographies of converts. The Group newsletter told members to ask local bookstores to stock them.[67] The books were also distributed by the Group's book room at Calvary, or were given away or sold at house parties.[68]

In addition to the press releases and the books, the Oxford Group produced the single-issue magazine called *Rising Tide*. In the spring of 1937 the Group's communications office in New York proposed a publication that would describe the "spiritual history" made by the movement. It would carry God's answer to the nation's problems "as it is being lived out in hundreds upon hundreds of revolutionary cells throughout the entire fabric of our national life."[69] The magazine copied

Life and *Look*, the new national magazines with their large pages and compelling photographs. Group members wrote the articles, took the pictures, laid out the pages, and oversaw the printing and distribution. The magazine had 50 pages and a first run of a half-million copies, at a newsstand price of ten cents a copy.[70]

Its message was a simple one: the world is a wonderful place, but it is overwhelmed with greed, selfishness, and hate. Although human wisdom has failed, God has a plan—new people building a new world. "Pictured in the pages that follow is a rising tide of men and women who are convinced that if you want an answer for the world today, the best place to start is with yourself." A country is only as good as its people, it continued, and when the ordinary man drifts, the nation loses its way. "Democracy without God-control means chaos." The solution lies in God-controlled people who "accepted from God the inner discipline which makes a nation great and democracy workable."[71]

Typical for the Oxford Group, stories made up the bulk of the magazine. It described the Group's work in Oxford, South Africa, Canada, and Norway. Several pages featured stories of changed work places, including mills and farms, describing the Group's answer to industrial strife. "These workers are part of a new industrial unity being forged throughout the world as Labor, Management and Capital become co-laborers under the guidance of God." Another section showed how the Group could help with conflict at home, too. The (most likely fictional) story tells of an executive whose life is changed by a friend; after his home life improves, he changes others. "Defeat in the home, disaster in the world. Faith in the home, security in the nation." The magazine concluded with the lyrics to a new Group song, "Wise Old Horsey."[72]

Group leaders saw *Rising Tide* as epochal. A consensus of newspaper people, they reported, called the magazine "just about the biggest news story in the history of the publishing business."[73] A British journalist supposedly called it "the finest bit of work since the Bible."[74] The editors encouraged Group members to market the magazine, because "Rising Tide is a life-changing vehicle for America." A powerful evangelical tool, it could create "a new moral and spiritual climate. In that climate God will begin to show us a new strategy for advancing toward a truly God-controlled nation."[75]

The Group advertised *Rising Tide* widely, with advertisements in newspapers and signs on streetcars. They put more energy, however, into getting endorsements from prominent people. A publicity agent for the magazine's distributor suggested that Group members in each city stage a picture with the mayor or the governor, looking at the first copy of *Rising Tide*. He also advised members to contact their local newspapers to "sell them the idea of pointing, editorially, to Rising Tide as a remarkable evidence of spiritual thinking on the part of an important portion of present population."[76]

Oxford Group members also created some innovative marketing techniques for *Rising Tide*, similar to what is today called buzz marketing, using word of mouth to spread the message. A mass mailing to Group members urged them to "talk-talk-talk-talk Rising Tide. Tell everyone you see that Rising Tide—the new fifty-page photo publication—is a knock-out." They should urge everyone they saw, even complete strangers, to order a copy. "Mobilize the tongue power of America for Rising Tide."[77] The New York office asked members to spread publicity postcards wherever they went, "like Hansel and Gretel." With their help, "Rising Tide will be entering every last home in the country."[78]

The Group's publicity outreach was not limited to print media. They also turned to visual means, producing several short films, including *Bridgebuilders*, which recounted its work in Denmark. It featured footage of large rallies as well as the impact of living Christianity "at work in a typical kitchen, in a factory, in a now happy home once threatened by divorce, a hospital, a business, a farm, and the cottage of an unemployed man."[79] In 1937 a group of young Group members produced a film, *Youth Marches On*, starring a singing cowboy, with volunteer writers and directors. A Group flyer called it a hit, noting "a five weeks' run on Broadway." The movie also marked the Group's first venture into music, including two new songs, "New Frontiersmen" and "Wise Old Horsey."[80] Drawing on movie and Broadway styles, the latter became a theme song for the movement, with its dialogue between cowboy and horse. They agree that the problems with the world are caused by its people. The cowboy believes that human nature is fixed, but the horse declares that God can change people, "but you gotta be willing...for God to hold the reins His way." The song concludes,

> So me and my wise old horsey
> We're taking new trails today
> For a brand-new country, you'll be proud to be in it,
> An' He shall have dominion from sea to sea in it,
> We're listening to God, every mornin' to God,
> And we'll soon remake the world that way.[81]

Such songs and films soon became an important part of the movement's outreach.

Independent of its own efforts, the Oxford Group also started appearing in popular culture. Rumor had it that the authors of *Anything Goes*, the Cole Porter musical of 1934, were inspired in part by the activities of the Oxford Group.[82] There is a clearer connection to *Susan and God*, originally a 1937 play, later made into a film starring Joan Crawford. The title character is as a wealthy woman, recently converted by an unnamed religious movement focused on the need for honesty and confession. "It's so *thrilling* and *alive* and *fun*," she tells her society friends, echoing Shoemaker and the others, "so people aren't *ashamed to be good*." Over the course of three acts she tries to convert her society friends by forcing them to be honest; she upsets their lives while ignoring the mess her own life has become. In the end she stays with her family rather than go off to a movement meeting at Newport.[83] And the Group was probably the only new religious movement of the 1930s to have its own limerick.

> There was a young man from Peoria
> Whose sins grew gorier and gorier
> By confession and prayer
> And *some* savior-faire—
> He now lives at the Waldorf-Astoria.[84]

The Oxford Group was entering the popular culture, showing its spreading fame.

It is not clear, however, whether the Group was becoming known for its accomplishments, or simply because of its publicity. The Group's own press releases make an impressive case for the movement's impact, but it is harder to get an objective assessment of the Group's work. Movement leaders quickly became masters of public relations, and used their connections to get their story told. But that effort often created to an echo chamber effect, with Group press releases quoting other press releases, all proving the movement's importance. They were making the Oxford Group a mass movement, but the size of that mass was and still is uncertain.

A Rolling Tide of Indomitable Power

The success of the Nazis inspired the Oxford Group to pursue another tool for building a mass movement—the large rally. The Nazi's 1934 Nuremberg rally demonstrated "the value of the large gatherings per se, both as a demonstration to the outside world and also as an inspiration to the one who attends it," Hallen Viney wrote. "The real lesson of Nuremberg to me was the personal inspiration of mingling with such a mighty, kindly and disciplined people all filled with a sense of real purpose."[85] Group members applied this lesson during the 1930s, as they turned their signature house parties—traditionally intimate meetings—into large rallies and week-long assemblies for thousands of people. These meetings became spectacles, with carefully crafted pageants, parades, and flags. Like Nuremberg, these events served two simultaneous purposes—giving rank and file Group members a feeling that they were part of a world-changing movement and catching the attention of the general public.

There were precedents for large parties, including the Louisville meetings in 1931 and the 1934 North American House Party in Banff, Canada. Those paled in comparison to the 1934 Oxford house party, which attracted nearly five thousand people from 30 countries for 18 days.[86] The daily program was like that of previous house parties: quiet time, Bible study, special groups, platform addresses, and evening group. To keep a more intimate feeling, the meeting separated into four separate house parties that came together for special events. "As house parties grow in numbers, we must keep the intimate idea of host and guest clearly in mind," the organizer wrote. Although efficiency was good, it was more important to be hospitable. "It makes for the difference between a 'conference' and a 'house party.'"[87]

The Group's house parties eventually turned into spectacles. At the 1935 Oxford gathering "representatives of 32 nations marched up the aisle of Christ Church Cathedral carrying the flags of their respective nations and singing, 'Like a Mighty Army Moves the Church of God.'"[88] At a youth rally in Oxford they marched in to the tune of the Battle Hymn of the Republic, "the arrayed youth of twenty countries. A steady tramp to the music of that great hymn thundering from two thousand throats as the young army steadily and like a rolling tide of indomitable power filed in its hundreds to the platform."[89]

These rallies echo—consciously or not—events like the Nuremberg rally. During a 1937 London luncheon for 800 people, "Dr. Buchman called out questions. The young men with the banners of their countries shouted their replies in unison."[90] At the 1939 World's Fair in San Francisco, one Group member remembered, "The youth marched with banners. Frank liked banners. European ideologies were using banners, and he wanted to compete."[91]

A landmark for the movement came on Easter Sunday, 1936. To celebrate the one year anniversary of its work in Denmark, the Group organized a gathering of 12,000 people in Ollerup, a small town 90 miles from Copenhagen. The plenary meeting focused on spectacle. "Music, movement and colour played as big a part in the meetings as the spoken word," a young Englishwoman told her California friends. "During these days we have been learning the secret of capturing men's imaginations through the eye as well as the ear. To see over three hundred Hollanders march in gave one a sense of national movement and Christianity on the march as no amount of talking about it could do."[92] A Group booklet reported that "the demonstration opened with a march of 1,000 youth bearing flags of the 20 nations who during the past year have sent 1,000 representatives to Denmark."[93] As they processed, Danish youth sang one of the Group's new songs:

> Forward march, forward march
> All we who would serve God.
> Discipline—discipline
> So that God can lead the army,
> One bond one spirit
> When we pray for guidance
> God alone gives orders here.
> Each single one must obey...
> The Weapon we conquer the world with
> Is His fine strong love
> God with us, God with us
> Then no power can stop us.[94]

The pageant concluded with an international series of speakers and Buchman's "Call to the Nations." The world needs to change, he told the crowd, but it needs to start with each individual. "Everybody can be a bridge-builder. Will it be you? Will it be your nation?"[95]

The Oxford Group brought this model to America for its first "National Assembly," held in Stockbridge, Massachusetts, in June 1936. Four thousand people attended eight house parties in outlying villages and participated in mass meetings; the smaller parties focused on personal work, while the larger rallies featured Group members describing their Christian experiences.[96] As sharing became spectacle, those who confessed their sins in the Stockbridge town hall included a British lord, the Protestant Episcopal Bishop of Arizona, a baker and a butcher, a Scottish communist leader, a French baroness and others.[97]

This meeting marked a shift from intimate religious experience to public performance; starting with Stockbridge, every word spoken at the Group's large meetings was transcribed and filed, and often turned into a press release.[98]

The pageantry developed at Ollerup was echoed in Stockbridge. The meeting opened with a Memorial Day ceremony, featuring a procession including Indians, former bootlegger Bill Pickle, the flags of the states and the nations, a covered wagon, and a group called "Youth on the March." Participants sang "America" and "Revere Is Riding Again." There were speeches from a former assistant secretary of agriculture, the Scottish communist, the French baroness, and several youth members. The highlight of the afternoon was a pageant first presented at Ollerup, "The Quest of Humanity." The choral play, "a product of the Artists' Section," described the despair of the world—ruler and citizen, rich and poor—transformed by God's word.[99]

Group members were excited by the impact of these large events. "Stockbridge marked a definite turning point," one wrote. "The news of the National Assembly was carried in every state and in every important city in America. It was filmed by all the principle [*sic*] newsreels, featured in magazine articles, and broadcasted on the radio." With all this coverage, the media had begun seeing "that the words 'Oxford Group' are—in the minds of the American public—beginning to be synonymous with national reconstruction."[100]

To further this process, Group members developed two specialized spectacles. The first was an Oxford Group holiday—Buchman's birthday, on June 4. Over the years, that day became a festival in every Group setting. In 1938, for instance, there were parties in London "where the children of the slums and the children of the privileged celebrate together the birthday of the man who, like Christ, has always time for the children. There is also a dinner in the House of Commons, where Lords and Commons together meet to honour one of God's statesmen." Across the Atlantic, others celebrated at a house party in Stockbridge. A thousand people bowed their heads "to thank God for the life and work of Frank Buchman, and to find their part in carrying on that work."[101] Buchman often used his birthday to make a major speech or announce a new initiative.

Another specialized type of house party was the New Enlistment camps of 1937 and 1938. These camps brought together hundreds of young people, usually in a rural area, for a week of spiritual experience and physical training; most were exclusively for men. They echoed Buchman's work on college campuses, trying to inspire the next

generation for the movement, the "militia" to lead the Christian revolution. They were not the moral equivalent of the Hitler Youth or
the British fascist group the Black Shirts, but offered some of the same
appeal.

Invitations to the camps set the tone, with inspiring language and
pictures of handsome young men. The brochure for the first camp,
held in Birmingham, England, in March 1937, offered "A Summons to
Enlist," with pictures of three buglers and of men jogging. The inside
text rehearsed the world's troubles, but proclaimed that "youths led by
God can remake the world." In Birmingham, it promised, "the vanguard of the New Enlistment will mobilize under God's Leadership to
bring about the greatest Revolution of all time, by which the Cross of
Christ will transform the world."[102] The brochure for a 1938 camp near
Toronto featured a poem.

> Vanguard of the New Enlistment, rise
> Marching with banners unfurled
> God-confident armies mobilize
> Free for remaking the world.
> Then break with our softness and lust!
> All false gods we'll trample to dust![103]

Many of these invitations included the same pictures of enthusiastic
young men.

The camps were like a rugged and casual house party. The schedule for the Australia New Enlistment (the only coeducational camp)
included physical training, quiet time, Bible study, large group meetings, and free time for sharing, special meetings, or writing articles
for the press team.[104] Sharing was crucial at the Scandinavian camp, in
Rørøs, Norway. "Young men [stand] up and announce in short, costly
sentences, or else with rejoicing, that at last they have found peace and
certainty and that they have decided from now on to live under God's
control and according to the four absolute standards." The witness was
casual, as it was at the house parties. "At one moment the hall rings
with laughter, at the next there is a straight and serious talk on the subject of sin. These are certainly unusual religious meetings," a journalist
commented; "young sun-burned men in sporting clothes talk objec-
tively, unaffectedly, concretely about their own sin and how they have
overcome it."[105]

The New Enlistment camps were physical as well as spiritual.
The Birmingham gathering featured the "New Fitness" led by a

South African international footballer and a Swiss skiing champion. Participants rose at 6 AM for a run and did calisthenics throughout the day.[106] This training was about more than just fitness. "The discipline throughout the camp in physical training, in food, in punctuality at meals and meetings, in loving and caring enough for each other to hold one another up to the very highest in the physical, mental, moral and spiritual spheres," declared a leader of the Australian camp, "demonstrated on a miniature scale the tremendous force Australia can be in world affairs, when she is freed from sins of casualness, pride, selfishness."[107]

Camp participants demonstrated their fitness to the public. During a British house party the "Youth Battalion" did their exercises and then marched through the streets of the town, singing "On the Revolution."[108] At the Scandinavian camp in Norway, the 275 men in the camp rose at six each morning. "From three different parts of the town through the empty streets run three troops of young men in shorts. Together on the sports ground of Rorøs they have twenty minutes of physical training."[109] At a public rally they had the entire crowd "repeat and repeat the 4 absolutes, till they knew them by heart."[110] These public exercises demonstrated the young men's—and the movement's—strength and power.

At the camps young men discovered the Group as a solution to individual and world problems, and learned that addressing one set of needs would solve the other. A speaker at the Australian camp stated that "every sin we commit is like striking a blow in the face of Australia. Our sin is no longer a personal affair, but is of significance to our nation. The quality of our life will either make or break Australia. The real traitor is the spiritual slacker, who has seen what he might be, but is just not bothered by it." In this work participants held each other to high standards. "There are no cushions in this revolution," another speaker declared. "Let us see that everything we do is revolutionary."[111] This challenge often came in military metaphors; one press released described the participants in an American camp as "an army in peace time to fight moral rot, disintegration, drift, and to assume day and night responsibility to rebuild America."[112]

The New Enlistment camps, like the other large house parties, show how the Oxford Group reshaped its practices to create a mass movement. The content of these events remained largely the same as the first house parties—platform talks, sharing, and recreation. But the larger events turned the traditional practice into spectacle, designed to energize the participants and get the attention of the public. The Group had once again reshaped the evangelical rally into something new, with the goal of transforming national and international politics and culture.

God's Answer to a World in Desperate Need

By 1938 Buchman and his colleagues had a core, a critical mass of people, for their movement. They had a message for a troubled world—listen to God and live the absolutes. They needed a better name, however. While "Oxford Group" had a certain cachet, it was also vague and carried with it a certain tone of elitism. In an increasingly media-centered age, the organization needed a name that captured the public's attention and summarized the movement's message. Starting in June 1938 Buchman and his friends began calling their work Moral Re-Armament. It was short, direct, and carried no class or religious baggage. It sounded like something everyone could support. Within six months the movement had an acronym—MRA—and a logotype. It had a new brand.

It was an anxious time for the world; Germany had annexed Austria in March, and the German-speaking regions of Czechoslovakia seemed to be its next target. As the crisis built, Buchman was resting in a small town in southern Germany. On a walk in the Black Forest, the phrase came to him: "Moral and spiritual re-armament. The next great move in the world will be a movement of moral re-armament for all nations." He told his supporters that the message "came straight from the living God."[113] "Moral" had two meanings, sometimes depending on the situation—both a commitment to correct behavior (the four absolutes) and the necessity of a unified society (i.e., morale).

Buchman made the public announcement as part of his sixtieth birthday celebrations. On May 29, Buchman kicked off the campaign for Moral Re-Armament at a public meeting in the London neighborhood of East Ham. He declared that the world's crisis "is fundamentally a moral one. The nations must rearm morally." The key was letting God change human nature so that people could follow the four absolutes. "We can, we must, and we will generate a moral and spiritual force that is powerful enough to remake the world," he concluded.[114]

The Munich crisis of September 1938 made the cause even more important. "Crisis is our opportunity," declared "Heralds of a New World Order," a MRA newsletter. "An increased response to Moral Re-Armament was the natural outcome of the September crisis. Many admitted to themselves that only a totally new spirit could save us and our civilisation." Group members had a special duty. "We who have experienced God's guidance in our own lives must teach nations to listen and find a united plan." No matter the disagreements, people agreed "that whatever else we do, we must at all costs re-arm our country morally."[115]

Munich also encouraged a new star to join the MRA forces. H.W. "Bunny" Austin was a mainstay of Britain's victorious Davis Cup tennis team from 1933 to 1936 and a regular winner at Wimbledon. He had long been a fortunate man, talented and happy, he wrote, but with the Munich crisis "we were all of us faced with the possible end of civilisation.... Tennis did not help much now." The crisis led him to a search for something offering "all the adventure and comradeship of war without the wastage; some aim which would give my whole life meaning, some cause by which the youth of Britain could create a new chivalry in the world." His contribution was writing *Moral Re-Armament: The Battle for Peace.* The bulk of the book was a collection of statements, letters to the editor, and other documents from across Britain and around the world, from politicians, labor leaders, and other prominent people, all supporting the movement.[116]

MRA members believed Austin's book would be a valuable piece of propaganda because of his celebrity. British group leaders told their national team, made up of almost 1,000 people, that the book "catches people's attention because it includes statements by people everyone knows about." The book was so powerful, the letter continued, "that local leaders and individual citizens in every part of Britain publicly demanded Moral Re-Armament." Members of the MRA British press team described it as "God's Christmas gift to Britain." It sold a half-million copies in Britain and was translated into eight languages. Group members in one county appointed MRA "wardens" for each community charged with publicizing Austin's book.[117]

The book fed the movement's publicity machine. The release of the American edition of Austin's book coincided with Buchman's arrival in New York in March 1939, which they hoped would generate front page news across the country. "You will want to have Frank's statement, issued to the press on his arrival, to think about in your morning quiet times and use it in your talks with people and in your touch with the press," the press office wrote. The book was "the most comprehensive survey of the development of MRA," deserving nation-wide publicity.[118] The press team asked for data about local coverage—"who has seen Bunny Austin's book, what has been the response, what plans have you? We would value seeing anything that has appeared in the newspapers."[119]

MRA publicity leaders developed other printed materials to spread the word. The British team produced 1.8 million leaflets, 4 million milk bottle caps, and 10,000 posters. "The poster shows the four granite standards of Moral Re-Armament (absolute honesty, purity, unselfishness and love), supporting the letters MRA against a blue sky." This was the movement's first logo; forms of it appeared in publications on both sides of the Atlantic over the next few years.[120] The American team printed up stickers for members to put on their outgoing mail. "Floods of MRA stickers going through Uncle Sam's mail will arouse the interest of the whole country," the New York office promised.[121] A sample bundle of publicity materials, including posters, leaflets, and book bands, cost $2.80 a set—over $40 today. "All these pieces of display will focus people's attention on Bunny Austin's book. Many of us find that it is the most timely instrument God has ever put into our hands. That makes it worth our best thought on how to get it as quickly as possible to the maximum number of people."[122]

Group members hoped that all this publicity would help them achieve their ultimate goal: making Moral Re-Armament official government policy. Garrett Stearly reported that Queen Wilhelmina of the Netherlands had "established Moral Re-Armament as national policy by official proclamation, posted in every city and village throughout Holland." Similar endorsements came from King Leopold of Belgium and the president of France, as well as leaders of Germany, Italy, China, and Japan.[123] The Group put great stock in these most likely symbolic proclamations.

Buchman's colleagues aggressively sought a similar endorsement from President Roosevelt. Just after Christmas 1938, Purdy wrote to Roosevelt, noting the publication of Austin's *Moral Re-Armament* and the movement's support from English nobility, the king of Belgium, and the queen of the Netherlands. Purdy suggested that in his next speech to Congress the president follow suit. "Such a lead on your part would certainly have a world echo and would be received with gratitude by responsible statesmen in England and throughout Europe, as well as by countless Americans who hold you in highest esteem."[124] A few months later a New York socialite urged Roosevelt to issue an endorsement like that of Stanley Baldwin. "Two such messages, yours and Lord Baldwin's, should inspire and encourage those who love true liberty and freedom throughout the world and unite them in a deserving peace."[125]

While they worked on Roosevelt, Oxford Group members aggressively sought other celebrity endorsements. This work reflected the movement's long-standing attraction to key men and its increasing sensitivity to the growing celebrity culture. They realized that in their media-heavy age, people paid attention to what famous people said.

A good example of this celebrity outreach is the Group's work with famous athletes. Austin asked 37 fellow British athletes to sign a pro-MRA statement in early spring 1939.[126] "What this country needs is a clean-up and more guts," a British boxer declared. "Moral Re-Armament is something every fellow can go all out for and we will need every sportsman if we are going to win."[127] A group of American athletes, including Babe Ruth, Don Budge, Joe DiMaggio, Bobby Jones, and Jesse Owens, signed their own manifesto on "Moral Re-Armament Through Sport." "To re-arm America morally is the greatest sporting challenge of our time. It is a game on a national field with Olympic scope," the statement declared. "Moral Re-Armament means sportsmanship everywhere. It means teamwork, fair play and clean living—personally and nationally.... We can train a world team of sporting nations to win the race against chaos."[128] The manifesto was placed as an advertisement in papers across the country. This outreach to sportsmen—and sports fans—was new for the movement, a logical tactic for a group seeking publicity in a sports- and celebrity-mad culture.

The Group also dipped its toe into an even bigger world of celebrities—show business. In 1939, in front of reporters and cameras, Buchman met with negligee-clad actress Mae West. West told reporters that the movement was "wonderful work...I owe all my success to the kind of thinking Moral Re-Armament is." Buchman beamed. "You are a splendid character, Miss West. You have done wonderful work, too." West encouraged Buchman to change co-star W.C. Fields. "Give it to him in a bottle and he'll go for it," West concluded. According to *Time*, however, Fields was recalcitrant. "I'll take anything in a bottle," he stated. "But I don't need rearmament."[129] Other stars did sign up, including actor Joel McCrea and dancer Ruth St. Denis.

The release of publications and recruiting of celebrities laid the groundwork for the movement's greatest publicity effort yet—a series of rallies across America in the summer of 1939. It kicked off with "MRA Week" in New York in May, including a rally in Madison Square Garden for 12,000 people, featuring both spectacle and oratory. It began with bagpipers and the flags of 50 countries and 48 states processing to a stage featuring four flood-lit pylons representing the four absolutes. There were speakers both in person and by radio from London, as well as messages from New York Governor Herbert

Lehman, Secretary of State Cordell Hull, 100 Canadian mayors, and 300 British mayors. Since it was Mother's Day, MRA had solicited statements from 3,500 British mothers and President Roosevelt's mother.[130] Sara Roosevelt declared by radio hookup that "moral rearmament is the price of peace. In this the mothers of America can take the lead. We cradle the future. We must preserve for our children the things we hold most dear—our homes, our families, our Christian faith." The *New York Herald-Tribune* wrote that "although Garden audiences have been stirred to more vociferous enthusiasm in the recent past, rarely has a New York mass meeting expressed such earnestness and conviction."[131]

A bigger meeting marked MRA's first anniversary—and Buchman's sixty-first birthday—at Washington's Constitution Hall. This time the celebrities were primarily political; among the 85 sponsors were cabinet officers and members of Congress. Meeting planners hoped this sponsorship would attract other publicity; one press team member asked the *New York Post* for coverage, noting that "six Cabinet members are now sponsoring Moral Re-Armament."[132] As always, *Time* was

Figure 2 The stage at the "Citizen's Meeting for Moral Re-Armament," May 14, 1939, Madison Square Garden in New York. From the Records of Moral Re-Armament, Prints and Photographs Division, Library of Congress.

less impressed. A few of the sponsors were dedicated supporters of the movement, the magazine said, "but a majority of the Hon. [*sic*] sponsors were bandwagon jumpers and politicians whose attitude was, 'Hell, it's not controversial, is it?'" House Minority Leader Joseph Martin said, "Sure I'm for Moral Re-Armament, whatever that is. It's just like being against sin."[133]

The Constitutional Hall meeting was an Oxford Group testimony meeting writ large, with broad statements alongside personal witness. A group of government secretaries and clerks declared that "Moral Re-Armament creates a new type of woman whose love of country is above love of self. She lives for the government, not on it." They promised to be honest, efficient, and not take office supplies. "Government workers, morally re-armed, can be the inoculation against the apathy which is sapping the strength of America."[134] Senator Harry Truman read the much desired—if somewhat noncommittal—statement from the White House, signed by Stephen Early, secretary to the President. "The underlying strength of the world must consist in the moral fiber of her citizens. A program of moral re-armament for the world, cannot fail therefore, to lessen the dangers of armed conflict. Such moral re-armament to be most highly effective, must receive support on a world-wide basis."[135] The first two sentences were written by an MRA member, with the last added by Roosevelt himself.[136] A reporter for the *Washington Star* was deeply impressed by statements from Britain, calling them "probably unparalleled in modern British history.... The popular reaction was spontaneous and moral rearmament overnight became a watchword of the hour."[137]

In his concluding remarks, Buchman said that MRA had "become part of the national policy of certain countries," and had gained overwhelming American response. "Some twenty governors sent messages saying that the need of this country is Moral Re-Armament," he declared. "Mayors, town councils, and city governments are responding." He then offered one of his favorite illustrations of a problem common to nations and individuals. "God gave man two ears and one mouth. Why doesn't he listen twice as much as he talks?" This remark drew applause. "There's your program for America; there's your program for the individual life; there's your recipe for tomorrow morning—to begin to listen twice as much as you talk!" He hoped that his influential audience, by listening twice as much as they talked, could "bring a message that will bring the new era to America!" The meeting concluded with a quiet time, the Lord's Prayer, and the Star Spangled Banner.[138]

The biggest and splashiest of the 1939 meetings was the Hollywood Bowl event, "A Call to the Nations for Moral Re-Armament." After the dramatic beginning described in the introduction, the Bowl meeting featured lots of speeches and messages, including Roosevelt's from Constitution Hall.[139] Among the speakers were the former president of the Los Angeles Chamber of Commerce, a group of Scots, a Nebraska school teacher, Louis B. Mayer, European nobility, and dancer Ruth St. Dennis.[140] The *Los Angeles Times* declared that it saw Moral Re-Armament in handshakes between a Japanese man and a Chinese woman, and between a Teamsters' leader and the president of a farmer's association. "Once enemies—admittedly—these men said they now understood each other."[141]

The program booklet for the meeting included "M.R.A. and You," a page-long summary of the movement's message. There is only one answer to the world's many problems, it declared, "a power outside yourself. That power is God." Readers should ask themselves if there was anything in their lives that was not absolutely loving, pure, unselfish, or honest, and then "let God take charge. Millions of people will tell you that if you make that experiment honestly you find new power to live and the answer to every problem. Then try listening to God every morning—try ten minutes at first. Let God direct your thinking." Through such listening you will find "the answer which you've been waiting for all your life, and never quite had the courage to try." Such listening with produce new people, and through them "we shall have new nations to make a new world. This is M.R.A. This is God's answer to a world in desperate need."[142] Although in grander language, it was the same message—the need for personal change and an experience of God—Buchman had preached for 30 years.

After the Hollywood Bowl meeting about 1,000 supporters of MRA headed to Del Monte, California, for the "Second World Assembly" of Moral Re-Armament.[143] "Everyone agrees that the need of the hour is for M.R.A.," Buchman declared in his opening remarks. In the current crisis, men and women in every nation should "enlist in the service of M.R.A. for the duration of this world war for peace." He summarized the Oxford Group's philosophy simply. "If people were different and had the power to change men and the nations, that would be the answer to all our problems.... Here in this philosophy is lasting peace, and only here. You will not find it in any other quarter."[144]

Like other Oxford Group and MRA meetings, the meetings at Del Monte consisted mainly of statements and witness. Most stressed the theme "Guidance or Guns." A 15-year-old student from Claremont,

California, declared that "unless God's guidance is put into practical use today—and every day—the fellows of my age inevitably are going to pay and I do mean pay." MRA members, he concluded, "set free by the guidance of God" will be able to "devote our mind, strength, and will to the creation of a New World Order and Culture." Scoville Wishard, a Buchman follower since the Princeton days, stated that "MRA is God's way of giving every man a chance to participate in world leadership. MRA reduces taxes, prevents crime, restores public health, inspires youth, creates national unity and reconciles nations. Enlist now. Tomorrow may be too late."[145]

On the last day Buchman challenged his audience. "Some of you come to a meeting and judge it. But you have no right to judge it. M.R.A. registers with you. You don't register with M.R.A. And your criticism is an index of where you are living." Echoing earlier calls for a unified society, Buchman stated that "America has to learn to have a group mind, and M.R.A. is that group mind.... Get a group mind in your community. Get a group mind in your state and in your nation, God-directed and controlled, and you'll have the new era. That's the group mind that America needs."[146]

Once again Buchman had reinvented his work, as he and his colleagues transformed their small, elite evangelical network into a mass movement. While less than two decades before Buchman sought anonymity, now he reveled in publicity. MRA writings brandished endorsements and statements from prominent people—athletes, businessmen, politicians, and even Mae West. Leaders saw history made in a tennis player's speech or a letter signed by some politicians. They highlighted symbolic actions, like the handshake between a Chinese man and a Japanese man, or the publication of a Buchman speech in the Congressional Record.

The movement's message had changed as well, downplaying its religious content. The big public meetings closed with the Lord's Prayer, but there were no other references to Jesus or the Holy Spirit. This muffling of explicitly Christian language may have been in part an attempt to attract people of other faiths, or as part of the bid for government support. The religious rhetoric was not totally eliminated. Group leaders did still talk about God, primarily the need to listen to God on a regular basis. Local cells, many of them led by clergymen, may have retained a Christian character. Most importantly, the movement retained its evangelical method, focusing on changing individual lives through sharing experiences. In the late 1930s, however, the focus of sharing in the large meetings shifted from "what God has done for me" to "what the movement can do for us."

Other Things to Do

The big summer rallies in 1939 were a high point for Moral Re-Armament. The movement was front-page news across the country and attracted tens of thousands of people. Over the next several years, however, MRA faced a series of challenges to its message and its leadership. While the movement survived, its work was once again forced to change.

The first challenge is the most obvious. Less than a month after MRA stated the choice as "Guidance or Guns," the world fairly decisively chose guns. On September 1, 1939 Germany invaded Poland, setting off World War II. Within nine months Germany controlled much of continental Europe. Meanwhile, Japan was seizing territory across Asia and the Pacific. By December 1941 virtually every country that had supposedly made Moral Re-Armament national policy was at war with another. The war Buchman wanted to prevent was under way.

Buchman and his colleagues did not immediately give up their hopes for peace. In late October the evangelist gave a world radio address from San Francisco on "Moral Re-Armament—a World Philosophy Adequate for World Crisis." "The world must declare a moratorium on hate and fear, personally and nationally," he declared. "I am speaking today to the millions across the world who in these anxious days are increasingly looking to Moral Re-Armament as the one hope for the future." He called on his listeners to "enlist for the duration of this war against selfishness." MRA's contribution to this war would be strengthening morale and restoring "God to leadership as the Directing Force in the life of nations."[147] Key to this strategy was a series of radio broadcasts in early December, calling for 100 million people to listen to God.[148]

Other group members, facing the reality of war, shifted their focus to national morale. A newsletter from the British team called each member "to win their special salient, and turn it into a base for further constructive advance. M.R.A. must be an impregnable line of advance everywhere in every community against the subversive force of greed, prejudice and self-indulgence which under-mine a country's true strength."[149] A California team member showed the same commitment to national unity. For her MRA "means I must have no self-pity, nor waste energy weeping for the world tragedy but dig in and work for the permanent cure. It means that we must all get into the same boat and pull together."[150]

As MRA called for national unity, it was facing its second challenge—disunity in its leadership. Since the mid-1910s, Buchman's closest associates were fellow clergymen, most notably Samuel Shoemaker and Sherwood Day. They led his work at Princeton and Yale in the early 1920s, and Buchman made Shoemaker's Calvary Episcopal Church his headquarters. Shoemaker was Buchman's most visible spokesman through the 1930s, writing books and making speeches across the country. "Judged by sheer depth of influence," Shoemaker wrote in 1933, "there can be no question that the Oxford group [sic] is today one of the mightiest movements on earth."[151]

In November 1941, however, Shoemaker told his parish that Calvary House would cease being Moral Re-Armament's national headquarters, effective immediately. He acknowledged the good the Oxford Group had done by encouraging vital personal religion within the churches, but concluded that "certain policies and procedures" on the part of MRA had given him "increasing misgivings." He had felt those misgivings, he wrote privately, "throughout almost my whole relationship with Buchman." Anytime he tried to raise them, however, "by the almost infallible process of the Group, the challenge has been hurled back at us again and again." He described the numerous times he had tried to talk with Buchman, only to be ignored or told that the problem was his own sin. Groups of other members would lay into him for hours at a time. He finally told Buchman that the movement was wrong in ignoring the church, that his temper was driving people away, and that his ambition was taking over. "He countered almost everything I said, very good-naturedly; but I knew he was using it all to diagnose me, not to find any real light upon himself or the Movement." Unity, Shoemaker felt, had become Buchman's "god—not Truth. And I see why—unity—on his terms, MRA unity, unity by everybody joining MRA—is the great way to build up the case for MRA, and especially the case for Frank."[152]

Shoemaker told Buchman in the summer of 1941 that he was concerned about the church—both the church universal and his own parish. While the early Oxford Group had focused on converting "pagans" and nurturing them into strong Christians, he worried that more recently it was only concerned with making people into a "spiritual Panzer division." There was no concern for helping young, weak Christians grow. Closer to home, Shoemaker acted to protect his congregation. The rector felt that the MRA team had been "using people [at Calvary] at the expense of developing them." Team members never came to worship, never received the sacraments, and took advantage of the parish's support. "We are in the intolerable position of being a church that is giving hospitality to a group that is against the Church," he declared.[153]

Shoemaker was saddened by his own decision. "Frank certainly had a great message when I met him, almost exactly twenty-four years ago to the day." Their relationship had been complex, with Buchman attempting to play father figure and Shoemaker often resisting. He concluded his memoir of the split by suggesting that Buchman was "a failure, trying to bolster up his reputation. I half-shudder as I write these words, [but] believe them to be true."[154]

Shoemaker was not the only clergyman to leave Moral Re-Armament. Sherwood Day, Frederic Lawrence, and Irving Harris, all early leaders, fell away in the 1930s. Most often they left because they wanted to focus their work on the church. Other clergy stayed because of their commitment to Buchman and the cause. Never again, however, would MRA have the close connection to the church that Shoemaker symbolized and encouraged.

The split with Shoemaker pained Buchman, too, his biographer writes. Shoemaker decided to work within a traditional parish, he argues, "while Buchman was convinced that he himself, and also the Church, must reach out into every corner of life, and that this would require a new and revolutionary attitude." While they had long been friends, Shoemaker "had never willingly accepted tutelage, and seems to have sometimes chosen to interpret Buchman's directness on personal matters as an attempt to dominate." The split caused Buchman "personal sorrow.... These difficulties caused his health to deteriorate."[155]

This was the third challenge facing the movement—Buchman's health problems. The evangelist had a long history of exhausting himself with work and then retreating for a period. He was a regular visitor, for instance, at John Harvey Kellogg's sanitarium in Battle Creek, Michigan. In his early sixties, however, things got worse. In the winter of 1941, Shoemaker remembered, Buchman had a serious heart attack and spent most of three months in bed at Calvary House.[156] He recovered for a busy summer of work.

In November 1942, however, Buchman had a serious stroke at Saratoga Springs, New York. Over the next several days his pulse waxed and waned. One night, convinced he was dying, Buchman asked for a funeral in Allentown and distributed the contents of his wallet. But after a vision of Christ he began to pull through. "The time is not yet. Your work is not finished. You have other things to do," was his guidance. His convalescence took four months; the stroke and heart trouble left him weak the rest of his life.[157]

These three challenges—the war, the loss of Shoemaker, and Buchman's health—were at most temporary interruptions in MRA's work. Almost immediately group members changed their focus from prevent-the-war to win-the-war. Other leaders rose to take Shoemaker's place. And Buchman's energy and determination overcame his illness. The outbreak of war left MRA slightly less confident that it could change the world, and it had only tenuous links to the church. Buchman's message, however, became a weapon in the coming war.

CHAPTER FIVE

Change! Unite! Fight!

In the summer of 1940, Frank Buchman and his closest devotees retreated to the shores of Lake Tahoe. A year earlier, Moral Re-Armament was the toast of New York, Washington, and Hollywood. Now, the movement's call for absolute love paled next to total war, and group members in Europe focused on survival rather than sharing. Buchman wanted to rethink the work for this changed world.

These new circumstances led to yet another recreation of Buchman's movement. Members turned their energies from prevent-the-war to win-the-war, strengthening morale in the allied countries. They concentrated this work particularly on labor relations in defense industries, trying to turn conflict into cooperation. Members created new media, especially musical revues, to spread its message.

The basic message, however, remained the same. In the time of war, as he had for decades, Buchman preached the necessity of social change through individual change, and the importance of absolute morality and following the guidance of God. These practices, MRA believed, would create the strong families and stable industries required to win the war.

A Unity of Commitment

Since the early 1930s, Buchman and his followers had warned against conflict and disunity—in homes, in industry, in national and international politics—and worked to bring about a unified and harmonious society. That unity was even more essential, they believed, in a time of war. An MRA flyer from 1940 declared that "every citizen can enlist in Moral Re-Armament to bring national unity. Begin with yourself. Are you a fear-free, hate-free, greed-free citizen? How many unselfish days will you give this year in the war to end selfishness?"[1]

Group leaders believed that their work for unified homes and conflict-free industry was essential to national survival. "The moral rearmament of our country may be the deciding factor in our national existence," a newsletter from the New York office declared. "It alone can create a strong, united nation behind our armed forces." This unity was particularly important in labor relations. Buchman and his followers had long worried that labor unions could foment discord and class warfare, a particular danger as America ramped up armament production. A Detroit union member serving as a soldier in Italy opined that "America's greatest need now is for men of moral stature who will make what's right and not who's right the basic principle for national teamwork." Such men would "foil the attempts of those forces whose aim is to foment class hatred," he declared. A changed labor movement, "morally rearmed and demonstrating teamwork and caring, can be the biggest bulwark against totalitarianism and class conflict."[2]

MRA workers in America took their message of unity to defense plants. Buchman told Charles Lindbergh that they had been invited by Seattle's mayor to work in the city, battling against what they saw as a communist conspiracy undermining production at Boeing and other contractors.[3] A member of the city council saw a new spirit in the city, "transforming homes, bringing trust, co-operation in industry, setting the public good above individual advantage on the part of civic officials and employees, creating new acceptance of responsibility by the Press as a builder of the community." A British member of the team reported from San Francisco that he "was called in by the Union chief and the ship owners to help settle a strike, and on the basis of honest apology got a satisfactory settlement. The Union leader had a Quiet Time and went and apologized to the boss, and the Federal Arbitrator has come out with a statement of the force of M.R.A."[4]

Movement leaders also addressed the general population. Buchman made radio addresses, calling for 100 million people to listen to God.[5] A booklet, "How to Spread a New Spirit," urged readers to "Study MRA, Live MRA, Apply MRA, Spread MRA." It declared that "all the troubles in the world can be traced back to unchanged human nature—selfishness, pride, bad temper, dishonesties, hates, fears and greed." Readers should "*Stop being little dictators* in the home. Live this new spirit there and everywhere. Start at the breakfast table. Learn to say *I am sorry.*"[6]

That message reverberated overseas. An MRA newsletter in September 1940 reported that people in East London had found that "listening to God in Quiet Times gives them courage in danger, fresh energy and the answer to tiredness." One block had worked together and become "an M.R.A. family. Air-raids were used for learning the Rising Tide songs, reading the Bible, and entertaining the neighbours to tea."[7] In the midst of the Blitz, the London office of MRA urged group members to "renew and deepen our commitment to our essential task. This means disciplined, hourly obedience to our Supreme Commander, and...faithfulness to the vision of a God-controlled world." The work would result in building "those moral and spiritual defences which no enemy can pierce."[8]

While MRA members labored to build morale, Buchman increasingly sensed that the movement's work lacked focus and discipline. In the summer of 1940 he invited a small team of supporters to a camp on the shores of Lake Tahoe; the group grew to include over 100. Buchman told John Roots that "dry rot had set in, and some of our leaders were called upon for tasks they were not able to carry through."[9] Years later, Howard Blake remembered that summer as "a time of complete spiritual overhauling. We took time to look at ourselves and our motives, to examine the places where we had sinned and apparently gotten away with it. There were lots of old hurts and wounds that for the first time were really brought to light and cured." It was, he said, a communal experience of the Cross.[10]

Members worked together in teams to do the cooking and cleaning; that collaboration itself changed the group. "Every daily act represented part of the force that can bind the community together and give everyone the sense of having a part," Purdy told Shoemaker. "How individualist we all have been, ever so slowly learning the lessons of cooperative living, the wisdom and economy of cooperative buying, the contribution to health, and the reality of the experience of continuous guidance that the whole program has brought." The team work revealed "the personal experience of Christ" as "every human alternative has slowly disappeared in the light of a working, sharing, constant fellowship."[11]

MRA's experience at Tahoe could teach the rest of the country a lesson, members believed. A newsletter declared that "behind ships and planes and guns lay three lines of defense—*sound homes, teamwork in industry,* and *national unity.* We sought to create a pattern of living that could stand as a demonstration for every home and community." In their careful budgeting and cooperative cooking "we saw the answer to America's wastefulness and self-indulgence." The community acted out

Buchman's maxim, "if everybody cares enough and everyone shares enough, everyone will have enough."[12] In the camp they glimpsed their millennium, their ideal world.

As Buchman hoped, the time in Tahoe gave MRA a new focus and discipline. He "believed that national will and effort in time of war depended on spiritual insight, personal sacrifice, and discipline," remembered one supporter. "Out of the daily informal meetings, conversations, and meditation there was borne a unity of commitment."[13] Participants talked about the war effort and their part in it. They held "MRA Industrial Round Tables."[14] They invited some of the people they claimed as supporters, including Senator Harry Truman. Purdy told the senator that they were "going over the practical details of our future program to make the spirit of Moral Re-Armament regnant in our political and economic life. As a result there is much on which we should like to have your mind and that of those who feel and see the fundamental need of this new and unifying spirit."[15]

You Can Defend America

The summer by the lake revitalized MRA and its message. The most important outcome was a musical revue. *You Can Defend America* was MRA's first theatrical production, setting the pattern for scores of plays and movies to follow, and the movement's next reinvention of the evangelical revival meeting. "Lots of Americans are tired of meetings, bored with speeches," a movement newsletter declared, echoing Buchman's scorn for traditional preaching. The song and spectacle were a more effective way of spreading the movement's message, as well as offering "an answer to the great American problem of 'what to do on Saturday night.'"[16] This show, and those that followed, combined the revival meeting, the patriotic tableau, and the Broadway musical into a new creation.

It started as a floor show at Tahoe, largely as entertainment for the summer evenings. Later MRA shows were plays with plots, but YCDA, as *You Can Defend America* became known in the movement, was a collection of skits and songs designed to build home front morale. MRA members wrote the songs, created the costumes, and played the parts. Each scene, comic and symbolic by turns, drove home the movement's message. The "Cowboy Scene," for instance, was broad and silly, complete with hokey accents and off-stage sound effects. A group of cowboys sit around a campfire, talking about how their lives have gone downhill, when formerly "ornery" Slim arrives and tells them about MRA. "I suppose you're expectin' the guys in the Army an' Navy, and them dudes in Washington to stick to their jobs and do 'em right," he challenges them, "while we are quiet and take things easy." Slim then demands, "when will some o' us ornery critters wake up and get it through our thick heads that bein' American means every man pulls his own weight, right where he is?" The cowboys mull Slim's words and admit that they are responsible for their problems and those of the world. They conclude by singing,

> Yo, ho, we'd like to know,
> Yo, ho, how to build nations,
> So, yo, ho, yippee hi ho
> We're all rarin' to go![17]

This ditty became a common refrain at war-time MRA events.

The show's finale was a tableau, with a figure of America surrounded by flags. On one side is a typical American family, quarreling instead of defending the country. On another side is labor and management, squabbling as usual. "And here are those politicians, still arguing about the nation's problems, talking, talking, talking." Meanwhile, rats identified as Gimme, Fear, Gossip, Waste, Greed, Graft, and Hate creep up to attack America. A lone voice cries out, "Americans! What's the matter with you? Don't you see what is happening? Wake up! Families unite! Or your homes will be undermined! Politicians, put your country first! Labour and Management—all of us—pull together or hate and greed will pull the country apart!" Awakened and unified, the Americans change Gimme to Give. "What we have just done is what every American must do," says the voice. "For when we can all change Gimme to Give, then we can really defend America." Together the cast points to the audience and says, "*You* can defend America!"[18] The show's title number drives the point home.

> You can defend America,
> You've got something to do;
> Clean up the nation from bottom to top,
> Start with yourself in the home and the shop.
> You can defend America
> Nobody will if you don't;
> So get going and give,
> We'll all learn to live,
> To defend America.[19]

Movement leaders quickly concluded that they had something special on their hands. The first public performance was in Carson City.
"The Governor was there and issued a special proclamation," Buchman
enthusiastically reported. "The comment afterwards was that we had
captured their hearts in a way no crowd have ever done."[20]

Inspired by that reception, MRA took *You Can Defend America* on
the road. Over the next two years a quarter of a million people in
21 states saw the show, starring full-time MRA volunteers in productions purportedly sponsored by unions, management groups, governors,
or service clubs. Behind the scenes MRA leaders carefully recruited
groups to sponsor a performance. An internal memorandum suggested
that invitations to a performance be sent in name of the sponsoring
organizations. "Use invitations liberally as they provide an excellent
background of information in the community. Use state or city seal
whenever possible." Echoing Buchman's focus on personal evangelism,
the memo suggested that invitations be targeted at community leaders.
The more personalized the invitation, the author suggested, the more
likely it was that people will come.

The movement claimed that their traveling revue had a real impact
on labor groups. A press release reported that YCDA "showed clearly
how every man and woman could play their fullest part for victory.
In many cities, opposing groups found new unity; industrial disputes
were solved, and apathy and complacency were replaced by alertness
and cooperation."[21] A chief welder at an auto parts plant reported that
workers in his plant were about to quit until the YCDA cast arrived.
They "spoke and sang a few songs. The spirit of what they gave broke
up the walk out. A few minutes later the boys went back to work."[22]
By the end of the war MRA claimed to have met 3,000 labor leaders,
and that over 10,000 workers had seen YCDA and its successor shows.
"In all of these plants there are now union leaders who look to MRA to
show them how build [sic] sound leadership and how to build teamwork
between labor and management."[23]

Reviews for *You Can Defend America* were mixed. The editor of
the Philadelphia *Daily News* attended an MRA banquet where he saw
some scenes from the revue. "The whole purpose of this affair was to
bring home to industry and to labor alike the fact that most troubles
surrounding war and peacetime production come from the fact that
men and management are not willing to clean up the devil that is in
them before accusing the other fellow." If everyone would follow this
philosophy, he concluded, "it would be a much nicer world in which
to live."[24] A reviewer in Columbia, South Carolina was less inspired.

"Somehow we didn't come away inspired, convinced that any member of Moral Rearmament campaigns or any numbers of productions of 'You Can Defend America' will give America 'guts' if America doesn't already have it." He thought it was a good show, with fun songs. "But wars aren't won that way. The show was too much like three easy lessons in how to be virtuous to convince us."[25]

To spread its message further, MRA leaders also produced a print version of *You Can Defend America*. The twenty-eight page booklet, illustrated with line drawings, warned readers that America could be endangered by weak morale. "Behind ships planes and guns stand three lines of defense: Sound homes, teamwork in industry, a united nation," it proclaimed. It called the nation to "Change, Unite, Fight!" by listening to God, working together, and fighting fear, hate and greed. "It is your job to make this country you love into One All-American Team."[26]

The movement worked to make a splash with the booklet. Copies were sold, like *Rising Tide*, and sent to everyone registered for the draft.[27] In anticipation of Buchman's birthday, members were urged to commit to selling a definite number of copies "as a gift beyond your personal gifts to Frank.... What is the guided number that God wants you to bring the book to?"[28] Always with an eye for the key men, MRA leaders solicited support for the book from well-known names, including Harry Truman, Richard Byrd, and Mary McLeod Bethune, and a preface from World War I hero John Pershing.[29]

With MRA's encouragement, teachers and school systems developed curricula around *You Can Defend America*. A syllabus for classes in the Detroit schools declared that "patriotism requires from each of us a determination to take responsibility for the men, women, and children around us. It calls for highest standards of unselfishness, honesty, clean living, self-discipline, and for Faith in a Wisdom greater than our own." In most of the ten sessions students wrote a short essay on a statement from YCDA about morale, such as "Morale is the winning weapon everyone can use." Students chanted together, "Together we will produce the arms and morale for victory." They also had a quiet time and built a "morale indicator." They sang songs from the YCDA show and produced their own dramatic skits.[30] In his essay for the class, one student confessed his selfishness—"my slate is very black," he admitted. "By reading and studying this little booklet that I only paid a nickel for," he wrote, "I have learned to fight for Uncle Sam and how to keep faith with that brother of mine who has left trusting us at home that we will carry on to help win this great tragic war."[31] The curriculum,

"Your Part in Winning the War," reportedly made both teachers and students more engaged and patriotic, improving their home life and increasing war bond sales.[32]

The editor of *United States News* held out something better than celebrity endorsement or classroom use—the suggestion that *You Can Defend America* "become the basis for the national philosophy of total defense for America."[33] This had been MRA's Holy Grail since the mid-1930s—to have its practices become national policy. One group member proposed creating "morale wardens," analogous to air raid wardens. They would be specially trained to build morale, to "deal with human nature in the form of jealousies, apathy, conflict, or lack of cooperation wherever it appears, in the Committee, on the block, in office, factory, or in a run on the grocery store." They would have to pass a written test describing morale, and—typical for MRA—tell the story of at least one experience in their lives that built morale. These wardens would use morale-building material, such as like YCDA and other MRA songs and skits. Their ultimate goal would be creating "such a united community that subversive forces are shown up and dealt with, that everyone has work, food and shelter, that the community lives for the State and Nation, and is a pattern for the New World."[34]

Group leaders built on YCDA's momentum in 1941 by organizing another summer camp at a disused resort, this time in Tallwood, Maine. They called it a "School for Home Defense," the prototype for similar schools across the country.[35] A "curriculum" called morale "democracy's answer to [communism and fascism]. With the right outgoing spirit we can out-laugh, out-work and out-strategy any crowd on earth. First we must get that spirit."[36] There were classes on "Morale and How to Build It," "Sound Homes; The First Line of Defense," "Teamwork in Industry," and "The ABCs of World Change." The only textbook was *You Can Defend America*.[37] The lessons were designed to "anticipate the strategy of the subversive forces, and create the community spirit in which these forces find it impossible to work; make preparations to face, and prepare the country to face, shortages of raw materials and consumer goods; lay the foundations for a better ordered postwar world, by training responsible leadership and citizenship now."[38]

While MRA did not mention religion in *You Can Defend America*, Christian language was inescapable at Tallwood, as speaker after speaker told stories of how MRA had changed human nature. "Day after day, week after week there was a steady flow of life-changing miracles in the lives of men and women who found in a simple experience of the Cross of Christ a new dynamic to give to their community and the nation."[39] The religious message was clear. "Does our national strength come from God, and does He have a plan for every man, woman, and child in America?" asked a presenter. "Is His guidance the basis for sound homes? Can we have morale without Him?"[40] For MRA, the answers were clear—Christianity remained at the heart of American morale.

The *You Can Defend America* campaigns gave MRA a new purpose; *Time* said that YCDA marked MRA's resurrection.[41] MRA leaders built on the experience by cloning the show, producing morale shows around the world. *Pull Together Canada* toured the Dominion, performing in labor halls and theatres and drawing much media attention. As always, there were numerous testimonies to the resulting decreased labor strife.[42] The cast of *Battle Together for Britain* sang

> Since the world we're looking for requires new men and nations,
> You and I may have to face some minor alterations SO!
> Let's all change and work as one
> Till the job be truly done,
> And the fighting men will come home again
> To a land they'll be proud to call home![43]

There were also shows in Australia, Barbados, Jamaica, South Africa, Kenya, China, and Switzerland, with language and rhetoric much like that of *You Can Defend America*.[44]

Meanwhile the American team wrote and produced another show focused specifically on war production and overcoming industrial strife. *The Forgotten Factor* told the story of conflict between a corporate president and a labor leader, caused by problems in their homes. Once that human issue—the forgotten factor of the title—was solved, the conflict evaporated. As an MRA press release puts it, the show's "simple but far-reaching theme is that human nature is the bottleneck in industrial relations and that disputes can be settled on the basis of 'what's right, and not who's right.' "[45] At a crucial moment, the cast sings that problems can be solved when mistrust and self-interest are banished.

> Ever since once in the Garden of Eden,
> When Adam said Eve was to blame,
> All down the centuries history shows,
> Human nature is just the same.
> THAT'S THE BOTTLENECK![46]

Unlike *You Can Defend America, Forgotten Factor* actually had a plot. The message, however, was much the same, just as Buchman learned at Keswick decades before—human nature can change.

As with YCDA, MRA aimed *Forgotten Factor* at labor, producing the show for union groups across the country. They presented it in Boston while the AFL convention was meeting there.[47] An MRA press release reported that 150 coal mines in the United Kingdom with 160,000 workers had seen the show, leading to more production and less absenteeism.[48] Employers supported this labor outreach. The National Association of Manufacturers asked for more showings in New York.[49] MRA leaders worked with three corporations to raise the required $15,000—$175,000 today—to bring the show to Philadelphia.[50]

MRA also planned a film production of *The Forgotten Factor*, starting with raising the required $200,000. "There was not an appeal for funds or subscriptions," John Roots wrote two supporters in 1945, "only a statement from several of us of our conviction regarding the urgency of the fight for industrial teamwork." He declared that the film would "play a primary part in swinging this nation to teamwork from conflict, breakdown, class-warfare and government regulation." He then made a nonappeal appeal for funds. "We thought you both would want to know of this great advance and have guidance as to how you would like to participate."[51] The movement finally produced the film in 1952.

The Fight to Serve

Moral Re-Armament spread its wartime moral message with its full-time volunteers. Keeping this force in the field became a challenge, however, as the war escalated and the American and British military wanted the same men for the military. This was particularly a problem for the movement's men of draft age, almost a generation younger than the founding cohort. The movement worked hard to keep these men out of the army. Buchman told Senator Harry Truman that there were many men who could be drafted, but the MRA workers were special. "I cannot believe that it is the part of wisdom that all this work should be set aside when the news every day graphically shows us where the real danger in our own country lies."[52] In another letter he worried that one of his key men, who "has the personal confidence of men like Firestone, Ford and other industrialists," would be drafted, leaving those businessmen without the leadership they need.[53]

MRA members saw dark forces behind the attempt to draft their workers. One leader believed that draft officials were being used by MRA critics. "There is no question that their avowed intent is to snuff out one of the strongest moral forces in the nation today."[54] Another attributed the attacks to "forces who do not talk outright Bolshevism, whether moral or political, but plan instead to confuse the thinking of both America and Britain." These shadowy forces wanted to keep MRA workers "from being the effective striking power that will give the needed Moral Re-Armament which is the inner strength of our democracy and the essential bastion of our war effort."[55]

This time, at least, their paranoia was not unfounded. Critics of MRA did call for movement volunteers to be drafted. *PM*, an unapologetically leftist newspaper in New York, called Buchman "the religious promoter and apostle of appeasement," and attacked YCDA as propaganda that did not condemn the Nazis or the Japanese. Most importantly, *PM* believed, MRA did not support the rights of workers. "The idea is that everyone should love everyone, love his job, love his boss, love his home, love his country, and love to work on Saturdays and Sundays with or without time-and-a-half for overtime."[56] Another publication, edited by leftist George Seldes, called Buchman an appeaser and cited his supposed statement about Hitler from 1936. "MRA in America is anti-labor. Disguised as an organization aiming to conciliate capital and labor, it is an organization subsidized by big shots of the National Association of Manufacturers for the purpose of making labor give in to capital."[57] Both publications called for the MRA men to be drafted.

MRA leaders responded to these evil forces by declaring the movement's patriotism and its value to the war effort. Reflecting their confidence in divine action, they promised that "the Superforce will shake many a citadel and make level the way."[58] More concretely, MRA leaders relied on lobbying to protect their men. Purdy wrote a group of labor leaders who had seen YCDA at work, encouraging them to contact draft boards.[59] An officer of Cramp Shipbuilding in Philadelphia told the chairman of War Manpower Commission that YCDA is "the most effective incentive yet found for increasing production, for it gets down to brass tacks in dealing with the basic human factor." He argued that MRA workers should be categorized as "key workers" by the Selective Service System, since they promote "harmonious labor-management relations."[60] MRA drafted a statement to be signed by clergy, asking that MRA workers be considered as clergy because their work "is both religious in character and significant in the present national effort."[61]

As usual, MRA used the controversy to raise its public profile. In 1943 it released *The Fight to Serve*, a book about its workers and their calling to doing morale work on the home front. It was largely a collection of statements and letters from industrialists and labor leaders about the value of MRA's work in building worker morale. Because of "opposition to Moral Re-Armament," the book noted, Selective Service stopped giving deferments to MRA workers, resulting in 21 workers taken into the army. "Thus was liquidated a major part of a force uniquely trained in giving the nation what it most urgently required." They did wonderful service in the army, "but the true function for which they had been trained was cast aside because of the misrepresentation and intimidation of a small but vocal group of officials.... The loss to the nation's war effort was keenly felt."[62]

An Assembly Line to Produce Men

In its first decades, Buchman's work was a movement rather than an institution. It had no paid staff, no corporate organization, and no property. It relied on volunteers, contributions, and rented rooms. These arrangements sufficed when the group's main activities were occasional house parties and assemblies, but shows like *You Can Defend America* and *The Forgotten Factor* and lengthy conferences like that at Tallwood required more support. In the early 1940s Buchman and his colleagues began developing resources for the movement's work, including training centers and a corporate budget. These resources also filled the gap created by the withdrawal of Shoemaker and his parish house.

The first base was its training facility on Michigan's Mackinac Island. According to Bunny Austin, Buchman toured Henry Ford's airplane production line at Willow Run in Detroit and asked, "How can we set up an assembly line to produce men who know how to work together, who can cure bitterness, increase production and supply the imagination for a new world to be born? Where can we find a Willow Run which will produce the ideas that will answer the isms?" Ford suggested Mackinac, in the strait between the upper and lower peninsulas of Michigan.[63]

MRA called the 1942 assembly at Mackinac "The National Training Center for Total Victory," making it sound like an official government program. Its goal was giving "further advanced training in the principles of teamwork in industry and in communities as illustrated by the Victory Revue 'You Can Defend America.'" Over 1,000 people attended, including "leaders in Labor, Management, Civilian Defense, Education, Civic, Government, Agriculture, and the Press." Most of the participants, however, were less prominent figures. The program included roundtables focused on teamwork, conquering apathy, and the importance of moral fiber, as well as the usual stories of how MRA fixed a home or a factory. Participants produced new plays, songs, and books, each focused on a national problem.[64] There were also worship services led by Buchman, "making the Cross a great reality in people's lives, and casting its shadow over the nations."[65]

Mackinac soon became one of MRA's permanent homes; by the late 1940s MRA was one of the biggest landowners on the island.[66] In the late 1950s the movement built facilities to accommodate ever larger crowds, including four dining rooms to seat 1,000, meeting and reception halls, two dormitories, an infirmary, and a theatre.[67] Guests were invited to join the housekeeping and cooking teams, a 1957 brochure stated. "This work gives an opportunity to test in practical ways the truths given from the platform and stage, and to draw on the experience of men and women from many lands who have learned to apply them."[68]

As soon as the war was over, MRA also developed a European training center in a bankrupt hotel in Caux, Switzerland, on the mountains above Lake Geneva. The location was not accidental, at the center of Western Europe, in a neutral country, and near the international organizations based in Geneva. The first assembly at Caux, in September 1946, brought 2,600 people, including 1,000 from Great Britain.[69] By 1950 Caux, "a world ideological training center for democracy," was drawing 4,000 "representatives" a summer from 80 countries.[70] As at Mackinac, the training center's guests did the cooking and cleaning. A Swiss journalist reported that he peeled potatoes with a Swedish bishop and an English lord. "It began always with a moment of silence, during which everyone thinks of the work as a whole and his own part in it."[71]

In 1948, MRA developed a third training center, in Los Angeles. They bought the former Women's Athletic Club, a six-story building with meeting and dining rooms for 500, plus bedrooms for 125.[72] While it kept offices in New York and Washington, MRA moved much of its leadership to the new facility, to support their growing work in making movies.[73] "This will enable us to have an adequate national center in a part of the country where Frank can live throughout the year," a leader reported, "and the hundreds of people in this area who have been changed through MRA in recent years are delighted with the prospect. It will prove a base for the making of movies and our other instruments which are urgently required in the increasingly critical war of ideas."[74]

Maintaining these three centers and all the full-time volunteers required money. Whenever critics of the movement asked where the money came from—and they often did—Buchman always said that MRA was financed by guided giving. "Where God guides, He provides," he noted in the mid-1930s. "Sharing" supported the movement.[75] Buchman and his colleagues, however, had solicited donations since the 1920s, and these solicitations became more organized and directed in the years after the war.

In 1952 the treasurer proposed creating a "national finance committee" from among the 60 or 70 people who had regularly given large amounts in the past. "They would undertake the guided enlistment of funds," he suggested. "They would encourage regular financial giving on the part of every participant in the MRA program. They would also enlist, as the guided opportunity was given, special donations from individuals, corporations and foundations." He also advised seeking support from industry. MRA had regularly shown "relevance and effectiveness in bringing an answer to industrial problems," but it had only received small donations from industry. "It is suggested that in the coming year every effort be made to secure corporate giving on the part of industry as industry's legitimate share in carrying forward the ideological answer for the democratic world."[76]

This fund-raising became increasingly specific. They sent a form letter to their mailing list, indicating the "Minimum World Needs of Moral Re-Armament." They needed money for Caux, for making films, and to support a task force of 500 people. "Millions must come from thousands of people; in cash, from income; from capital, from the enlistment of others, from the gift of real estate which can be done tax free; gifts of food and commodities, of personal jewelry; and the national commitment of national teams." The letter told stories of people who had given sacrificially, including some who had given their homes.[77]

MRA critics had long suspected that the movement was supported by wealthy donors and industrialists, but movement leaders replied that their money came in sacrificial donations from donors with small incomes. Both were correct. In 1951, for instance, MRA received almost a million dollars in donations. Half came from 40 people or corporations who gave over $3,000, and the other half from 10,000 contributions less than $3,000.[78] The same was true in 1961, when the total contributions were $3.7 million; 905 people gave over $100, 98.7 percent of the total gifts, while 5,000 people gave less than $100, 1.3 percent of total gifts.[79] As with most nonprofit organizations, a lot of donors gave small amounts, but most of the money came from a small number of large donations.

Through such solicitations, MRA's income grew significantly in the years after the war. In 1941 the U.S. organization received $51,000 in donations, which trebled in the following year. By the late 1940s donations were regularly a million dollars a year, and in the extraordinary year of 1958 reached seven million. Expenses and assets—mainly the training centers—increased proportionately, but MRA remained comfortably in the black.[80] The 1958 treasurer's report noted that MRA had 1,500 full-time volunteers; with an assumed salary of $5,000 each, which was equivalent to an annual gift of $7.5 million. The greatest expenses were in the US, at almost four million dollars, with British expenses of about a million. MRA owned seven million dollars worth of property in the US, two million in Britain, and 2.5 million in Switzerland.[81]

Labor Led by God

The post-war years were a boom time for labor. Wages surged in thriving American industries while several European countries had governments led by socialist or labor parties. MRA responded by strengthening its labor outreach, building on *You Can Defend America* and *The Forgotten Factor*. A 1942 memorandum noted that labor unites millions of people, a valuable asset for a movement focusing on creating national and "supernational" unity. "No other worldwide organization has so great an opportunity to give every nation a common aim." American unions have a special calling in this work, MRA believed, fighting "to see that sound unionism brings true democracy to every industry and so create a sound national life." Unions must unite "against those forces which incite class warfare and division, undermine the moral standards of the workers and plan the break-up of family life." MRA could offer labor "a superior idea that will capture people's minds just as completely as our arms capture their territory."[82] At the first Caux assembly, Duncan Corcoran—regularly identified as a Scottish shipyard worker, even though he had worked full-time for MRA in the United States for many years—declared that "labor led by God can lead the world." MRA saw itself as an alternative to communism, building harmony between worker and management instead of conflict.[83]

MRA used a variety of methods to achieve its labor goals. It took its shows—notably *Forgotten Factor*—to factories around the world. It brought union leaders and managers to Mackinac and Caux for intimate discussions and enthusiastic speeches. Perhaps most importantly, it did personal work—just like Buchman had done in China decades before—with the "key men" in labor circles. In 1948, as MRA developed its labor work, Roots proposed that they should "concentrate on a few strategic men whose means would allow them to give something really significant, and who with the right approach on our part could, I am sure, be moved to action."[84]

One example of this personal work is MRA's intervention in a strike against the Miami Transit Company in 1952. Over the course of several weeks MRA met the president of the union local, the company's general manager, the owner's son, and the owner himself. Some friends brought the local president to an MRA play in Miami Beach, and then to a Bible study session. Simultaneously the owner's son was brought to an MRA training meeting by his sisters and to tea at Buchman's Miami house. Influenced by their experience, the union official and the owner's son invited the owner to meet MRA, which led to the settlement.[85]

Another example of this approach is the story of John Riffe—a story MRA told often. Riffe was coal miner who helped to organize the United Steel Workers in the 1930s. He served as the last executive vice president of the Congress of Industrial Organizations before it merged with the American Federation of Labor in 1955. As often happened, Riffe came to MRA through his wife, who had met Buchman in 1940.[86] As Buchman told it, Riffe and his wife acknowledged their sins to each other. "The kind of teamwork you create with Rose and the children from the quiet time in the home and reading the Bible," Buchman said, "is the kind of teamwork you can create with management and labour and take into your office, conference rooms and negotiating tables."[87] Riffe told a Miami audience of how he looked for the answer to life's problems in unions and in politics, but "now in MRA I have found the answer." He "apologized to management for the bitterness he had shown in previous negotiations." Riffe testified to the value of guidance and declared that he negotiated "from the heart on the basis of not who is right but what is right."[88]

Riffe became an important part of MRA's labor outreach. He tried to persuade AFL–CIO president George Meany to be supportive of the movement.[89] Before he died at Mackinac in 1957, he supposedly said on his deathbed, "Tell America that when Frank Buchman changed

John Riffe, he saved this country's industry $500,000,000."[90] After his death Riffe became a labor saint for MRA, the subject of a book and a musical.[91]

Using this personal work, the movement claimed, MRA settled several airline strikes, increased labor-management teamwork in Pacific ports, created a new labor-management understanding at Boeing, and thwarted Communist strategy in the French textile industry, all in one year.[92] A British dockworker told a gathering at Caux that MRA had "saved the whole British waterfront from being controlled by the Communist Party."[93] During the federal intervention in the United States steel strike in 1952, both sides conferred with MRA. According to Roots, a federal official said that even after the strike "we will need the spirit of Moral Re-Armament to achieve anything lasting." Roots told Buchman that "this week has brought MRA to the heart of the nation's chief crisis center, and that many, both in government and industry, look to us as the best hope of any permanent solution."[94]

One of the movement's showcases was Germany's Ruhr Valley, the heart of Europe's coal industry. In 1948 Communists controlled 72 percent of the work councils in Ruhr mines, and strikes paralyzed the industry. MRA organized a campaign through the region, with large rallies and intense personal work; it also invited non-Communist miners to Caux.[95] By 1952 Communists controlled only eight percent of the work councils, leading to a reduction in conflict. The miners became celebrities in the MRA world, speaking at conferences in Europe, Asia, and North America. They even wrote a play about their experience with MRA. In 1960 *Hoffnung (Hope)* played for 155,000 people in 48 cities in twelve countries, including 150 performances in Washington and two telecasts in Japan.[96] It is not clear whether the men still mined coal.

The airline industry was MRA's big American success story. In the late 1940s, strife between management and the unions at National Airlines almost led to the closure of the airline. In 1950, however, management and labor leaders both attended an MRA assembly, reported a devotee, "and heard people of opposing interests speak of their enmities and their reconciliations—French and German, Communist and anti-Communist, management and labor." The next day the company president went to the union president and said, "I've been an SOB. I don't expect you to believe what I say, but I saw something which just might be an answer for us." The union leader replied, "And I'm just fool enough to believe you!" They found a way to settle their problems.[97]

That same fall a United Airlines pilot attended an assembly at Mackinac and acknowledged his responsibility and shame for his bitterness against the company. "I realize now that I as an individual have a great responsibility in this world. I have a responsibility to fight Communism, to fight for an ideology that is positive, to fight for the human dignity of the worker, to fight to eliminate all bitterness and hatred wherever I may encounter it." His apology was welcomed by the company's management, which acknowledged its mistakes. The pilot urged his union to set an example. "Let's show them how the intelligent application of some basic Christian standards can solve labor-management differences."[98]

Over the next six months MRA leaders worked intensively with airline personnel, primarily based in Miami. They concentrated their training "with the key men," intensely personalizing the work. Twitchell told Buchman that the MRA team saw "the need for getting down to moral standards and personal change from the drop of the hat."[99] A pilot announced that "MRA is an official part of [the] Eastern Air Lines training program" and offered it as answer to morale and customer service problems. Company president Eddie Rickenbacker told his staff that "You'll be better, the company will be better, the world at large will be better."[100] At training sessions in the Pan American cafeteria, MRA members told stories about changes in France and at Lockheed Corporation. "It is an impressive sight to see the tough down-to-earth working men and their foremen gripped by the Holy Spirit as they begin to take in a worthy ideology," Twitchell told Buchman. Other group members visited pilots' homes, talking with their wives.[101]

Not everyone was impressed. A United pilot told the press that "this movement has no place in our representing organization." He argued that MRA was "basically against unions"; in MRA doctrines, he said, "the employer gets what's right and the employee gets what's left."[102] MRA's work at United did lead to negotiations, which eventually broke down.[103]

Airline leaders, nevertheless, endorsed MRA's work. A vice-president of the Airline Pilots Association told a reporter that he would "refer to MRA as a wonder drug that makes real human beings out of people."[104] The airline executives urged management and labor in the steel industry, facing conflict in 1952, to come to a meeting at Mackinac. "Our experiences in making available the atmosphere in which vital disputes have been settled supports our conviction that there is an inspired settlement to the steel issue on this basis—a solution of ideological as well as economic problems."[105] Their support also helped the movement's bottom line. Rickenbacker gave MRA $10,000, as did a vice-president of Pan American, who said "that the change in one labor leader had more than justified their investment," Twitchell reported.[106]

As with the Ruhr miners, the airline story became an important part of MRA's publicity. The movement produced a booklet and a movie about the airline initiative, both called *An Idea Takes Wings*. It showed the movie around the country, and Pan American distributed the booklet on board its planes and across Latin America.[107]

MRA claimed other successes in the labor sector. Roots reported that a campaign in Hartford "left a real dent on the industrial and labor life of the city," including the settlement of a strike.[108] After MRA changed the owner of a Maryland factory he raised salaries, put out a suggestion box, and changed his workers. The foreman told an MRA youth rally that "the general atmosphere of the whole factory has changed. Swearing and foul stories have been eliminated. My work is easier because of the new cooperation." The president declared that he did not fear labor organizers. "The answer lies in a new spirit of understanding and cooperation between me and my men. That is the answer to labor wars." If both sides would each keep to the four absolutes, he concluded, "as well as demand it of the other, they would be able to solve all their problems."[109] These claims are hard to evaluate; they were trumpeted in movement publications or corporate newsletters, but MRA's labor work was rarely mentioned in the independent press.

To fill this press silence, MRA created a press service for labor issues to tell its own story. The World Labor Information Service was created, its director said, "because of a demand by editors on a world scale for a central agency which would give news of the advance of a positive ideology that is uniting labor on a world scale."[110] The service's stories never mentioned its MRA link, but its agenda was clear. One release called Buchman "one of organized labor's best friends," and declared that after visiting Caux a group of Italian workers replaced pictures of Stalin and Lenin with one of Christ on the cross.[111] The agency made sure that MRA's story was told the way it wanted.

Organized labor had mixed impressions of MRA. In 1951 an American Federation of Labor report cited "numerous instances" in which MRA "contributed more or less to the development of a more friendly and cooperative understanding and relationship between organized wage earners, their trade unions and management." It noted that most of its funds "come largely from retired persons," not business. The author concluded that it was not up to the union "to advance or retard its influence or prestige to any greater or lesser degree than any other moral movement seeking to advance the good of all in our varied relations."[112] The AFL, a coalition of trade unions, was traditionally the more conservative of the large American labor groups.

Other unions were hostile to MRA, however. The St. Paul, Minnesota, Congress of Industrial Organizations condemned the movement as fascist, citing Buchman's supposed praise of Hitler in 1936 and his links with Henry Ford and other industrialists.[113] The International Confederation of Free Trade Unions warned members to avoid MRA, accusing it of engaging in "anti-trade union efforts" and denying MRA's claimed success in the labor arena.[114] That message carried weight; George Meany declared in 1961 that the AFL-CIO "in keeping with policy of ICFTU regards the Moral Re-Armament unfavorably."[115] A British labor journal warned workers that those who went to Caux were "falling into a new capitalist trap." It alleged that "the activities of M.R.A. are directed to undermining the workers' power of resistance to any inroads the employers make on their standards or rights." The movement's aim was "to 'keep us in our proper stations.'"[116]

MRA had sympathies and connections with management as well as labor. James Newton and Charles Haines, both involved with Buchman since the 1920s, had been executives in the steel industry. As they watched the rise of the Congress of Industrial Organizations in the 1930s, Newton wrote, they suggested that management develop "a similar, united leadership." The goal would not be opposing labor, "but teamwork with the unions to achieve the harmonious expansion of industry, for the benefit of all."[117] Among Buchman's long-time supporters were the Seiberling family, owners of the Goodyear Company. During the war a family matron told Buchman that she had enjoyed seeing *The Forgotten Factor* at Mackinac, but she asked the evangelist "to look into the serious consequences of the demands of labor for the *closed shop.* That means tyranny to free men, who do not want to join the union—and there are many varieties of men in that category. There must be some elasticity to labor regulations."[118] These connections fed labor's suspicions of the movement.

★ ★ ★

For two decades the men and women of Moral Re-Armament worked to settle labor disputes in the United States and around the world, by producing movies and plays, hosting conferences, and encouraging face-to-face contact. They believed that these means would create changed people, workers and owners, able to cooperate rather than fight. This cooperation, MRA felt, was the key to a more harmonious world.

This labor work was part of MRA's larger battle. The world, Buchman believed, was caught in a battle of ideologies. On one side was materialism—fascism and communism. On the other was Moral Re-Armament itself—fighting for the Western Christian tradition. Buchman had hated communism ever since his China days, but starting with World War II the battle against the alien ideology became the main purpose of his movement.

CHAPTER SIX

Ideological Warfare

On August 15, 1945, Buchman met with the team gathered at Mackinac and announced the surrender of Japan. They had a quiet time and sang the Doxology. That night they met and "re-dedicated our lives to the battle for a new world. Frank's guidance was, 'There is just one war left—the war of ideas.'"[1]

During World War II, Moral Re-Armament reinvented its work yet again, repackaging its message to fight that war. Movement leaders called that message an ideology, putting their preaching on par with rival ideologies and making evangelical Christianity relevant for hot and cold wars alike. It called its work ideological training, and produced propaganda—plays and films members called weapons—to spread its ideological message. MRA members believed that their message was not just the preaching of an American evangelist, but an ideology, superior to communism or capitalism, and the path to a better world.

The Thing that Really Commands Your Life

"Ideology" has a variety of meanings in philosophical and political contexts, but true to form MRA developed its own. It defined ideology as a comprehensive belief system that explains the world and demands complete loyalty from the believer. Douglas Cornell, executive secretary of the National Academy of Science and a Buchman convert, told a MRA audience that an ideology is "the set of ideas that actually governs what you do, how you live with the next man you meet, what you give to the difficult person, what you give to your own wife, or your own children." Reflecting Buchman's commitment to experience over theory, an ideology is "the thing that really commands your life—not the thing you say you believe in."[2]

This definition of ideology gave MRA's work an existential purpose, making their message something to fight for. A British man in the American army told his fellow soldiers that they were fighting "a War of Ideas, of rival philosophies," and called for "ideological supremacy. We need the force of arms plus the Superforce of an unconquerable spirit."[3] Kenaston Twitchell's brother Hanford grudgingly admired the communists' dedication to their cause. For them, "it is a philosophy of life, felt so keenly that it is lived out with passionate commitment," while the West is divided and confused. "When we know what we are fighting for," Twitchell concluded, "our friends join us in the fight and we win our battles. When we fight only to defend our materialism, our right to do as we please, we tend only to defend."[4]

Like the theology of the Oxford Group, however, Moral Re-Armament's ideology was never systematic. In place of philosophy, political theory, and economics, its ideological writings consisted largely of stories and well-turned phrases. Most of the movement's books on ideology are collections of stories, recounting how MRA changed the lives of individuals and nations. One anonymous document declared that America's ideology was encapsulated on its Great Seal. "Liberty—E Pluribus Unum—teamwork—the guidance and providence of God.... These are the ideas the world is hungry for. They can be America's greatest export."[5]

The ideology expressed in these stories and phrases was essentially a repackaging of Buchman's evangelical message. The movement sought to restructure all aspects of a society's life—government, business, and international as well as interpersonal relationships—by his core principles: societies can be peaceful and unified if human nature changes, and if all actions are guided by God and evaluated by the four absolutes. In MRA's eyes, this message was inherently Christian. During a session at Caux in 1948 on "How to Live Your Ideology," a South African told the assembly that "the Cross means to identify myself with God's battle for the whole world." The work of Moral Re-Armament, he concluded, "is very simply identifying ourselves with the outstretched arms of the Crucified."[6] John Roots told the Dutch Minister of Justice that MRA's ideology "was the Christian Faith, which was the only philosophy that counted to-day," including the idea "that human nature can be changed, and that God can guide."[7]

Movement members distinguished their ideology from Christianity as it is practiced by most Christians, which they saw as soft and undemanding. In 1954, one member dismissed the traditional evangelical Christianity because it is "filled with piosity [sic], personal drive, personal care, and in the matter of commitment does not demand everything." It is sentimental and soft, "unrelated to the hard realities." The ideological approach, on the other hand, "demands a complete abandonment of self, self-made policies and plans. It puts the will of the group before the will of the individual." It is Christian, led by "a fearless, favorless fellowship at the Cross" and "accepts, as Christ did, total blame for the sins of all men."[8]

Christianity remained prominent in MRA conferences and in private correspondence, but members played down religious language in other settings. Contradicting his words to the Dutch minister, John Roots told a contact at the State Department that Moral Re-Armament was "not a religion, an organization, or a political party. It is an ideology for all men everywhere." The message was not sectarian, but "the ideology of freedom. Its roots are the same as those of the United States. It gives the strength that makes democracy effective."[9] The speaker at an ideological training session argued that "Frank takes all the old basic truths of the Cross of Christ, the guidance of the Holy Spirit, redemption, the Kingdom of God, old truths in Biblical language and turns them into the language of the Ordinary Man." Devotees should use whatever language—secular or religious—that would work for the target audience. "Use the language that the person understands and give it the content that changes them."[10] Calling their message ideological rather than religious allowed MRA members to expand their audience, seeking government endorsement and reaching out to non-Christians.

MRA also called itself an ideology to put it on the same level as other, competing ideologies, chiefly communism. Buchman had disliked communism ever since his days in China; the ideological campaign turned that opposition into war. Communism was bad, MRA believed, because it was materialist, focused on economic and political systems rather than people. "Communism and Fascism are built on a negative something—on divisive materialism and confusion," Buchman said. MRA, on the other hand, was positive, the "rightful ideology" for America, sprung from "her Christian heritage." Such an ideology was America's "only adequate answer in the battle against materialism and all the other 'isms."[11]

MRA claimed that it would create a harmonious society, unlike materialistic philosophies which cause selfishness, individualism, and class conflict. An ideological training class in 1948 learned that "materialism teaches us to draw a battle-line which divides people." The problem in industry, for instance, was not labor versus management, but "subversive labor and reactionary management. The real battle-line is never between Left and Right, but between Right and Wrong."[12] During the war a Canadian soldier told an assembly at Mackinac that a subversive minority "born of class war" had disrupted production at a Canadian coal mine. In response the movement was working to "restore to the community the family spirit that it used to have."[13] An English worker criticized capitalists, on the other hand, for running an unjust system.[14] The movement advocated a well-regulated, organic society—a family—in place of a conflictive system of individuals.

Materialism triumphs, MRA argued, because of immorality. In 1948 a woman told a youth gathering in Los Angeles that "the heart of the problem is moral. If you have love first, then you want to share your goods, but the Communists know people are selfish and it is organized materialism."[15] Communism both caused and benefited from immorality. "Moral defeat is its greatest ally. That is why the Communists begin to have a hold in America. Not because of the economic system but because of moral defeat."[16]

MRA's key to defeating materialism was absolute morality, long a key theme for Buchman's work. A 1943 letter to MRA team leaders warned that "alien philosophies thrive on the break-down of our homes, the break-down of our morals, class conflicts, race riots. When the inner discipline of a nation breaks down, chaos or dictatorship takes over." Only MRA, the movement believed, could provide the new spirit that would keep democracy alive.[17]

Purity remained the most important of the four absolutes. At the first assembly at Mackinac in 1942, speakers bewailed the impurity in American culture. In American movies, one said, "lust is glamorized, marriage something to joke about, divorce is accepted as part of the American way. Evil is organized."[18] The proper response, Kenaston Twitchell said at Caux in 1948, was positive purity. "It is concerned not only with what we do not do, but also with what we do. It is far more pleasurable than impurity. It means discipline." Twitchell called for sexual sublimation, dedicating one's "affectional power" to the movement's work. One could indulge or repress sexual energy, "but the real way is redirection under Christ. It means freedom and health." Decisions about conception were an important example of purity for Twitchell. If marriage "is ruled by fear or human planning, then God's gift of creation is interfered with and there is always tragedy." Children conceived under guidance, however, are part of God's plan.[19]

Absolute purity, MRA believed, meant strong families. The nation needs "a common purpose between husband and wife," a speaker at Mackinac declared in 1942. "There is nothing more powerful than people who are united and will sacrifice for each other." Communism and fascism, on the other hand, "make a beeline for the homes," Twitchell said. "They have to have a mass production of their philosophy, determined that the things associated with a close, warm community life have got to be broken if they are going to win."[20] An ideological training session in 1948 focused on family life, called "Families Can Be Fun." The leader and his wife told how their lives changed when she admitted that she was a nagging wife. "It was absolutely black one moment and change the next," she declared. "It was a glorious experience."[21]

Since its founding at men's colleges, Buchman's movement had largely been led by men; it had a substantial female membership but talked little about roles or rules for women. Gender became more important, however, as MRA talked more about ideology. An ideological course for women called the participants to "recognize the real enemy within ourselves that softens, and makes absolute moral standards impossible." Materialism, the women learned, leads them to "put things ahead of people and personal plans before a real and unselfish care for others." Instead of following fashion or demanding affection from their husbands, women should aspire to "the glamour of purity, honesty, unselfishness and love and the guidance of God."[22] Marion Twitchell, Kenaston's wife, called women to "create a framework of living that makes statesmen, a sound family life that creates inner strength, trust, peace, backing, and fun." Resisting feminist claims, she declared that women should provide silence, support, and gracious service, to support men in their important work. "Frank has given a pattern to us women, and restored to America the real dignity and grace of service."[23]

MRA believed that the postwar world was a time of almost cosmic crisis. Twitchell's son Kennie told a group of fellow soldiers in 1953 that "we are living at a turning point in history." The war of ideologies "will affect our lives, those of our children, and of our children's children. In fact, I believe it is safe to say that the outcome of the conflict may well determine the course history will take for a thousand years to come."[24] An unnamed member anticipated that MRA would bring about one thousand years of "Inspired Democracy based on change," with a "world family of God guided free men." Buchman, he concluded, was chosen for this time of crisis.[25] This is millennialism—the conviction that MRA's work would bring about a better world, a perfected millennium, maybe even the kingdom of God.

An Effective World Answer Documented

In June 1944 Kenaston Twitchell told Buchman that the postwar world would need ideological training "We shall need to train people quickly, it seems to me, in the truths we have known through the years related to the national and world scene, in terms of America's ideology."[26] Over the next several decades MRA organized large conferences and small sessions for such training. Just as its ideology was a repackaging of evangelical Christianity, these training events resembled the Oxford Group's house parties and cell groups.

The most important ideological training events were its assemblies, which echoed the large house parties of the 1930s and the rallies of nineteenth century evangelical Christianity. The biggest were the months-long assemblies held every summer at Mackinac and Caux; participants came for a few days or stayed for weeks. They sometimes had as many as 1,000 people at a time, with over 5,000 over the course of a summer.[27] The programs at Caux and Mackinac featured plenary sessions, special discussions with smaller groups, and ideological films and plays.

The plenary sessions featured lengthy speeches from MRA leaders about the nature of ideology and the challenge of communism, including some of Buchman's favorite evangelical bromides. "Sin the disease. Christ the cure. Result a miracle," said one speaker in 1946. "Sin Binds, Blinds, Multiplies, Deadens, Deafens."[28] There was also music, with choirs or congregations singing hymns, MRA songs, or Handel's "Hallelujah" chorus. A visiting British journalist admitted that the façade of a Caux assembly was impressive, "but behind it one finds glorified YMCA meetings and juvenile amateur theatricals putting over uplift."[29]

Testimonies played an important role at the conferences, as they did at Oxford Group house parties. The first Caux assembly concluded with a "pageant of nations" as "representatives from all over Europe and the East spoke of what the assembly had meant to the future of their countries." Among the speakers were a British journalist, a hero of the French underground, and a Norwegian soldier.[30]

The plenaries also featured repentance. Just as young men shared their sins at early Buchman gatherings, speakers at MRA conferences confessed their nations' sins and offered apologies to those who had been wronged. At the Caux assembly in 1952, for instance, an Indonesian woman apologized to Dutch, Japanese, and Muslim people for her hatred. At the same meeting, a person from Ethiopia embraced a person from Italy.[31] In 1957, on the anniversary of the Japanese attack on Pearl

Harbor, Masahide Shibusawa, the son of a former Japanese finance minister, told a MRA gathering, how sorry he was "all suffering my nation caused in war. I am giving my life [to] restore and together with you build [a] new world under [the] control [of] God."[32] MRA made a great deal of such apologies, implying that such individual actions represented policy changes on the part of their nations, reflecting the movement's belief in the power of an individual's actions.

MRA also organized smaller ideological training sessions for a variety of audiences. In fall 1949 MRA hosted a series of ten "Informal Evenings" on "An Ideological Strategy for Democracy" at a Washington hotel. The syllabus promised answers to questions about making peace and uniting humanity. "They will be treated—and evidence of an effective world answer documented—by means of informal lectures, colored slides, films and music, as well as by distinguished speakers from overseas." The sessions included definitions of ideology and a discussion of the "Dilemma of Democracy: Freedom versus Order." As always these sessions included many "illustrations," stories of MRA's success around the world.[33]

A special audience for ideological training was the military in the United States and Europe. One of the MRA veterans suggested that Mackinac Island, a military base a long time ago, should be reactivated and made the base for "an Army of life-changers," with active soldiers sent for ideological training. The army could be "a force for the moral re-arming of the nation," creating "soldiers who believe that their Army exists to serve God and Country and therefore that anything which is guided by God is in the interest of the Service."[34] In March 1947 they ran a program in London for fifteen Danish army and navy officers, with sessions on ideology and morale, field trips to British military camps, a reception with British officers, and a concert by the Mackinac Singers.[35] In 1953 Kennie Twitchell, now a second lieutenant in the army, told a group of officers that "the guy who wins in this war of ideas is the guy with the better idea." Soldiers with strong moral standards and a fighting faith "would give us a superior ideology." Their morale, he concluded, "would be of the highest because every last soldier would know and believe in what he was fighting for."[36]

Weapons

Concerned with the communist bloc's "tremendous propaganda for a false idea," MRA developed a collection of tools—explicitly called weapons—for the world-wide ideological war.[37] These tools included plays and movies in the tradition of *You Can Defend America* and the pre-war pageants, which reflected the growing role of media in American society. They spread MRA's message in new ways, yet another reinvention of its evangelical method.

To lead this propaganda war MRA found a new spokesman, to assist the weakened Buchman and take the place of Shoemaker. Peter Howard brought a lot of assets to the movement. He was a celebrity; virtually every reference to Howard in MRA literature identified him as a "well-known British journalist" and a national rugby star. He was fiercely loyal to Buchman and an effective writer. He had a clear ideological vision, framing the Cold War as a battle between the forces of evil and the forces of good. Howard served as the movement's most effective propagandist for over two decades.

Howard wrote the movement's first postwar show, *Ideas Have Legs*, in 1945, later renamed *The Good Road*. A review from a Michigan paper described the spectacle. "The opening curtain rises upon an illuminated globe. Lightning flashes and thunder rolls as 'voices from the past' echo the great ideas and ideals that have shaped the course of history." An amplified voice asked, "Is there an idea for democracy which you and I, the ordinary people of today, can give legs in our homes, on our farms, in our industries—big enough to remake the world?" Like *You Can Defend America*, the play featured a series of scenes showing how problems are resolved by self-examination, confession, and apology.[38] It included a search for "the true America" guided by God, featuring Swiss yodelers, Joan of Arc, Lincoln, Washington, the Magna Carta, a G.I. on Okinawa, and an average family.[39]

The Good Road received mixed reviews. A group of British young adults, touring the United States with the show, reported that the New York run "was a fortnight of head-over-heels success." Everyone in the New York theatre community loved it, they said. "Even the most go-getting side of America responds to people who give their hearts without asking for reward. One chorus girl from another show said: 'Our show makes people forget; yours makes them think.'"[40] A columnist for the *Washington Daily News*, on the other hand, called *The Good Road* "a strange mixture of uplift musical revue and old fashioned morality play with overtones of amateurism, corn, hokum and the Communist doctrinal type of drama intended to inspire the comrades to do and die for the dear old Soviet Union."[41] A British journalist saw a production at Caux. "I don't know what visiting statesmen and politicians made of them all, but the Buchmanites seemed to be whipped into ecstasy by such items as 'Sorry is a magic little word' and 'If You Harnessed All the Heart-power in the World.'"⁴²

You Can Defend America and *The Good Road* were revues, a series of musical scenes around a theme, but *Jotham Valley* was a full scale musical, with a plot and a large cast. It was based on the true story of two feuding brothers in the American west. One brother ended the feud when he admitted that he was wrong and his wife gave the other a spice cake. *New York Times* theatre critic Brooks Atkinson said the message was "a sane way of approaching insoluble problems."⁴³

MRA saw the musical as part of a cosmic struggle. A press release called it "far more than a play. It is the focus of a battle in the world war of ideas." Although set in the west, "it might be the Ruhr or your office or Washington." With its all-MRA cast, "it has real people playing a real story. But it is an act in a bigger drama—the fight between good and evil that will settle the future of us all."⁴⁴ When it received bad reviews, they blamed cultural decay. John Roots declared that MRA was "challenging the dictatorship of a degenerate clique over the cultural diet of America." Another member reported that "our real opposition on Broadway comes from the brethren and the Commies." The "brethren" most likely refers to homosexuals.⁴⁵ In the face of meager attendance MRA defiantly extended its run and moved into a new theatre, declaring that its "box-office response indicated that there was a place in the New York theatre for a clean, wholesome show suitable for theatregoers who do not depend upon the average Broadway offering."⁴⁶

Several MRA productions were written by people outside the MRA inner circle. At the Mackinac assembly in 1956, a group of Africans presented *Freedom*, about the challenges facing the continent as it decolonized.⁴⁷ The following summer saw the New York premiere of *The Next Phase*, written by six members of the parliament of Ghana, designed to answer the ideological problems of their time. The answer, of course, was the need for the four absolutes, presented through "scenes of African parliamentary, political, business, and home life." The cast of 54 came from 15 African nations, including William Nkomo, founder of the African National Congress Youth League.⁴⁸ Buchman said that *The Next Phase* was a smash. "It had an immediate success in Washington, went to the South, where the racial conflict is at its bitterest, and has caught the imagination of New York."⁴⁹

The ultimate MRA show was *Pickle Hill*, which premiered at Mackinac for Buchman's eighty-first birthday in 1959 and opened in Washington that winter. Written by Peter Howard, it was a musical if not always accurate account of Buchman's Penn State years.⁵⁰ The first scene was set in State College in 1909, with the students drunk and the faculty godless. Bill Pickle, the town's bootlegger, after confronting and being converted by Buchman, dedicates himself "to be a fighting, fighting, fighting American!" His change convinces the whole campus, and the students proclaim they have taken their "battle stations, we are living to set men free." In the epilogue various international figures—Carl Hambro of the Norwegian parliament, a Japanese official, and a leader of Cyprus—talk with Buchman about their own experiences with him, with Pickle, and with each other.[51] The show retold Buchman's Penn State story for MRA's ideological agenda.

In time Moral Re-Armament produced 36 plays and musicals. The early productions were written by and starred MRA volunteers, but in the 1950s the plays became slicker, recruiting professionals both on stage and behind the scenes. Some plays were the work of a single author—14 by Howard alone—while others were purportedly written by groups inside or outside the movement.[52] In addition to the traveling and Broadway productions, many of these shows had long runs at the Westminster Theatre in London, bought by MRA supporters as a memorial to British soldiers lost in the war.[53]

MRA leaders realized early on that their plays could reach a broader audience if they were also made into movies. In 1948 Kenaston Twitchell told Buchman that "we may be at the beginning of considerable film production. It is conceivable that God might give us a set of technicians who by their spirit and teamwork challenge the industry in what they do with our material." Such films would lead to "far greater recognition than we have yet achieved." The first play to be turned into a film was *The Good Road*, released in 1949.[54] A decade later MRA built a television and film production studio at Mackinac, declaring that the expense was necessary because Moscow devoted 11 percent of its budget "to the creation of plays and films to advance the cause of Communism." The men from 24 nations who worked through the winter to build the studio "demonstrated an ideological incentive which is the free world's answer to Moscow's boast of superior technological progress, an incentive which lies not in dictatorship but in the wills of free men."[55]

Movement leaders were particularly proud of the film version of *Freedom*, which came out in 1957. A member of the group invited congressmen to the Washington premiere, declaring that "this film will do for Africa and Asia what 'Uncle Tom's Cabin' did for America. I believe you will be interested to see this film in the light of its being used by America as a potent weapon for freedom in Asia and Africa."[56]

MRA leaders were convinced that their plays and movies were world-shattering. Buchman told a long-time financial supporter that MRA was showing several plays in Washington "and they are having a great impact on American opinion." Diplomats and members of Congress were attending. "Night after night the theatre is crowded out and on the opening night there was a ten-minute standing ovation."[57] They were very proud when a Los Angeles newspaper declared that "the plays of Moral Re-Armament are giving the answer to the Peking Opera and the Moscow Ballet."[58]

Like other armaments, however, ideological weapons did not come cheaply. Two members wrote a strategy memorandum in 1953 laying out the movement's financial challenges. The demand for MRA programs was growing, they argued, but so was the expense. In 1951 its budget in the United States was over a million dollars, which included the traveling and living expenses for 200 full-time workers in America, and "World Assemblies" in Washington, Mackinac Island, and Los Angeles. That budget also paid for media productions, including one musical, two plays, literature, radio, TV, and a documentary film. Veterans had given their bonuses, a typist gave two dollars a week, and a congressman gave 50 dollars a month, but MRA needed more money for a new Asian initiative, including a tour and conferences in the region. "It may be decisive in winning the war of ideas. If we are to seize an opportunity so timely to meet a need so urgent, further substantial funds will be necessary."[59] Another proposal called for a campaign in Long Beach, California, which would create sound homes and industrial teamwork on the docks. The program would include presentations of *Jotham Valley*, 150 or more workers providing ideological training, screening of documentary films, performances by the Mackinac Singers, speakers, and books. That campaign would cost almost $9,000.[60]

To support this work, the movement sought government money for its ideological weapons. In 1961 Ray Purdy drafted a letter to a State Department official who had attended the assembly at Mackinac. He noted that the assembly had seen "weapons, the effectiveness of which have been tested in action across the world. Other plays and films are available as ideological weapons, provided the necessary funds can be secured." He proposed that the U.S. government provide funds "to mount and distribute the plays and films of Moral Re-Armament," and that "United States Missions overseas should be advised to cooperate to the fullest extent with the forces of Moral Re-Armament in their countries." Purdy concluded with a list of weapons immediately available, and "the convictions of national leaders as to the effectiveness of this work."[61] There is no evidence of a response to this appeal.

Buchman and his colleagues also solicited funds from several leading American foundations. A 1959 proposal sought almost $7 million dollars—the equivalent of almost $50 million today—from the Carnegie Corporation of New York, the Ford Foundation, and three other foundations for a "Program to Bulwark the Free World Against Communism in 4 Vital Areas." The funds requested would support ideological campaigns in Germany, Japan, Nigeria, and Iran, "four hot-spot countries where Communism and anti-moral pressures are severe and where a defeat of the free world would lead to disastrous consequences and possibly even to war." MRA would use "ideological plays, motion pictures and other communication means. Previous experience has shown this is highly effective in switching the minds of people from an ideology of hate and stubbornness to an ideology of cooperation and friendliness." The proposal declared that MRA "is NOT a religious organization. Espousers of the principles of Moral Re-Armament come from all religions of the world." Signatories included "a Catholic, a Protestant, a Jew, a Hindu, and a Moslem."[62] The proposal was not funded.

Battlefields

The world situation looked critical in the years after the war. "In Europe today there is hunger and hate and hopelessness," Alan Thornhill, a long-time British member, told the Washington team in 1947. MRA's message must be "a colossal love that will burn out hates like that." The assembly at Caux, he said, showed "that the hurts and hates of generations can be healed by the Spirit of God and by the infection of a family that gave everything." Thornhill concluded that Europe's fate would be either dictatorship or the message of Caux.[63] Europe was not the only battlefield. In 1960 Peter Howard wrote Buchman from Bombay that "it is MRA or Communism, and the issues are unfolding fast."[64] MRA fought the war of ideas around the world, using its conferences and its weapons to spread its message.

The most important battlefield directly after the war was Germany. People were despairing, and the country was being flooded by materialistic propaganda from the east. In November 1945 John Roots argued for a team to visit Germany "with a constructive policy because if we wait too long it will be too late."[65] Buchman insisted on inviting

Germans to the first Caux assembly; under the guidance of MRA, a
small group of Germans drafted a manifesto for their country's ideological recovery. It blamed Germany's problems on materialistic ideologies and unguided democracy. "Democracy without an ideology
is like a ship without a rudder, tossed aimlessly here, there and everywhere by the waves of materialistic ideologies." In its place, the manifesto argued, Germany needs "a *genuine* democracy where God stands
on the bridge and everyone carries out His orders. Then democracy
will also have a passion, a philosophy, and a plan—an inspired democracy." It called on Germans to test their actions by the four absolutes,
and to listen for God's guidance. It included many of Buchman's favorite phrases, including a quotation from William Penn: "Men must be
governed by God or they will be ruled by tyrants."[66]

In addition to bringing Germans to Caux, MRA also organized meetings throughout the conquered country. In 1952, at a public meeting
in Essen, they met the Ruhr miners who became an important part of
their labor work. The meeting featured songs and speeches from miners
and government officials. A communist student declared, "My Marxist
faith is shattered. We must win the East for this ideology."[67] MRA had
a tougher time when an audience at Stuttgart University started asking
questions. "The opportunity was used by the Communists to confuse
the issue on the question of peace," a British member told Buchman.
"We had to review our policy about allowing questions at the end of
such meetings." Such questions turned the focus of the meeting from
stories of change to intellectual discussion. "You could feel the morale
indicator falling fast. This was a lesson for all of us."[68]

The movement also worked in other European countries. Members
organized large campaigns in Sweden, Denmark, and Finland, reminiscent of the 1935 Denmark campaign. Paul Campbell, Buchman's physician and advisor, told him that Scandinavia was in a unique position.
"These Nordic countries morally re-armed could well be a pattern of
the third way to which both East and West could look. You feel that we
have on the one hand people who know that they are in desperate need,
and on the other an openness on the part of leaders of all sections of
the nation to our message and program."[69] Buchman told a meeting in
Copenhagen that cooperation had reduced Denmark's unemployment
from 20 percent to nothing, because the root cause of unemployment
was not economic but moral. With God's guidance, honest employers worked with laborers to open up new jobs. "Thousands of Danes
decided to clean up their lives and motives and take responsibility for
the nation," he said.[70]

MRA put a lot of energy into Asia as well. Kensuke Horinouchi, who had met MRA in Washington before the war, led a Japanese delegation to Caux in 1948. He offered apologies on behalf of the delegation and all Japanese people for all the wrong they had done.[71] The summer of 1950 saw the grandly named "Japanese Ideological Mission to the World Assembly for Moral Re-Armament and the Western Democracies." The 74-member group included parliamentarians, mayors of cities including Hiroshima and Nagasaki, labor and industrial leaders, and young people. They visited Caux and other sites in Europe, as well as New York, Washington, Mackinac, and California. They exulted over all the important people they met, including the pope, and offered testimonies of their experiences. At Caux former communists gave them "first-hand understanding of the strategy, tactics and ultimate objectives of Communism, and the requirements for counteracting it with a democratic ideology." At the end of the trip they declared their desire "to make amends for our mistakes of the past by constituting our country a trusted partner of the United States in building a regenerated Asia."[72]

MRA leaders saw the trip as "one of the greatest events in the history of the United Nations," "a major world event."[73] In Washington the Japanese "apologized to America and the world for the tribulation which their country had brought upon mankind and pledged themselves and their nation to work with us for a free and peaceful world."[74] Roots observed to Buchman that "God's ways are wonderful indeed, and you see in an event like that how fast the world could change if people would listen and obey. No one could possibly have planned humanly to have the Japanese here in Washington at this particular time. God brought them here."[75]

China was an even more important battlefield in the ideological war. Thanks to Buchman's missionary work there three decades before, he had long-standing connections to China's Christian community, including Chiang Kai-shek. Movement members were thrilled when a Chinese representative told a Paris conference that "Chiang Kai-shek is guided by God. China is not led by a single man, but under God."[76] As Chiang's government struggled to defeat the communist forces, Twitchell complained to Buchman that Chiang, "the greatest Christian statesman of the age," had been betrayed by Roosevelt and George Marshall. "A group of liberal-left[ists] in State do not really want the Chinese Nationalists to survive." He believed that the press was anti-Nationalist and had convinced American public that Chiang was fascist and corrupt.[77]

John Roots, who grew up in China as the son of the Anglican bishop of Hankow, wrote a long memo on US policy in China, arguing that just as the Marshall Plan saved Europe, "America can take the initiative and save the China situation." The answer was a new approach, "ideological, rather than only political, economic, or military." The Soviet Union had pursued such an approach for over 25 years, leading "as many Chinese as possible to dedicate their lives to the communist faith, with a view to enabling that faith to triumph in China and ultimately in the world." The west's method, on the other hand, was ineffective. In mission schools "our curriculum has not been calculated to turn out zealous and disciplined agents of the ideology of freedom in any way comparable to the dedicated graduates of the Comintern."[78] Roots suggested to a contact in the State Department that the United States create a "Presidential Commission on Ideological Aid" that would "popularize democracy among the masses; deal with grants among officials; create a spirit of teamwork among military and political leaders; broaden the base of responsibility in military and political affairs; [and] win key communists to the democratic faith." Roots believed that the movement's plays would be effective ways of overcoming communist propaganda. The State Department official replied that "you people certainly seem to be functioning as the Comintern of the democracies," advocating for the west as the Communist International did for Marxism.[79]

MRA organized assemblies in Asia to spread its message. Perhaps the most important was the "South-East Asian Assembly for Moral Re-Armament," held at Baguio in the Philippines in 1957. MRA leaders planned the assembly to serve as "an answer to the Communist-inspired Afro-Asian Conference going on in Cairo."[80] As at Caux, apologies were an important part of the agenda. A "Supreme Advisor" to the Japanese government saw the conference as "the only way in which Koreans and Japanese could get together."[81] Within days, a press release headlined "Japan and Korea Reconciled"—or at least some Japanese and some Koreans.[82] At another session a Japanese senator apologized to Philippine and Korean delegates. "I want to take full responsibility for what my nation did and for this I ask your forgiveness." He was inspired by a Philippine cabinet minister who lost her bitterness after meeting Japanese war widows. She said, "I realized that I must wipe out the bitterness in my heart because the world is full of it. What better way is there to bring peace and friendship in the world than through Moral Re-Armament. Gathering like this is the answer to the problems in the world today."[83] In these ritual acts individuals apologized on behalf of their countries, although it is unlikely that these apologies carried any official weight. The closing address at Baguio was given by a rising star in MRA, Rajmohan Gandhi. Again reflecting MRA's use of celebrity,

Gandhi was always identified in MRA publicity as "grandson of the Mahatma."[84]

This Asian outreach led MRA into non-Christian countries. One of Buchman's supporters acknowledged that the evangelist spoke out of his Christian experience, but Buchman "believed that every man should live the highest that his own faith taught him. On that basis, as each one searches for the inner light with all his heart and mind, men of faith can move together and learn from one another." The world was divided, the supporter believed, "not between the great faiths, but between men whose allegiance is to God and spiritual values and those who are dedicated to their destruction."[85] This approach is reflected in a press release from a 1953 Asia conference quoting the endorsement of a Thai Buddhist abbot. "If the Lord Buddha were still alive, I am certain he would be most pleased. The absolute moral standards correspond to the principles of Buddhist Dharma. People who practise them, practise Buddhism."[86]

MRA also reached across faith lines in the Middle East. In 1959 the Caux assembly marked the birthday of Mohammed with Muslims from many nations among the participants. An Egyptian told the gathering, "When we Muslims live what God has told us to live we find unity with all those of other faiths and nations who truly live their faiths too." He noted that Muslims need to live the four absolutes as well. "In Moral Re-Armament the Muslim and the Christian World is united on a platform unique in the world today."[87] A group of Britons, including journalists, military men, and members of parliament, wrote to Egyptian president Gamal Nasser, thanking him for a statement supporting MRA. "We hold with you that this materialist ideology can be met and mastered by a greater moral ideology based on a revolutionary change of heart and issuing in radical change under God in the political, economic and social order, uniting all classes, races and faiths." The writers expressed their regret for what the United Kingdom had done against "the liberty and dignity of the Arab people," and invited Nasser to send a group to Caux.[88] In 1959 the Shah of Iran made Buchman a Commander of the Royal Order of the Crown. "Our greatest need is a superior ideology," read the proclamation. "Moral Re-Armament has accepted this great challenge. It has succeeded and has evoked a deep response throughout the world." Rajmohan Gandhi, "grandson of the Mahatma," told the gathering at Mackinac that "with MRA Iran will expose 1,500 miles of Russian border to a supreme ideology."[89]

As Africa went through the complex process of decolonization, MRA leaders and surrogates crossed the continent preaching its message. Buchman reported on a 1954 return to South Africa, where blacks and whites spoke on the same platform. William Nkomo, founder of the African National Congress Youth League, reputedly disavowed revolution and declared himself free from hatred of Afrikaners. "I saw something greater than nationalism at work. I saw an ideology which is superior because it is an ideology for everyone, everywhere." Government officials invited MRA to visit Nigeria. "We are doing this with the realisation that a self-governing Nigeria must be built on a firm moral foundation, and with the conviction that MRA by its performances in Europe, Asia and other continents can give to our people and country the moral revolution which is the only basis of survival in a world of conflict and chaos."[90]

MRA reveled in the world-wide attention. The movement's corporate report for 1956 described "the need and the expectancy for this answer" as "embodied in invitations of historic significance from heads of state and national leaders, as the idea of a world-encircling force took shape." Movement leaders received "invitations" from the Shah of Iran, Chiang Kai-Shek, Gamal Nasser, and the presidents of Philippines and Viet Nam. The "Statesmen's Mission" featured many speeches and the movement's earnest plays. "Holding forth as it did a conception of freedom based upon the will of God and absolute moral standards, this Mission drew from leaders and people alike in the lands of Asia and Africa a heartfelt and authentic response."[91]

Movement leaders continued to believe that true change would happen only if Moral Re-Armament became official government policy. In the movement's corporate report for 1955 Buchman shared his birthday wish that "Moral Re-Armament becomes the normal philosophy of every cabinet, every race, every class and every individual throughout the entire world."[92] If it didn't, Campbell warned, the results could be dire. "I feel the national leaders in Europe must be told that they choose MRA as national policy or accept Communism. There is no other choice. And my other conviction is that the time is come when we take over nations with the same magnitude of planning and action and statesmanship as the materialists have been doing."[93]

Resistance

MRA reveled in attacks on its work. Adolphus Staton, a retired admiral and MRA supporter, revealed with pleasure that "MRA has been discussed in the top echelons in Moscow and Peking and made a high priority target of world Communism." According to intelligence sources, the Communists were upset that MRA had gotten to Africa ahead of them. A visitor to the Kremlin had been told "that the greatest obstacle to the advance of Communism was MRA."[94] Buchman "has been the target of attack by world Communism and the organized forces of immorality and perversion for 40 years," noted one movement member. "They have attempted to destroy the force of Moral Re-Armament by their attempt to blacken the name of its founder." Communism attacked MRA only because "MRA is militantly turning the tide of Communism on a world scale."[95]

Party publications saw MRA either as the vanguard of fascist reaction or as a figure of fun. In 1952 a commentator on Radio Moscow described MRA as one of "the ideological arm-bearers of U.S. imperialism, an international religious and political organization" that was "created for the benefit of monopolies." He called Buchman "a U.S. missionary with fascist tendencies." With the support of the U.S. "secret police," he declared, the movement infiltrates unions, breaks strikes, and engages in espionage. "Together with the bourgeois political parties and right-wing socialists, mercenary bourgeois science and Americanised literature and art, this propagandist and espionage organisation is attempting to fool the people and paralyze their will for the struggle for peace and democracy."[96] An article in a Finnish communist paper mocked MRA, calling it simple and straight-forward, "like the best soap advertisement." MRA conferences "are short striking speeches and personal witnesses, in between the MRA dance orchestra plays 'Tico-Tico,' then a chorus sings or there is a MRA play." Meanwhile the movement works to break down worker solidarity.[97]

Communists often asserted that Moral Re-Armament worked hand-in-glove with Western governments, especially their intelligence agencies. MRA denied such accusations, claiming its independence from governmental influence. There is no denying, however, that MRA leaders sought closer connections with government officials and financial support for its work. The movement often sent its task forces where anti-Americanism was particularly intense.[98] Any records of this link remain classified and may never be public.

MRA was also criticized by the church. A leading example was a report written by the Social and Industrial Council of the Church Assembly of the Church of England, which did an extensive study of MRA at the request of business and labor leaders in Britain. Its report, rooted in liberal politics and neo-orthodox theology, appreciated MRA's commitment to living a practical faith, but found it theologically thin, with little understanding of the nature of God or the causes of sin. The authors also argued that MRA's politics were simplistic and utopian.[99] On the other side, fundamentalists in Britain and the United States had distrusted Buchman's work for decades, seeing it as heretical at best and morally dangerous at worst.[100]

Others in the church praised MRA's work. A British vicar argued in 1946 that MRA had given the church and the world a strong set of standards against materialism. "Some of the most effective ministries today, and not least in the Church of England, owe their distinctiveness to what the Oxford Group has given them. Evangelicals above all should rejoice that the Group has done so much to demonstrate a conception of evangelism adequate to the needs and special conditions of the age."[101]

The Catholic Church had equally mixed views of MRA. The Congregation of the Holy Office forbade priests and religious from participating in the movement; even if its objectives were praiseworthy, it "possesses neither the patrimony of doctrine or of spiritual life, nor the supernatural means of grace which the Catholic Church has." It could lead Catholics to "syncretism and religious indifference." The Bishop of Marquette, the see that included Mackinac, warned Catholics that MRA "assumes the role of spiritual direction and guidance for which it does not have a divine authority," endangering "the purity and integrity of the faith of Catholics who participate in this religious movement."[102]

Other Catholics supported Moral Re-Armament. French Catholic philosopher Gabriel Marcel regularly endorsed the movement, an opinion that carried some weight with the Catholic press.[103] In the 1960s Cardinal Richard Cushing of Boston called MRA a "noble cause" as the church became more open to Catholic participation in ecumenical activities.[104] MRA received the ultimate endorsement in 1950, when Pope Pius XII called it "*a good thing. We must, above all, give the world peace. We must also abolish Communism by giving those people something better and the Church and Moral Re-Armament can do this. I give Moral Re-Armament my Blessing.*" A member suggested using those words whenever the "bad falsehood" of Catholic objections to MRA came up. "His blessing to MRA will, I am convinced, have a great influence for good."[105]

One church leader made a useful argument for MRA. The Bishop of Lausanne, Geneva and Fribourg, the see that included Caux, concluded that Catholics could participate in MRA because MRA was not a religion. Catholics within MRA should continue their involvement in the church and check their guidance "according to the traditional rules for the discernment of spirits." A member will be safe "if he lives his Catholicism intensely, if he is really of the Church," but he must remember that "Moral Re-Armament is not a religion and cannot satisfy our religious needs."[106] The Abbot Primate of the Benedictine Order agreed with this distinction, saying that MRA's "standards are universally valid. It is not a religion, nor a substitute for religion."[107]

MRA made this distinction when it was helpful. Because it was not tied to a creed, a movement report noted, "Frank Buchman and Moral Re-Armament have been effective with men of all faiths and men of no faith." Many Christians have returned to their churches after meeting MRA, and non-Christians have found a new faith, "but the aim of MRA has steadily been a faith in action—an ideology for the world that barred no one and gave every last man and woman a destiny."[108] This distinction was particularly useful when working with governments.

Although they occasionally downplayed MRA's religious nature or explicitly Christian roots in public, among themselves members still believed their work was millennial, bringing about a better world, the kingdom of God. "1960 is going to be the most monumental year for MRA the world has yet seen," Howard told Buchman that January. "It is God's purpose to win the world and for this MRA has been created."[109] This conviction made their every action world-shaking. Twitchell told Buchman in 1958 that one of his speeches was "a superb and historic document. It is so timely it will burn through the consciousness of this country. We are very grateful for it."[110]

In this millennial vision, Buchman became the world's savior and suffering servant. In the dark days of 1941, just after Pearl Harbor and Shoemaker's withdrawal, a woman noted that "the enemy" had focused its attack on Buchman; "their aim is to smear him with the American public. I feel we should work for a flood of statements from prominent men testifying to the integrity and true greatness of Frank Buchman, once and for all putting him in his rightful place in the rank of Great Americans." She felt that Buchman "should be advising the heads of our government as to policy instead of having to work under cover. His guided word, said at the right moment, might save our nation from collapse if he only had the opportunity and the backing."[111] As the war ended, Twitchell despaired to Buchman over the trials ahead. "The awareness of what we are up against in Europe is almost nil." The government was weak and riddled with leftists. MRA was clearly the only answer. "There is certainly no other crowd on the horizon within miles or years of giving an answer." "We need you," he concluded, and underlined that phrase 23 times.[112]

★ ★ ★

In 1920, Frank Buchman was the leader of a small religious movement, with teams planted on college campuses in Britain and the United States. Forty years later, Moral Re-Armament was active around the globe, with assemblies drawing thousands of participants to conference centers in Switzerland and the United States. It spread its ideology of world change through individual change via movies, plays, and publications. Millions of dollars in donations, large and small, paid for the work. Buchman's movement had gone through a series of reinventions—with different names, different approaches to publicity, and different organizational structures. The basic message, however, remained the same, and it was led by the same cohort of men, who met the movement as college students in the early 1920s.

At the peak of its visibility and influence, however, Buchman's movement began to face a new set of challenges as the leadership cohort aged and the surrounding culture changed. The next reinvention was going to be the hardest.

CHAPTER SEVEN

Tomorrow's American

Life on Mackinac Island was idyllic, but the young people meeting there in the summer of 1965 knew that the world beyond the island was troubled. They discussed the protests on their campus and the riots in the cities. Finally, an Iowa State track star challenged the crowd. "The loud-mouthed, pacifist minority scream about what they're against. Why don't we stage a demonstration of what we're *for?*"[1] This, according to the MRA legend, was the birth of Up With People, the last and best-known stage of the movement's life. Within a year, three casts of young people were traveling the country and the world, sharing their positive message through song.

In the 1960s Moral Re-Armament once again reinvented itself, this time as a youth-focused initiative to change the world. It was responding to the rise of the baby boom generation, as well as the priorities of new leaders. It also hoped to create a new cohort of leaders for the movement to replace the founding generation that was nearing retirement.

By 1970, however, MRA in America was largely out of business. This rapid decline in fortunes reflects the limits of reinvention. Tensions in MRA circles over the rise of Up With People, were exacerbated by a sudden leadership vacuum. In the end, MRA did not respond fast enough to the rapidly changing society around it.

The College of the Good Road

Echoing Buchman's work with college students 20 years before, Moral Re-Armament targeted much of its postwar ideological training on young people. For a brief time it focused that work through a new institution called the College of the Good Road. The idea began in the spring of 1948, when a leader in London proposed incorporating "our youth round the world into a college or university which could be called 'The University of the Good Road.'" He based the name on one of the movement's first plays. Such a school would meet the needs of an ideological age, he suggested, needs untouched by traditional universities. "It would give us a great opportunity to write a charter of our conception of true education and enlist the support of our friends all over the world."[2] The college, which enrolled many children of MRA's founding generation, might also pass the movement's message on to a new cohort of leaders.

The college's founders looked to two very different models for its work. The first was the elite military academies of America and Western Europe. "West Point and Annapolis, Sandhurst and Saint-Cyr were founded to provide officers for the war of arms," declared the prospectus. "The College of the Good Road is being founded to provide officers in the war of ideas. It recognizes that this is an ideological age and that the instant need of the age is a rising generation trained both to understand the conflict of ideologies and to equip their nations with a superior ideology."[3] The second model was communism's youth movements and cadres. One MRA document noted that while totalitarian powers train their youth, there are no comparable programs for "Inspired Democracy."[4] By creating this new school, "pioneering in a completely new field," one of the first proposals noted, MRA would "steal the march on the Communists, as far as creating and copyrighting the concept of degrees in 'ideology,' and in establishing standards and definition of such degrees. For they are the only ones operating in this field."

The college would also give MRA's ideological training a patina of intellectual authority. It would have a faculty and offer bachelor, master, and doctoral degrees in Ideology. One early leader warned his colleagues that "it is important that we do not let our standards down, if we are to win any respect or recognition from the academic world." Only through such recognition would the college "have an effect on educational thinking in this country or the world. The very existence of such a school, if a recognized institution and worthy of being looked into, will revolutionize educational thinking."[5]

Despite such trappings, however, it was not a traditional college; its only purpose was teaching the MRA message and method. The college's goal was to "make each student a revolutionary," declared the curriculum committee. Graduates would understand "why he is part of this force of MRA and what the destiny of this force is in the life of this nation and the world." Serving the movement's practical goals, the college would also help students to "articulate to the business, labor, government and educational leadership the needs of this nation so that these groups, especially business men, will play their full role in financing this revolution on a world scale."[6] Students were evaluated not by grades—which might feed student ambition, taboo in MRA—but through meetings with faculty. Students would be dropped only if they demonstrated emotional unsuitability, ineptitude, or "off-the-ball-ness."[7]

When the college began in the fall of 1949, an important part of the curriculum were the daily lectures, which often resembled the platform talks from Mackinac or Caux. There were sessions "on economics, industrial leadership, history, the struggle of ideologies in the world today," noted a report from Caux. "The ideology of Moral Re-Armament was clearly presented as the answering ideology in all these fields."[8] Almost all of the lecturers were MRA devotees, dedicated students if not always scholars of their subject matter.[9] Lectures in the Department of Ideology included "Is the New Testament Ideological?", "Frank Buchman and the Ideological Age," and "The Ideological Problem of Yugoslavia." College sessions sometimes overlapped with the Caux conference, with students attending conference platform talks as part of their study.

These lectures distilled the MRA message. "The knowledge that we are living in an ideological age, that a sound ideology is based on absolute moral standards, and that we must move together on a plane above national frontiers or class barriers, is rapidly growing," Principal Roger Hicks told students at the end of the fall term in 1949. "We are called to a great destiny. Our task is nothing less than to remake the world under the power of God," another lecturer declared. "Your task as youth is first to *train* the statesmen of the world and then to *be* the statesmen of the world. And statesmanship involves study. Statesmen are out-thought before they are ought-fought. In order to change the world you must understand and interpret it."[10]

Students at the College of the Good Road did more than listen to lectures, however. They worked in small tutorial groups to apply their lessons, learning to become spokesmen for MRA's message. Each group accepted "responsibility for a situation or an area; to plan what to say to an editor, a mayor, shop steward or housewife; how to train spokesmen and how to use them."[11] They then put their skills into operation, traveling around Europe and the United States to tour factories, meet leaders, and speak to workers. Students in Los Angeles, for instance, toured defense industries in Southern California "to see at first-hand conditions in industry, to hear stories of the war of ideas at work and to discuss with industrial leaders and workers the answering philosophy." They wrote and produced musicals "and other weapons in the war of ideas."[12] Students lived and traveled in family-like groups, which helped "to break the individualistic streak that is so strong in many of us," wrote Hicks. "They have taught us how to identify our hearts with something outside ourselves and something that goes far further and deeper than simple loyalty. You can be loyal to a movement, but you have got to give your heart to a family. A movement is made up of families."

In the fall of 1949 there were 314 students from 18 countries in the College of the Good Road, with big groups from the United Kingdom, the United States, Switzerland and Norway, and a few from Asia.[13] Among the students were several children of MRA leaders, as well as veterans of World War II from both sides, including a former member of the Hitler Youth.[14] They met at Caux, Mackinac, Los Angeles, and a new center outside London.

Students and faculty alike drew sharp contrasts between the College of the Good Road and other universities, which Hicks felt were too specialized and too focused on research. They "lack self-confidence and any agreed sense of direction and purpose. Because they increasingly lack this and are aware that they lack it, they are part of the spiritual confusion of the age." The College of the Good Road, on the other hand, had a clear purpose, to change human nature. "Education needs to get back to the place where we start with the surrender of our will, mind and heart to the creative and controlling mind of God. That is where the College of the Good Road is different from other colleges and universities."[15] A German theology student reported that he was studying under the guidance of God, not just from duty. "Only a burning passion in my heart for God's plan not only for myself, but also for my nation and for her true destiny, is adequate to give me the right impulses for my study at the College of the Good Road." Lecturers and students cooperate rather than compete. "The aim is not an examination but a world revolution."[16]

As with its other initiatives, MRA started the College of the Good Road on faith, trusting that the money would be available. It found, however, that running a college was expensive, and invited contributions from "corporations, unions, service clubs, foundations, as well as private individuals who are concerned that the youth of their nations receive such training."[17] Hicks also arranged for students to receive benefits through the new G.I. Bill in January 1950.[18] By then, however, it was too late. The college faded away in spring 1950, after a year of operation, largely due to the lack of money. Dean Howard Blake reported, however, "that the College had achieved its objectives of giving academic training to students and that they were better prepared to give what they learned as an answering ideology to the nation than the people they meet in education, government, industry, farm and other phases of life."[19]

Transitions

Despite weakness resulting from his stroke in November 1942, Frank Buchman remained at the heart of his movement. As he aged, however, Buchman's health increasingly limited his travels. In 1958 he established a base in Tucson, Arizona and let his guests come to him. By 1960 he was usually in a wheelchair or bed.[20] This long illness, his secretary Morris Martin believed, made the movement more rigid and less creative as his devotees tried to fill his shoes. "In less experienced hands, his teachings about the guidance of God, of obedience, of self-examination of motives and actions had unforeseen effects," Martin wrote years later. "Guidance masked human control; obedience bred a form of dictatorship; and self-examination became a probing for the motives of others." Buchman tried to get his closest followers—the converts of the 1920s—to take more leadership, Martin remembered, but the world "was a more complex place than it had been when he saw it through the eyes of his youth and had passed on that vision to so many others. He could neither recapture the vision nor could they relate it to that different world."

In the summer of 1961, Martin wrote, Buchman was frustrated "with his inability to inspire those closest to him as he wished." Sick and tired, the evangelist left Caux and returned to Freudenstadt, Germany, where he had first conceived the idea of Moral Re-Armament.[21] He hoped for rest and restoration, but his strength faded. On August 7, 1961 he drifted in and out of consciousness, talking with his closest friends and the inevitable visitors when he could. "I want to see the world governed by men governed by God," he said between moments of pain. "Why not let God run the whole world?" That evening he died.

Upon Buchman's death, Peter Howard became MRA's international leader, changing its tone and style. Buchman, Shoemaker, and the other early converts were clergymen and structured Oxford Group activities like evangelical campaigns. While Howard was a Christian, he was at heart a political journalist; his MRA work was basically propaganda for the movement's ideology. He gave speeches around the world and wrote a series of full-page newspaper advertisements. Under Howard's leadership MRA moved to broaden the reach of its publications, the *MRA Information Service* and *New World News*, designed to be weapons "in the hands of an ever-increasing force of Americans and Canadians who will draw a clear line between right and wrong in their homes, communities, government, press, entertainment, and every phase of national life." They aimed to "give ideological insight to the head-lines of the day."[22] Under his guidance the movement published several ideological tracts, including *America Needs an Ideology* (1957) and *Ideology and Co-Existence* (1959).

Howard was more provocative than Buchman, particularly on issues of morality. In one college speech he decried the "propagandists" who "if you don't drink, or dope, or sleep with people, or do as they do, try and push their ways down your throat and call you a 'square' if you refuse. I am not going to be told what to do by that kind of person."[23] A 1963 newspaper advertisement declared that MRA was for "God's standard of absolute purity," and against "homosexuality, lesbianism, pornography, adultery, lies which say sin is no longer sin when enough people come to like it. Preoccupation with dirt which robs a nation of sweat and skill and helps to lose its markets."[24]

Reflecting his political roots, Howard highlighted the ideological rather than the explicitly Christian aspect of MRA's message. Speaking to a college audience in the early 1960s, he called for "one nation God-centered—or if you don't believe in God, a nation centered on the morality and spirit and character of men—teaching men to accept absolute values of honesty, purity, unselfishness and love, and to obey that inner voice which distinguishes all men from any beast."[25] This focus on ideology rather than Christianity or religion helped to reach non-Christian audiences, but was a shift from that of Buchman and other clergymen in the movement.

Howard's most important initiative as MRA's international leader, however, was an increased outreach to young people. "Howard had large ideas for transforming MRA into a truly contemporary move-ment among the youth of the world," Morris Martin wrote, "a concept that found more acceptance in the United States than in London."[26] He went on a nation-wide blitz of college campuses, speaking to stu-dent groups about the challenges they faced—and MRA's answer.

"Every single day people in Peking and Moscow are planning for you," Howard told one group. "They want to take over this country. They're not wicked people. They're people with an idea they believe is right. What is your plan for the masses of China, for the masses of Russia, for Asia, Africa, the entire world? What is your plan to build a world that really works?"[27]

MRA was hit with its second leadership change in less than four years when Howard died suddenly in Lima, Peru, in March 1965—ironically just after finishing his last play, *Happy Death Day*. After years of leadership by one man, first Buchman and then Howard, the movement became more decentralized. Blanton Belk, a young American who had worked alongside Howard doing youth outreach work, told a reporter for London *Sunday Times* that "in every country there are men trained in leadership and in charge of Moral Re-Armament, as I am here in America, who have worked shoulder to shoulder with Peter Howard for the last four years."[28] In place of one international leader, Belk was to direct the work in America—a split in responsibilities that was to lead to diverging fortunes for the movement.

Passionate, Imaginative Builders of a New World

Howard's youth outreach started paying off before his death. In the summer of 1964, over 2,000 young people, high school and college students, gathered at Mackinac for the "Conference for Tomorrow's America." In a blend of boot camp, revival meeting, and hootenanny, those students learned MRA's ideology and ways to spread it. With the conference and another the following summer, MRA tapped into the energy and enthusiasm of the rising baby boom generation and—they hoped—recruited new leadership to replace the founding cohort that was about to retire.

MRA believed it was competing for the allegiance of the world's youth, above all with communism. The movement's annual report promised that the 1965 youth conference would "raise a force of young Americans more disciplined, more revolutionary, more dedicated to building a world that works than any Communist is to Communism or any materialist to his materialistic way of life."[29] In this new age, however, MRA was also competing with hippies and other rebellious youth. The editor of *Dare*, MRA's new youth magazine, argued that hippies were "disillusioned, pessimistic and have experimented with sex as the source of truth and satisfaction. They are listless, irresponsible and social casualties." MRA youth, on the other hand, "are enthusiastic and have experimented in the spirit as the source of truth and fulfillment, turning them into passionate, imaginative builders of a new world."[30]

As with other postwar conferences at Mackinac and Caux, these events focused on ideological training. Publicity for the 1964 conference promised that the youth "will consider how to build homes in which families learn to live together; how to build industries in which management and labor learn to work together; how to build a nation in which all races, colors and classes learn, together with other nations, to lead the world forward into the next stage of human evolution."[31]

The schedule echoed the big Oxford Group house parties of the 1930s, running from dawn to almost midnight every day. The participants rose every morning at 6:30 for twenty minutes of calisthenics. A plenary session followed breakfast, and then students split into workshops. After lunch there were seminars focused on particular issues, such as poverty, African affairs, or education. Following two hours of sports and dinner, participants gathered for a Peter Howard play or a concert of new MRA music.[32] As with other MRA meetings, teams of young people took turns preparing the meals.

These conferences had a different feel than other MRA events, however. "Take the excitement of a political convention, add it to the physical exertion of a basic training camp, the beat of a hootenanny [*sic*], and the urgency of a summit conference," one young man wrote, "and you begin to get an idea of what is taking place on Mackinac Island."[33] The gathering was entertained by "The Thundertones"—"America's reply to the Beatles"—and a Trinidadian steel band, reported a journalist. "American delegations waved their state and regional placards, competing in voice and enthusiasm for the crowd's appreciation and the television cameras. It was evident that the so-called beat generation was setting a new tempo and tone for America."[34]

A central part of each conference day were the speakers—similar to the platform talks at Oxford Group house parties or MRA conferences. Speakers at the 1964 conference included a member of the Massachusetts State Senate and the mayor of Phoenix, the presidents of Sheraton Hotels and the Rockefeller Institute of Science, and representatives of the State Department, the NAACP, and the Urban League.[35] The 1965 conference heard many of the same speakers, as well as Michigan congressman Gerald Ford, baseball star Stan Musial, an Air Force officer, and the ubiquitous Rajmohan Gandhi.[36]

The most important speakers at the youth conferences were Peter Howard and Blanton Belk, who delivered the keynotes for the summer. In July 1964 Howard told the participants that they had a task "more adventurous, formidable and urgent" than the one that faced the Founding Fathers. "You have to save a corrupt society from self-destruction, and to bring sanity back to a civilization that is becoming a moral and spiritual nuthouse." He said that civil unrest and racial protest were just distractions while Khrushchev and Mao were taking over the world.[37] Belk set as the 1965 conference's goal the creation of a "modernized" man, "a man whose heart belongs to the whole world because it has been freed of hate and fear and greed. He has a passion for the whole world because his heart is pure. And his commitment is never to abate until every nation is governed by men governed by God."[38]

Behind the hootenannies, the message at these conferences remained traditional MRA ideology—the path to national and international change was personal morality. How can we bring hope to the world, Howard asked the young people in 1964, "if we give in without a fight or thought to sex temptations, liquor temptations, or me-first temptations?" The country needs a passion, he told them, and "only passion for the will and way of God in our personal life can meet the passion for the will and way of the anti-God of Communism and Fascism in our national life." If you choose wrong, he declared, "you become part of the deathknell of democracy, the disease of Materialism that is food for Fascism."[39] Later that summer Howard told a Canadian reporter that the older generation had been too permissive, and the youth hated their softness. "They hate permissive parents, they hate a permissive society. They want to be shown how to live, told how to live, and given the discipline to live for something greater than themselves. And that's what we try to do for them."[40]

Given inescapable teenage hormones and the blossoming sexual revolution, speeches at Mackinac inevitably discussed one of MRA's favorite issues, purity and sexuality. Howard told the youth that "America needs a passion for what is right, rooted in absolute purity." To bring about world change, the young people needed to have a passion for God, not a passion for each other. "No man or woman run by sex can answer the needs of somebody run by hate of color, class or race."[41] That same summer Paul Campbell, Buchman's personal physician, talked with the young people about directing energy properly, including sexual energy. "There is a much better and more exciting way of using our energy [than petting]. If we are committed to a revolutionary program for the nation, we need every ounce of energy we've got."[42]

After the lectures the young people participated in workshops where they developed ways to spread the MRA message. Publicity for the

1964 conference promised that the "workshops will combine practical training with creative production in journalism, drama, film making, music, painting, photography, international cooking, secretarial work and nursing." The youth will produce feature films and TV shows "under the direction of Hollywood professionals." Musical and variety shows, "as well as a repertory theater, will explore a new role for popular entertainment in the modern world."[43] In afternoon seminars, participants worked to "create moral weapons to deal with specific areas of the country and the world." One group, for instance, wrote a paper for President Johnson "offering a workable solution to world poverty." Another group studying Indonesia set out to "prepare a policy for Southeast Asia." There were other seminars on China, Africa, Japan, and education.[44]

MRA kept the young peoples' bodies as disciplined as their minds. They were asked to dress conservatively, including coat and tie for men at meals.[45] A reporter visiting the island noted that none of the girls wore lipstick. "Shorts are not seen, on either sex, except on the athletic field. Few students smoke."[46] They also exercised, like the New Enlistment camps of the late 1930s. One leader told the conference newspaper that the goal was creating "2,000 young Americans this summer who will not only be physically fit, but through sports and vigorous competition will learn the quality of character and determination for victory so sadly lacking in our American sports programs today." There were team and individual sports in addition to the morning calisthenics.[47] A sports columnist for the *Tomorrow's American*, the youth-produced newspaper, noted that energy and enthusiasm "are the mark of a man with some burning purpose in his life." The conference offered both an ideology and the physical conditioning to carry it out. "With a simple exercise before breakfast each morning we might get into such good shape we will make a better impression when we meet new people."[48]

Articles in *Tomorrow's American* show that the participants learned MRA's lessons well. In a prize-winning essay, a high school boy argued that a clear ideology was necessary to guide the proper use of freedom. "The root of freedom is the choice to do what is right," he wrote, echoing Howard. "For the choice to do what is wrong does not issue in freedom but in exploitation, and finally in enslavement. Compromise with moral standards is the mortal enemy of freedom."[49] Another young man challenged others at Mackinac to do more than just have fun. "A few say they are going to do this or that when they are home. The time to do something is now," he declared. "This Conference is ours. We will get from this Conference what we put into it. Unless we do our part now in this Conference, we face no hope of victory in morally rearming this country and the world."[50]

Their experience at Mackinac convinced these young people that MRA's message was the answer to the nation's woes. Reflecting the movement's long-time goal of shaping national policy, a group of students sent a letter to President Johnson about the urban riots of 1964. They had "been trained during the last six weeks to create a change of heart without which no legislation will work," they wrote. "The hatred and division in our own lives has been replaced by an idea greater than any racial question. That idea is Moral Re-Armament." In that election year, they declared that "the nation's leadership belongs to the party and to that man who will challenge America to this destiny under God."[51]

Some of the young people took MRA's purity message to heart. In a *Tomorrow's American* article, Steve Cornell declared that youth were concerned with the nation's falling moral standards. "Films and books are saturating us with nihilism, sadism, sexism and anti-Christ." This impure culture, Cornell argued, has consequences for the nation's future. "Barnyard morality termed 'art' is producing a generation of potential suicides and military rejects. It is producing a people who no longer have the will to fight but for personal gain, whose energy is being drained by self-indulgence." Young America, he promised, will fight against this flood of filth. "We of Tomorrow's America are no longer willing to bow down before altars of perverted sex and blood lust." Cornell vowed to make films and theatre "a monument to America's talent and heart."[52]

Belk told the conference newspaper in 1964 that the 2,000 youth at Mackinac would become 200 million youth dedicated to MRA. "Give me one per cent of the youth, self-disciplined and militant for a cause far greater than themselves," he said, "and they will determine the policy of this country in spite of the 99 percent who are neutral."[53] With Belk's encouragement, conference participants brainstormed ways to spread MRA's message. They produced several films and plays about what they learned at Mackinac, and took the message home to their schools. The student body president of a Seattle high school pledged to lead "a different school this year—a school with bigger goals than painting or destroying other schools' property. What I see is a school hard-working in class and as hard-playing on the field."[54]

Music was an important part of this outreach, much of it led by the Colwell Brothers, a young trio with long MRA ties. Steve, Paul, and

Ralph Colwell become folk music stars as teenagers in the late 1940s, and started including "positive" songs on their records after meeting MRA in Los Angeles. In 1953, Buchman invited the Colwells to travel with MRA for the coming year. They wrote songs for each of the places they visited, and always had their instruments at hand, in case Buchman called for a song among the MRA testimonies. They were on the road for eight years, including a year in the Congo, where they played positive music during that country's civil war.[55]

The brothers discovered American rock when they returned home in June 1964. They bought electric guitars and started changing their style. The Colwells were also just in time for the 1964 youth conference at Mackinac. They organized song sessions and hootenannies for the conference, and even created a showboat that toured the region around Mackinac, performing new MRA songs. They called it "the happiest, hard-hittingest show afloat."[56] During the next year the Colwells toured college campuses, singing songs and recruiting students for the 1965 conference.[57]

As the Colwell Brothers traveled the country for MRA they made plans for the 1965 conference, with weekly musical "happenings" that would be showcases for musical expression. Over the course of the summer these performances developed into full-blown variety shows, with weekly themes and stage lights, hosted by the brothers.[58] These shows became the model for MRA's last reinvention, Up With People.

Dare

The first "Colwell Hour" at Mackinac was in late June 1965, featuring international songs and dances, as well as some of Peter Howard's writings set to music. "Through dance, song and dialogue, the ideas of Moral Re-Armament came across strongly," the conference newspaper reported. "It was fun! A jam-packed audience in the Film Studio was seeing the birth of a world weapon." The Colwells said that their summer goal was "to raise an 'army' to spread the ideology of Moral Re-Armament through the international medium of entertainment." They promised their audience a sing-in for the next week—a response to the sit-ins and teach-ins then sweeping America's campuses—with songs about "the truly critical issues facing our world today."[59] The program that second evening included a mass chorus, a medley of military and marching songs, Japanese singers, and Korean dancers. Most importantly, *Sing-In '65* premiered several new Colwell songs, including

"Up With People," "What Color Is God's Skin?", and "Freedom Isn't Free."[60]

Before the end of the summer, Belk and the Colwells sensed that they had something remarkable on their hands, and made plans to take the show on the road. They called it *Sing-Out '65*, an intentional contrast to the sit-ins and teach-ins of the time. Paul Colwell said that they wanted "to show America the secret of unity at home, how to win friends abroad and offer Moscow and Peking a more revolutionary way of life than Communism." One woman in the cast saw the goal as rousing the whole nation. "We want to give President Johnson something positive from the youth of the country instead of all the pacifism, protests and non-involvement that have been coming from the campuses. And we are going to back this idea with the discipline and sacrifice of our own living."[61]

After a try-out at several Michigan resorts, in early August the 66-member cast headed to New England, where they performed in towns in Connecticut and along Cape Cod.[62] Following the MRA pattern, the show was then "invited" to Washington by 96 senators and congressmen and the "Dean of the Diplomatic Corps." Before the performance at the Washington Hilton, the Colwells said that they were "working to show a new type of America—more dynamic, disciplined and dedicated than anything produced by the Communist world. Judging from our experience abroad, this is a voice the world will not only listen to, but follow."[63] The invitation to the performance called Mackinac "a staging area where policies are being formed to answer Washington's need."[64]

Sing-Out '65 then traveled to California for a performance at the Hollywood Bowl, returning to the site of a previous MRA triumph. While on the west coast the cast performed in an unlikely setting— the riot-torn Los Angeles neighborhood of Watts. "We are grateful for what Moral Re-Armament has given us in Watts and there are thousands of us here who are going to give a new image of our community to the whole of America," one resident told *Tomorrow's American*. Another declared that the children of Watts did "not want the moral disarmament of the pacifist protestors of Berkeley. What American youth want is Moral Re-Armament."[65]

MRA believed that the world's youth wanted Moral Re-Armament, too. *Sing-Out '65* went to Japan and South Korea, invited by Rajmohan Gandhi. The show performed at "the traditionally anti-American universities where it received a tremendous acclaim." There were also shows for US troops.[66] "You have shaken and shocked the major universities of Tokyo," a student at Waseda University supposedly said. "You have changed entirely our idea of what young Americans believe and stand for. If this is America, we are for it."[67]

Like early MRA productions, such as *You Can Defend America*, *Sing-Out '65* featured inspirational songs sung by an earnest and enthusiastic cast. Unlike them, however, the music was inspired by folk and rock, not Broadway, trying to capture the energy of the rising baby boom generation. A program for the show called it "alive with color, bursting with hit tunes, dazzling in its speed and what one newspaper described as 'almost frightening pace.' "[68] Reminiscent of the "New Enlistment" of the 1930s, *Sing-Out* casts ran everywhere, embodying the vigor of youth.

Each performance began with the cast running onto an empty stage to sing the National Anthem. Then they broke into a Colwell song, "Design for Dedication," inspired by a Peter Howard book title.

> Hay-yay, ev'rybody come!
> We're gonna play-yay,
> We've got a swinging drum,
> We're gonna sing about a new idea,
> We're gonna need-yeed ev'rybody here,
> In a Design for Dedication.

Another song urged young Americans to "stand up. Don't be afraid. Show America that she belongs to you…Don't you know by your choice you will bless or blight mankind for a thousand years to come?"[69] The program also featured comedy and satire, as well as "authentic Indian and folk dances; audience participation, including special songs written for every city in which the show appears; musical tableaux of our historical heritage; and songs written to feed hungry minds and hearts with a new sense of purpose."[70] The best-known song in the show was the first act finale, "Up With People."

> Up! Up with people!
> You meet 'em wherever you go!
> Up! Up with people!
> They're the best kind of folks we know.
> If more people were for people,
> All people everywhere,
> There'd be a lot less people to worry about,
> And a lot more people who care![71]

Many of the songs in the first show were written by the Colwell brothers, who took center stage at the performances, while others were first written for *The Good Road* in 1947. As the show developed the cast members started contributing songs as well.[72]

The music may have been inspired by folk and rock, but the performers did not look like rock stars. Reporters always described the cast as "clean, well-scrubbed, fresh," in contrast to others of their generation. At a street performance in Harlem, the *New York Times* noted, "the girls [wore] bright jumpers and long-sleeved blouses and the boys in various colored blazers and striped ties."[73] The show was also deeply patriotic. Herbert Allen, the musical director, said that the casts wanted to speak up for "love of God and country, and are prepared to pay the price of discipline, hard work and sacrifice to preserve freedom. It is a revolt against the cynicism and moral relativism which have diluted the country's traditions and represents a determination to take a responsible part in the task of society and nation building."[74]

The show's creators contrasted these young people with their hippie contemporaries. A program for the show declared that "the generation of the 1960's has begun to talk back. For too long the headline-makers in the hot city streets and the brawling campuses have spoken for America." But against this "brilliant cynicism, sophisticated filth, superannuated defeatism and unbelief," there is a new "generation that *does* believe—first of all in the future," but also in work and sacrifice. "They dare to run, to work long hours, to move fast, to live straight, to speak out and, at the drop of a hat, any time of day or night, to sing out for their love of liberty. Finally they believe in faith."[75] When Vice-President Hubert Humphrey visited Germany, he was often greeted by protests, but also by *Sing-Out* participants, "young Americans who voiced their lively support for honest, sane, firm and positive action by men in public life. They made it plain that they, and in fact the decent but usually silent majority of their generation, are patriotic young Americans, searching for new ways to take responsibility."[76]

This majority, MRA declared, would be silent no longer. One adult leader declared that if the young people were "going to debunk the myth of a soft, indulgent, arrogant America and show the world that we care about tomorrow, we've got to sing out our convictions, loud and strong!"[77] A concert program noted that "the world knows what the young Chinese live for. They know what the young Russians live for. They have not been very clear what young Americans live for." *Sing-Out* showed "the world that free men and women can be the most convinced, most enthusiastic, in fact the most revolutionary people on earth. We want to see people rise up out of their rocking chairs of cynicism and complacency and ride with us whole-hog for a new tomorrow."[78]

The young cast members came to *Sing-Out* seeking many things. Many hoped to change the country and the world. One young man wrote that he had been scornful of the show until he saw it and "realized that there was more to life than me. The world is real. Its problems are immediate. And their solutions depend on the integrity of individual people to recognize their responsibility to carry it out." The world needs young people that "have the guts to stand up and say what we know to be right in the world, and we need to have the courage to live the answer convincingly in our lives. Lust, hate, and violence aren't very convincing exports for this country to other nations."[79] Parents of cast members testified to the show's impact on their children. "It might be the answer to the problems that we as parents have created. It is making a real contribution to restore a God-fearing life to the nation," one said.[80]

Being part of *Sing-Out* gave meaning to these young lives. A young woman from Atlanta said that she was drifting until the show came to her high school. The cast showed energy, enthusiasm, responsibility and dedication. "I knew I wanted to do something with my life, and I knew this was it." She learned to be honest with others, and got used "to hearing, in a very loving manner, things you need to change about yourself."[81] A man from Boston had read about *Sing-Out* and Moral Re-Armament, "and found that this was the exact purpose I needed for my life." He wanted to help bring about "an era of creativity by promoting absolute honesty, purity, unselfishness and love among the world's people."[82]

The show worked to change the audience, not just the cast. A blurb that appeared in almost every program for several years warned that "many normal and responsible people do the most unexpected things" after seeing the show. They badger others into seeing the show. "They grin and laugh and break into song. They whistle around the house. They may start talking with total strangers." Parents and children start to understand each other. Young people "often get their hair cut, start to dress in a sensible way, and even offer to do the dishes."[83]

In its early days *Sing-Out* casts kept up MRA's spiritual practices. The show was not religious, the Atlanta woman said, but she did stress the importance of seeking guidance.[84] The cast had quiet times before performances, "when we are quiet and listen for God's direction, when we are straight about our own needs, when we are united in a great purpose, when we pray for strength to forget ourselves and do the job to be done." MRA veterans had told the young people that the practice "keeps you on your toes, it keeps you young at heart and it lasts as long as you keep moving. We believe them."[85] By 1968, however, there were fewer mentions of the absolutes in *Tomorrow's American*, and none of guidance or God.[86]

MRA reveled in public praise for its show, excerpting gushing reviews in all its publications. The *Santa Fe News* welcomed youngsters who "break into your heart instead of your store window; they set fire to your conscience instead of your home; they march with a smile and a song of hope in lieu of grim, unreasoning demands and a club."[87] Entertainment guru Walt Disney was often quoted as calling the show "the happiest, most hard-hitting way of saying what America is all about that I have ever seen or heard."[88] MRA used these quotations to demonstrate the show's impact—and, by extension, its own.

Many supporters praised the *Sing-Out* kids for challenging the stereotype of their generation. Jesse Helms, then the editorial director of a Raleigh, North Carolina, television station, exulted that "none of these youngsters has burned a draft card, or participated in a sit-in, or marched in a protest against efforts to stem the tide of communism. These are clean-cut talented young people with an unshakable faith in God and a love of country."[89] A Texas woman was overjoyed after watching the show on television. "It is the most wonderful thing that has happened to us in a long time, to sit in front of the TV and hear such evidence of a growing Moral Tide!" If nothing else, "it was just plain pleasant to hear *pretty music* coming from sweet and pretty and wholesome young girls, and good looking, clean cut young men with their hair cut!!!"[90]

The creation of *Sing-Out '65* transformed MRA in America. After years of stasis the movement quickly developed programs, recruited volunteers, raised money, and bought property. MRA's report for 1965 noted that it had "seen explosive growth in the range of its activities, the effectiveness and outreach of its programs, the increase of manpower, the expansion of facilities and the enlistment of support." It had trained 9,700 youth in Michigan, California, New York, and Colorado, and sent the performing troupe on an international tour of almost 20,000 miles. Eventually there were five casts constantly touring, each performing largely the same show. While in the 1940s and 1950s the movement had done its programs for unions and corporations, those audiences faded into the background in the 1960s as the new show went to colleges, high schools, and public auditoriums.[91] Up

With People—the program took the name of its best-known song—was eclipsing the parent movement.

On almost every tour, Up With People (UWP) did free shows at military bases and academies, reflecting the group's increasing focus on patriotism and its alliance with the military. The commander of Fort Hood thanked the cast for a 1966 performance, which he called an inspiration. "In talking with members of the group after each of the sing-outs, I was most impressed by their enthusiasm for freedom and their willingness to stand up and be counted." He made the cast honorary members of his command.[92] A group of Marines wrote that thanks to the show they had a reason for going to Vietnam. "We now have the desire and will to really give it a go and fight for the best darn country in the world. Not just for ourselves." The show made them realize "that this country really does have something worth fighting for."[93] The relationship went both ways; the Air Force used an UWP film as part of its orientation, while the Infantry allowed the movement to sing "Follow Me," the official song of the United States Infantry. A sizable number of UWP alumni went into the military after completing their tour with the show.

Up With People was not strictly an American phenomenon. The U.S. casts toured internationally from Europe to Australia, reported *Tomorrow's American*, and "electrified the new generation they have found with a picture of militant, enthusiastic U.S. youth."[94] Within a year there were local shows in countries around the world, including the *Springbok Stampede* in South Africa, *Harambee Africa* in Kenya and Uganda, *Sing-Out Korea*, *Sing-Out Finland*, *India Arise*, and *Let's Go* in Japan.[95] Most of these shows followed the U.S. model, with choruses and solos, even starting their shows with the cast running onto the stage. They also performed many of the same songs; *Sing-Out Australia* included Australian folk songs and Asian dances alongside "What Colour Is God's Skin?", "You Can't Live Crooked and Think Straight," "Freedom Isn't Free," "Which Way Australia?", and "Up With People!"[96]

In many American and international cities these tours left behind regional "Sing-Outs" to perform the same songs, complete with costumes and music. These troupes resembled the Oxford Group's cells. Within a year there were 150 Sing-Outs in the United States, with 100 more around the world.[97] The worked to spread the Sing-Out message far and wide. "We are determined to demonstrate this idea to America and the rest of the world," a student declared in December 1965. "We decided to make Sing-Out the most up-to-date and fastest moving demonstration of not what we are against but what we are for. This is the pace for America."[98] Many of these groups also planned events to improve their communities.

Participants in these "Sing-Outs" gathered for regional and national assemblies that resembled MRA meetings of the late 1930s. At a Connecticut conference "delegations rushed on stage and one after another sounded off their convictions, telling how they themselves had changed and had brought answers to their communities through Moral Re-Armament." One young man said he had had long hair and belonged to a motorcycle gang, "but then I saw Sing-Out. There is something completely different about it that grabbed me."[99] At a meeting in the Southwest, a college student declared that "the basis of Sing-Out is Moral Re-Armament. Any who take this on have got to live it. We don't want just a social Sing-Out because it would be only a fiasco unless it is backed by commitment in our own lives."[100] It was a new generation, but the MRA influence was unmistakable.

The national "Sing-Out" meetings, like the "Action Now Demonstration" in the summer of 1966, echoed the Mackinac youth conferences. Youth from 250 colleges arrived in Estes Park, Colorado, "on the run" equipped with "guitars, drums, typewriters, drawing boards and electronic equipment." The conference was a month-long "multiplication of the Sing-Out explosion which has rocked America in the last ten months."[101] At the conference the young people would form task forces, create films and Sing-Outs, and learn new skills. "It takes a tough new breed of moral man to create a moral society. Our generation can be the first to be free from the divisions of hate, fear and greed and reach out with a new aim for all peoples across the globe."[102]

Blanton Belk's opening address at the Estes Park conference reflected both MRA's long-standing millennialism and its new focus on the energy of youth. "The world's eyes and hopes are on young America and what you will explode from this Demonstration for a generation around the globe," he told the young people. From the conference will come "an idea from the heart of the land that can yet bind up the world's wounds and set nations free." The young generation, he continued, "will not be blackmailed by the secular, satanic, sensory view of some parts of our society who say that human nature cannot change, that man is the highest authority, that right and wrong are old-fashioned, that God is dead, that nothing new can happen that has not already happened."[103] MRA's belief in personal change gave individuals power to perfect the world.

Up With People soon became more than just a stage show. MRA
sold recordings and sheet music from the show, as well as instructions
on how to create your own Sing-Out.[104] In the summer of 1966 the
NBC network carried a half-hour television special, hosted by singing
star Pat Boone—the first time the show was officially called *Up With
People*.[105] *Pace*, a monthly magazine resembling *Life* (previously named
Dare), also spread the Up With People message. *"Pace is the product
of an idea: that as well as work for his hands, man's spirit quests greatness and his mind a far-reaching challenge,"* declared MRA's annual
report. It claimed that the magazine was "recognized as an authority
on world youth, a source of new thinking, a projection of the future
and light on the controversial. *Pace* is not a presentation but a dialogue with this generation, who want to make their lives count, who
want creative involvement, and who want to demonstrate for a better
world."[106]

Belk told donors in 1966 that all this activity led to the greatest
expansion in MRA's history, "whether in terms of numbers reached,
manpower involved, number and variety of activities, or public impact
in the United States and, from the U.S., overseas."[107] A movement
that for years lived out of Buchman's suitcases now had five traveling
national casts and over 1,000 full-time volunteers. MRA bought or
leased buses, trucks, and airplanes to move those casts, and several new
offices to house them. It established a traveling high school to serve the
hundred cast members who had not yet graduated. The school superintendent said that at the Sing-Out High School "students with a big
purpose, absolute standards and inner fire and discipline clearly learn
better, live better and give better to their country."[108] The movement
also bought 775 acres in the Sierra Nevadas as a permanent conference
center for youth. "Bear Creek Ranch is striving to develop tough, ver-
satile leaders for all fields of business, government, and agriculture,"
Tomorrow's American declared. "The ultimate goal is a permanent training center for the youth of every nation."[109]

Supporting this expanded work required money. Income came
from student tuition, ticket sales, and sales of books and records. More
important were donations. The program at each performance solicited
money from the audience. The cast had made sacrifices, a note declared,
"given up university scholarships, sold cars and personal possessions,
and postponed plans for college education." Supporting their work,
it concluded, "is a chance for every man, woman and child to express
what freedom means to him."[110] Friends of MRA organized fund-
raising events, and corporations and foundations added their support.

More than a College

While *Up With People* rocketed around the world, MRA members were also quietly building a very different institution for young adults on Mackinac Island—a liberal arts college. Like the College of the Good Road, Mackinac College embodied a critique of American higher education and an attempt to plant MRA ideas in an academic setting.

Howard proposed creating a new institution in November 1964, five months before he died. Since the MRA conference centers at Caux and Mackinac sat unused eight months a year, Howard suggested using them "as a school for modern languages, international relationships, theater, T.V., radio, journalism, art. It could be the education of the 21st century," he told Morris Martin. "The aim would be to train youth to take on the key places in nations, to get the right young men instead of the wrong ones into places of influence in public affairs."[111]

A year later the new college received a formal charter from the state of Michigan and the Mackinac center as a gift from Moral Re-Armament.[112] The board hired S. Douglas Cornell, an MRA convert and executive officer of the National Academy of Sciences, to serve as president, and Martin as dean.[113] Unlike the College of the Good Road, which focused on teaching MRA ideology, Mackinac College planned to offer a liberal arts education and preprofessional degrees for government and public life, law, education, business, journalism, industry, theater, films, labor, television and radio.[114]

Mackinac College was born at a time of upheaval in American higher education, as students and professors alike rebelled against a system they saw as antiquated, bureaucratic, and irrelevant. The mid-1960s saw the foundation of several new institutions, most prominently the University of California at Santa Cruz (1965) and Washington's Evergreen State College (1967), that tried to make education relevant. Mackinac's founders shared this critique. Belk told the "Sing-Out" conference at Estes Park that education "is no longer exciting. It is not creating history. It cultivates spectatorism and non-involvement." He promised, however, that Mackinac College "is going to be the most exciting, creative, new kind of academic training America has ever seen. It will be dynamic and it will propel you into action now."[115] At their first meeting the Mackinac trustees declared that the college would "equip students morally, spiritually and intellectually to answer the pressures of fear, hatred and greed, prejudice and apathy which threaten to negate man's spectacular advances in knowledge and skills."[116] While MRA was generally critical of the counter-culture of the 1960s, it joined in the radical critique of traditional higher education.

Some of Mackinac's critiques of American higher education, however, reflected uniquely MRA themes. Cornell told *Tomorrow's American* that higher education had lost its moral foundation, but the new college would be led by those who understand something "that institutions of higher education appear often to have forgotten—that knowledge is power, and that the way in which power is used is as important as the power itself." If an institution "confers such power without looking at the same time to questions of character and moral quality" it is irresponsible and a menace to democracy. Mackinac graduates would "recognize the eternal verities not as historical curiosities, but as determinants of the rise and fall of civilizations, men and women with the fullest opportunity to find the reality and the adventure of God's governance in their lives."[117] This call for a moral education echoed Buchman's message, although without its Christian particularity.

The 120 students in Mackinac's first class—a third of whom had MRA links—shared the founders' convictions.[118] As she applied, Ellen Hodges anticipated that "at Mackinac we will be able to demonstrate something positive to the nation—how men and women live as God means them to, and how the great society can be built by the greatness in men." Another early applicant, Peter Carey, wanted "to study under a faculty that is as interested in developing character and responsibility as it is in giving academic training to its students."[119]

Later classes shared the same enthusiasm. William Henry wanted to make a difference in racial issues and was frustrated with his experience at Purdue University. He felt that Mackinac students were "a bunch of people who seemed to be going somewhere" and the college was going to train leaders.[120] Like many applicants, Michael Redman had traveled with UWP. He "was hoping to find myself in an academic setting with people interested in living with the kind of intensity we did in Up With People. I was very interested in learning and being with others who shared that excitement. My previous academic experience was limited to job preparation and drinking beer."[121]

Many, but not all, of the faculty members were committed to the college's mission. Dean Morris Martin remembered that about half of the faculty had an MRA affiliation, a quarter were supportive of its idea, and another quarter were at the college simply to have a job.[122] Many of them, like Cornell, had left prominent jobs elsewhere to teach at Mackinac. The chair of political science, for instance, was Daniel

Yu Tang Lew, former Nationalist Chinese ambassador to the United Nations.[123]

While Belk proclaimed that Mackinac would be "the most exciting, creative, new kind of academic training America has ever seen," these faculty members taught a relatively traditional liberal arts curriculum.[124] Its most distinctive element was its interdisciplinarity. The dean told *Tomorrow's American* that Mackinac had replaced "the traditional majors with integrated programs of study, enlisting student initiative in drawing for their content upon all departments of knowledge represented in our curriculum." Instead of departments, classes were clustered in four areas: Man and His World, Man and His Society, Man and His Environment, and Man and His Values.[125] This arrangement, one student wrote in 1967, trained students "to approach a problem in its totality, to understand its essentials, evaluate it and decide how to tackle it. It means being able to deal with all kinds of people in every kind of situation, on the basis of seeking what is best for them. It means an involvement in the world and not just in myself, my own fulfillment, my future."[126] Katherine Minton remembers that at Mackinac she "began to see the world where all the pieces came together." The way professors taught "and got us to go out and dig up our own information, enabled me to see things from many different viewpoints— rather than having blinders on and being a specialist."[127]

Students found the college an exciting academic experience. A member of the charter class described "a sense of questing" on campus, "looking for facts, but also for the ideas behind the facts; of understanding what produces creative thinking. A term paper on China cannot be merely an exercise in research and exposition. It must include understanding of the spirit of the Chinese people, instilled by their ancient civilization."[128] Many of the students had transferred from colleges or universities where the students were focused on drinking or making money, while at Mackinac they found colleagues committed to ideas. Brian Marshall says that the students were "optimistic and terribly idealistic." It was socially acceptable to be smart; it was "a school of nerds."[129] Redman remembers that "most were as excited as I was about learning because they saw education as a tool for living well, for changing the world by changing your little piece for the better."[130]

The sheer newness of the college also made the experience compelling. The college's viewbook promised that charter class members would be "the pacesetters for those to follow," involved "in the shaping of an educational venture as no other undergraduates in any other college setting."[131] At the end of the first year a student said his head was still spinning. "Exciting is too drab a word for Mackinac. We're vibrating, we're alive and involved."[132] A visitor felt "an atmosphere of extreme dedication—dedication of the faculty to more than training minds and of students to more than acquiring knowledge." Students told him that they were "preparing themselves to be leaders of tomorrow by training not only their minds but their whole selves."[133] In May 1967 President Cornell reported that the students of the charter class have "responded to high intellectual challenge [and] pioneered the life of an institution that is 'more than a college.'"[134]

The college was legally independent of Moral Re-Armament, but MRA's influence was inescapable. In words that could have been written by Peter Howard, one student stated that Mackinac students were "acquiring a sense of responsibility for their nations and the world; the knowledge of how to evaluate, not just learn; and a realization of the creative power they can and need to unleash to solve the problems which will otherwise destroy humanity."[135] Meanwhile, some of the MRA-affiliated faculty members tried to control student behavior, concerned about smoking, drinking, dancing, and dating.[136] Dean Morris Martin declared, however, that the college was not out to "indoctrinate, to make students fit any mould, no matter high-minded. Our task was to give an education."[137]

A New Age

Blanton Belk, now executive director of MRA in the United States and chair of the MRA International board, believed that Up With People was the key to the world's future. Around the world, he wrote in 1967, people saw crisis and searched for an answer. "They want to participate, sacrifice and live for big aims and purposes. It is for this reason, I believe, there has been such an overwhelming response here and abroad to Moral Re-Armament's Up With People program."[138] A headline in *Tomorrow's American* put it more concisely: "A New Age Opens for All Mankind."[139] Echoing Moral Re-Armament's longtime millennialism, Belk believed that UWP offered the answers to humanity's problems.

Up With People began to see MRA as a liability for this vision rather than as an asset, however. Belk, the Colwell brothers, and others within UWP started "outgrowing the limitations that MRA had placed on their vision," Martin remembered. "They stepped out together into the swiftly changing sixties and seventies."[140] Stewart Lancaster, an MRA board member, felt that the movement was tied to religion, while the younger generation was "looking for a new means of expression." In that context, he believed, "affiliation with MRA was a handicap."[141] Belk told a youth conference just after Christmas 1968 that UWP was "expanding, broadening, evolving with the times. A form or structure that serves today's needs is obsolete to meet tomorrow's necessities." He concluded that "the tides of history sweep past those who cling to a form for its own sake," perhaps referring to the traditions of Moral Re-Armament.[142]

The old guard of MRA, on the other hand, wanted to keep MRA as it was under Buchman, Martin believed. This reinvention of the movement made no sense to its long-time supporters, especially in Britain. They "accused Up With People of watering down the 'message,' of relaxing standards, of throwing out the baby with the bath water." British MRA leaders saw the popularity of the show "as a typically superficial American glamorization of generalities and a straw-fire that would soon burn out." Martin countered that Buchman's tight control of the movement's people and program had prevented new thinking, much to the frustration especially of younger members. "This had resulted in the frustration of the very aims to which MRA was committed."[143] MRA had run up against the limits of reinvention.

In 1968 Belk decided that UWP should break away from MRA. He created a new corporation, which received as a gift many of the older organization's assets, including the Los Angeles headquarters, Bear Creek Ranch, and the buses and airplanes. Many younger members of the MRA board also moved to Up With People. Kenaston Twitchell Junior, the executive director of the remnants of MRA, described the move as an evolution of the movement. "Moral Re-Armament since its beginning has aspired to carry mankind forward for a new age. In pursuing this goal, MRA has moved as an evolving expansive force relating itself to the live issues of the day, using fresh forms for its truth, developing new channels of action and communication." The spin-off of UWP would allow that program to develop its "unique educational potential, and facilitate its further rapid expansion." It would not, however, "replace, supplant or be a substitute for Moral Re-Armament or any of its other activities."[144]

As it pursued its independent path, Up With People used less MRA language to describe its work. The program for a 1969 performance, for instance, described UWP as "an evolving experiment in a lifestyle, an education that involves totally the young men and women who participate in it, uniting the best of academics with relevant action to build a just, new society." The show no longer included "Which

Way America?" or "You Can't Live Crooked and Think Straight."[145] Articles in *Tomorrow's American* talked less about patriotism or communism, and more about rethinking education, being creative and being a maverick. It even featured a positive review of a Janis Joplin record.[146] Some MRA language, however, continued. At a conference held over New Year's Day 1969, Belk told his young people that "we are going to have to discipline ourselves more than ever before, if we are going to produce this leadership; we are going to have to have standards like never before; we are going to have to have faith in God like never before."[147]

The summer youth conferences also continued, but with different form and content. With a theme of "Action Education," the 1969 conference taught participants about the world and equipped them to spread the UWP spirit.[148] The format was somewhat different from the conferences at Mackinac, but the content was similar. *Pace* editors taught communications, "proliferation of an idea, song-writing, 'instant learning' and how to operate in a foreign country." Meanwhile "delegates were preparing detailed reports expressing the deepest convictions of American students about the future and their ideas for specific changes that can be put to work without the pressure of violence and disruption."[149] They did not call it ideological training, but these sessions continued the same work of preparing young people to spread a message.

Up With People quickly became a national institution, performing at political conventions and in presidential inaugurations. It also performed four Super Bowl half-time shows, including the national bicentennial in 1976. Perhaps most surprising for a program created by deeply anticommunist Moral Re-Armament, UWP casts went to China in 1978 and the Soviet Union in 1988. By 2000 more than 20,000 young people from 65 countries had traveled with UWP.[150] Up With People suspended its traveling program in 2000, but it was resurrected by a program alumnus in 2005, with a stronger focus on community service and cross-cultural education. Participants still sing and dance, and the executive director still describes it as a leadership program.[151]

Mackinac College's story, unfortunately, did not have such a happy ending. It was a lively atmosphere for learning, Martin remembered, but its isolation meant that the college never approached its target enrollment, and it struggled financially. Like Buchman and his colleagues, the founders started the new initiative with the expectation that God would provide. "We had the great faith and financial naiveté of enthusiasm—something which we had brought with us from MRA," Martin wrote. "Difficulties were to be brushed aside, friendly warnings were suspected of being attempts to deviate us from our inspired course." At end of second year in 1968, however, it had become clear that even with their desired full enrollment of 800 students, the college would still be a million dollars in the red.[152] Non-MRA donors were wary of the college's connections, the college's business manager reported, doubting "its independence of Moral Re-Armament despite separate incorporation."[153]

Meanwhile, MRA leaders, especially those in London, were "fundamentally opposed" to the idea of the college, Martin remembered. "There was a streak of anti-Americanism and a streak of obscurantism that led them to believe that education itself was not an objective of MRA, and especially not American education." From this perspective, anything that distracted the organization from what they understood as Buchman's and MRA's main goals, "to offer individuals an experience of God," should be closed down. "They washed their hands of the college." American MRA leaders continued to support the college, but more of their attention and funds were going towards Up With People.[154]

Belk offered the struggling college a lifeline. At Up With People's annual winter conference in December 1968, he announced that Mackinac College would become part of UWP, offering an undergraduate degree to participants in the traveling program. Most Mackinac students—including those who had participated in UWP themselves—rebelled.[155] In the end MRA and the college's board decided to close Mackinac. While most students transferred elsewhere, 31 members of the charter class stayed on to graduate in the summer of 1970.[156]

Since Howard's death, MRA in America had focused most of its energy on youth outreach, organizing the Mackinac conferences and creating Up With People. Its property, staff, and resources went towards supporting the new initiative. Once UWP split off, MRA was left much smaller, with fewer resources and a board largely made up of older members. After downplaying specifically Christian language in service of ideological training and youth outreach, the change did allow the movement to return to its earlier message. In the 1968 annual report, young Twitchell, now the executive director, committed the organization to "an active program of literature and film distribution. It plans the early publication of two new books which will stress Moral Re-Armament's emphasis on the power of person-to-person Christianity to transform the lives of men and women."[157] MRA was freed to return to its evangelical roots.

The context had changed, however. MRA's traditional message had less resonance with America in the late 1960s than it did in the 1930s. Stewart Lancaster, a former MRA board member who joined the UWP board after the split, told the *New York Times* that MRA had "seen its day. MRA activity now is nothing but a drop in the bucket compared with its heyday." The organization and its views were too rigid, he said. "Many true-believer causes are dwindling today. Many are worthy but dogmatic and opinionated."

Recognizing this reality, Twitchell announced in August 1970 that MRA was "sharply curtailing its operations in the United States." While UWP flourished, he said, contributions to MRA had declined for several years. It was selling all its offices and training centers except for a small New York office, and was planning no new publications or plays. The proceeds from the real estate sales went to the men and women who had served MRA as full-time volunteers for decades, and thus had no savings for their retirement.[158] MRA's American operations, long its largest and wealthiest, were out of business. Twitchell urged followers to continue practicing the four absolutes and converting others.[159]

EPILOGUE

Remaking the World

One May night in 1921, Frank Buchman was bicycling through Cambridge, England, after visiting with a group of students. Suddenly a thought came to him: "You will be used to remake the world." He was so astonished, he remembered later, that he almost fell off his bicycle. He didn't tell anyone this story for quite some time, but it shaped his ministry for the rest of his life.[1]

Buchman's goal must have seemed close at hand during the 1939 rally at the Hollywood Bowl. Searchlights lit the sky and flags filled the stage. Actors, athletes, and politicians testified to how Moral Re-Armament had changed their lives and told how it could change the world. MRA had become a mass movement, with billboards and milk bottle caps all across America telling citizens the same basic message: listen to God and lead an absolutely moral life.

Thirty-one years later the world was very different indeed. After a world war, America was now caught up in a cold war, civil strife, and a sexual revolution. MRA, however, had not remade the world; the world had left MRA behind. Up With People continued its youth explosion while the earnest world-changers met at Caux. People around the world still listened for God's guidance and followed the four absolutes, but MRA was no longer a mass movement.

In the almost 50 years between Buchman's Cambridge experience and the closure of MRA's American offices, his movement was reinvented several times. He changed his target audience from college students to adults. He and his devotees broadened their efforts to change the world as well as individuals. MRA's message was still evangelical— bringing about changed lives through religious experience—but they called it ideological instead of Christian. In the 1960s it repackaged its message to reach the rising baby boom generation.

MRA reinvented itself in response to changes inside the movement and in its environment. Buchman's early converts, many of them clergymen such as Sherwood Day and Samuel Shoemaker, saw their work as an extension or reformation of the church's ministry. Their ministry changed as they aged, paralleling their maturation from college student to young adult to middle age. Later leaders such as Peter Howard were more interested in world affairs than in ministry. Other reinventions responded to new circumstances, as cultures changed and wars raged. Buchman, Shoemaker, Howard, and the rest reshaped their gospel for new audiences and new media, offering the same basic message for new contexts.

In the late 1960s, however, reinvention failed. American culture was changing so much and so quickly that MRA could not keep up. Buchman had died, and the founding generation was retiring. Younger members embraced Up With People, which fled the constraints of MRA's history and practices. Older MRA members, meanwhile, scorned the youth initiative and clung to the movement's evangelical Christian tradition. Without strong leadership, no one reinvention could satisfy all of MRA's constituencies. The mass movement fragmented.

But Moral Re-Armament was not dead. People continued to follow Buchman's practices, including sharing, guidance, and the four absolutes. There were still operations in other countries, with conferences at Caux and plays in London.[2] In 2001 MRA changed its name to Initiatives of Change, reflecting its commitment to transforming society through personal change. Its literature calls for spiritual renewal from an interfaith perspective, no longer rooted in Christian evangelicalism but still using the tools of guidance and absolute moral values. Headquartered in Geneva, with representatives in 60 countries including the United States, Initiatives of Change sponsors conferences on multiculturalism and peacemaking at Caux and in Asia and Africa, and still gives Buchman pride of place in its history.[3]

MRA has other descendents, including Alcoholics Anonymous and other 12-step recovery groups, the best-known legacies of Buchman's movement. While they avoid explicitly Christian language, these groups still follow the practices of confession, sharing, and making amends that they learned from Buchman and Shoemaker in the 1930s. They have grown quickly in recent decades, and for many people have become a spiritual community more important than the church.[4]

There are also echoes of Moral Re-Armament in religious small group organizations. In many communities there are small house churches that resemble the Oxford Group cells, with people gathering around practices of witness and prayer.[5] On the other end of the spectrum, extremely large evangelical churches—sometimes called megachurches—have created small groups where members can build intimate spiritual connections in the midst of a huge congregation. A recent variation on this theme is the Alpha Course, a program designed to teach the basics of the Christian faith in small congregation-based groups. Founded in Great Britain, it is now active in churches around the world. Like the Oxford Group, Alpha includes a special focus on the work of the Holy Spirit, but it is more focused on teaching doctrine than was Buchman's movement.[6]

MRA roots remain visible in Up With People, which takes young people around the world, with the goal of building connections between people and between cultures. This latest incarnation of UWP no longer talks about ideology, but still works to change the world through individual actions.

Individuals still follow Frank Buchman's practices, too. Although this book has focused on the activities of the leaders, at its best Moral Re-Armament was a network of people rather than an organization. As Buchman often said, it wasn't something that you could join or resign, but a way of life.[7] There were—and may still be—individuals and cells practicing Buchman's teachings all over the world, perhaps unnoticed by the MRA leadership. These men and women observe the four absolutes and listen to the guidance of God, some not knowing that they are practicing Moral Re-Armament.

All these activities—from AA in the church basement to the Alpha Course in the pastor's office, from the Up With People kids with their guitars to individuals with their guidance books—show the richness of Frank Buchman's movement. It generated practices and beliefs that are useful in a variety of cultures and contexts.

No one activity, however, embodies all of Buchman's work. Alpha focuses on the Christian language that AA plays down. The house churches build an intimate community while individual practitioners go it alone. None of these groups has every piece of MRA's bricolage—its combination of practice and beliefs. It fragmented as times and leaders changed. These successor organizations and individuals perform their own bricolage, using the pieces of MRA's heritage that best suits their needs.

They do all have one thing in common, however—MRA's essential evangelical belief in personal change. From the most secular 12-stepper to the most Christian Alpha participant, they all believe that human beings can change. College students in Up With People get a new view of the world. People in Alcoholics Anonymous find sobriety. Alpha students discover a more vital Christian faith. People in house churches build a new kind of community. They may not remake the world, but they remake *their* world, and that may be enough.

ABBREVIATIONS

A note on sources:

This book draws heavily on collections of primary documents from several libraries. To simplify the notes, these collections are represented by abbreviations. The full citations are below.

FB #: Papers of Frank Buchman, Folder #, Archives, Hartford Seminary Library.

HAS #: Papers of H. Alexander Smith, Box #, Princeton University Archives, Department of Rare Books and Special Collections, Princeton University Library.

MRA #: Records of Moral Re-Armament, Box #, Manuscript Division, Library of Congress.

MWJ #: Papers of Melancthon Jacobus, Folder #, Archives, Hartford Seminary Library.

PSCA: GVF Religion/Penn State Christian Association, Penn State University Archives, The Pennsylvania State University Archives.

SCA #: Records of the Student Christian Association, Box #, Princeton University Archives, Department of Rare Books and Special Collections, Princeton University Library. (*Note*: The Student Christian Association records were reorganized after this research was completed, so box numbers are approximate.)

SMS #: Folder #, The Papers of Samuel Moor Shoemaker. Reprinted by Permission of the Archives of the Episcopal Church.

NOTES

Acknowledgments

1. Frank Buchman to Samuel Shoemaker, January 1923 [?], MRA 83.

Introduction

1. Text of "A Call to the Nations," Hollywood Bowl, July 19, 1939, MRA 389.
2. James E. Bassett, "M.R.A. Rally Draws 30,000 to Bowl," *Los Angeles Times*, July 20, 1939, 1.
3. The best-known book on Buchman and MRA is Garth Lean, *Frank Buchman: A Life* (London: Constable, 1985), written by one of Buchman's closest aides. Other useful if dated books are Walter Houston Clark, *The Oxford Group, Its History and Significance* (New York: Bookman Associates, 1951); Tom Driberg, *The Mystery of Moral Rearmament: A Study of Frank Buchman and His Movement* (New York: Alfred A. Knopf, 1965); Allan W. Eister, *Drawing-Room Conversion: A Sociological Account of the Oxford Group Movement* (Durham, NC: Duke University Press, 1950); and Basil Entwisle, *Moral Re-Armament: What Is It?* (Los Angeles: Pace, 1967).
4. Howard Blake, "The Growth of MRA in America," April 27, 1950, MRA 284.
5. Ray Purdy to Shoemaker, August 7, 1940, MRA 216.

One   The Soul Surgeon

1. Lean, *Buchman*, 9.
2. Buchman, "The College Hero," ca. 1895, MRA 4.
3. Lean, *Buchman*, 10.
4. Buchman to father, July 26, [1899?], MRA 4. (Emphasis in original.)
5. Buchman to parents, May 19, [1900?], MRA 4.
6. Frank H. Sherry and Mahlon H. Hellerich, "The Formative Years of Frank N.D. Buchman," *Proceedings of the Lehigh County Historical Society* 37 (1986), 250.
7. J.F. Ohl, "Report of the Philadelphia City Mission," *Minutes of the Annual Convention of the Evangelical Lutheran Ministerium of Pennsylvania and Adjacent States,* 1905, 76.
8. Lean, *Buchman*, 24.
9. Ohl, "Report of the Philadelphia City Mission," 80.

10. Lean, *Buchman,* 26–27.
11. Theophil Spoerri, *Dynamic Out of Silence: Frank Buchman's Relevance Today* (London: Grosvenor Books, 1976), 23.
12. Driberg, *The Mystery of Moral Re-Armament,* 32.
13. Lean, *Buchman,* 29.
14. *The Message of Keswick* (London: Marshall, Morgan, and Scott, Ltd., 1957), 33, 42.
15. Lean writes that the woman was evangelist Jessie Penn-Lewis, while Pollock states it was one of General Booth's daughters. Lean, *Buchman,* 30, and J.C. Pollock, *The Keswick Story: The Authorized History of the Keswick Convention* (London: Hodder and Stoughton, 1964), 143.
16. Lean, *Buchman,* 30–31.
17. *The Message of Keswick,* 36.
18. The classic history of the YMCA is C. Howard Hopkins, *History of the Y.M.C.A. in North America* (New York: Association Press, 1951).
19. Hopkins, *History of the Y.M.C.A. in North America,* 179, 381.
20. Mae Phyllis Kaplan, "The Oxford Group: A Sociological Study" (M.A. thesis, Pennsylvania State College, 1934), 105.
21. Lean, *Buchman,* 82.
22. Clarence P. Shedd, *Two Centuries of Student Christian Movements: Their Origin and Intercollegiate Life* (New York: Association Press, 1934), 281.
23. Kaplan, "The Oxford Group," 93.
24. Walter Houston Clark, "The Oxford Group: Its Work in American Colleges and Its Effect on Participants" (Ph.D. dissertation, Harvard University, 1944), 42.
25. Elston John Hill, "Buchman and Buchmanism" (Ph.D. dissertation, University of North Carolina, 1970), 114.
26. Princeton's YMCA, the Philadelphian Society, practiced the "Morning Watch" before World War I. "A Religious Program for Princeton," undated [1915–1916], SCA11.
27. "The Y.M.C.A. Campaign," (Penn State) *Alumni Quarterly* 2:2 (January 2, 1911).
28. J.M. Willard, "Report of Advisory Committee," State College Christian Association, March 1, 1911, PSCA.
29. "Indications of Usefulness," State College Christian Association, undated [1909?], PSCA.
30. "Report of the General Secretary for 1913–1914," 1, MRA 150.
31. Frank Buchman, *The Making of a Miracle* (New York: Moral Re-Armament, 1952), 18.
32. Buchman to H. Alexander Smith, January 26, 1928, HAS 45.
33. Paul Campbell and Peter Howard, *America Needs an Ideology* (London: Frederick Muller Ltd., 1957), 158–159.
34. Fred Lewis Pattee to Hermann Hagedorn, December 7, 1933, January 5, 1934, MRA 150.
35. "The Campaign at Pennsylvania State College," *The North American Student,* April 1914.
36. Kaplan, "The Oxford Group," 88.
37. Lean, *Buchman,* 35.
38. "Report of the General Secretary for 1913–1914," 8, MRA 150.
39. Buchman to H. Walton Mitchell, November 11, 1913, MRA 150.
40. Buchman, *The Making of a Miracle,* quotation at 5.
41. Lean, *Buchman,* 46.
42. Howard Walter, *Soul-Surgery: Some Thoughts on Incisive Personal Work* (Oxford: Oxford University Press, 1932). The YMCA of India published Walter's book in 1919; the 1932 edition was published for Buchman's organization. Unless indicated otherwise, the quotations below come from *Soul-Surgery.*
43. Lean, *Buchman,* 46.
44. Christian Endeavor was founded in 1881 as a nondenominational evangelical society for young people. Francis E. Clark, *Christian Endeavor in All Lands* (Philadelphia: Christian Endeavor, 1906).

45. Lean, *Buchman,* 78.
46. Samuel M. Shoemaker, "The Crisis of Self-Surrender," *Guideposts,* November 1955, 6. (Emphasis in original.)
47. Buchman to John R. Mott, November 10, 1915, MRA 63.
48. Howard Walter to E.W. Capen, June 3, 1918, MRA 155.
49. Lean, *Buchman,* 49.
50. Clark, "The Oxford Group," 49.
51. Walter, *Soul Surgery,* 37.
52. Edward Perry, cited in Lean, *Buchman,* 84.
53. Buchman to Douglas Mackenzie, April 26, 1917, FB 27/349.
54. Billy Sunday to Buchman, February 28, 1923, MRA 88; Buchman to Billy Sunday, May 30, 1918, MRA 88.
55. Douglas Mackenzie to E.A. Burnham, October 9, 1916, FB 27/349.
56. Buchman to Melancthon Jacobus, October 24, 1917, MWJ 299/4196.
57. Walter, *Soul Surgery,* 26–27.
58. Buchman to Mr. and Mrs. Fletcher Brockman, November 20, 1917, MRA 141.
59. Mark O. Guldseth, *Streams: The Flow of Inspiration from Dwight Moody to Frank Buchman* (Homer, Alaska: Fritz Creek Studios, 1982), 98–99.
60. Buchman to Mr. and Mrs. Fletcher Brockman, November 20, 1917, MRA 141.
61. Lean, *Buchman,* 65.
62. J. Dwight Dana, ed., *Five Year Records of the Class of 1911* (New Haven: Yale University, 1916), 87.
63. "The Alumni," *Princeton Alumni Weekly* 17:5 (November 1, 1916), 126.
64. Samuel Shoemaker to Miss Evans, June 12, 1917, Shoemaker Alumnus File, Princeton University Archives, Department of Rare Books and Special Collections, Princeton University Library.
65. Helen Smith Shoemaker, *I Stand By the Door: The Life of Sam Shoemaker* (Waco, TX: Word Books, 1967), 19.
66. When Shoemaker protested that he knew nothing about insurance, the principal told him, "You read English faster than these Chinese schoolboys; so you're going to teach insurance." Shoemaker, "The Crisis of Self-Surrender," 6.
67. Irving Harris, *The Breeze of the Spirit: Sam Shoemaker and the Story of* Faith-at-Work (Hantsport, Nova Scotia: Lancelot Press, 1980), 4.
68. Harris, *The Breeze of the Spirit,* 5. (Emphasis in original.)
69. "Extracts from S.M.S. Jr's. Journal," SMS RG101-2-16.
70. "Extracts from S.M.S. Jr's. Journal," SMS RG101-2-16.
71. Shoemaker, *I Stand by the Door,* 26.
72. "Extracts from S.M.S. Jr's. Journal," SMS RG101-2-16.
73. Shoemaker to Buchman, February 2, 1918, MRA 83. (Emphasis in original.)
74. Buchman to Shoemaker, May 23, 1918, MRA 83.
75. Buchman to Shoemaker, September 28, 1918, MRA 83.
76. Lean, *Buchman,* 65–69. (Quotation at 68.)
77. H.W. Austin, *Frank Buchman As I Knew Him* (London: Grosvenor Books, 1975), 23.
78. Hill, "Buchman and Buchmanism," 78, 81.
79. Spoerri, *Dynamic Out of Silence,* 55.
80. Helen Hawkes to Sherwood Day, November 18, 1919, MRA 24.
81. Douglas Mackenzie to Shoemaker, November 29, 1922, MWJ 58/1050.
82. Buchman to Douglas Mackenzie, January 12, 1922, FB 27/349.
83. Douglas Mackenzie to Day, March 24, 1922, FB 27/350.
84. Buchman to Melancthon Jacobus, May 30, 1917, FB 27/349; Melancthon Jacobus to Charles Thayer, July 29, 1920, FB 27/349.
85. Buchman to Melancthon Jacobus, July 10, 1919, MRA 49.

86. Edwin Knox Mitchell to Douglas Mackenzie, February 16, 1922, FB 27/349.
87. Day to Douglas Mackenzie, March 20, 1922, FB 27/350.
88. Day to Buchman, October 25, 1919, MRA 24.
89. "Herman Hagedorn's Notes on Hartford Seminary," MRA 139.
90. Campbell and Howard, *America,* 165.
91. Clark, "The Oxford Group," 55.

Two   Men Want Something Real

1. C. Irving Benson, *The Eight Points of the Oxford Group: An Exposition for Christians and Pagans* (Melbourne: Oxford University Press, 1936), xiv.
2. S.M. Shoemaker, Jr., *Children of The Second Birth: Being a Narrative of Spiritual Miracles in a City Parish* (New York: Fleming H. Revell, 1927), 10.
3. Helen Lefkowitz Horowitz, *Campus Life: Undergraduate Cultures From the End of the Eighteenth Century to the Present* (New York: Alfred A. Knopf, 1987), ix. See also Paula S. Fass, *The Damned and the Beautiful: American Youth in the 1920s* (New York: Oxford University Press, 1977).
4. See George Marsden, *The Soul of the American University: From Protestant Establishment to Established Nonbelief* (New York: Oxford University Press, 1994) for one analysis of this history.
5. R.H. Edwards, J.M. Artman, and Galen M. Fisher, *Undergraduates* (Garden City, NY: Doubleday, Doran, 1928), 244, 243.
6. Nelson Burr to H.L. Burr, March 5, 1924, Nelson Burr Papers, Box 2. Department of Rare Books and Special Collections, Princeton University. (Emphasis in original.)
7. A.D. Britton, Jr., "The Church a Non-Essential," *The Churchman,* August 27, 1927, 15–16.
8. Harold Begbie, *More Twice-Born Men: Narratives of a Recent Movement in the Spirit of Personal Religion* (New York: G.P. Putnam's Sons, 1923), 126.
9. For this Establishment network, see William R. Hutchison, "Protestantism as Establishment," in *Between the Times: The Travail of the Protestant Establishment in America, 1900–1960* (New York: Cambridge University Press, 1989), 9f.
10. Buchman visited Princeton fairly often; see J. Nevin Sayre to Buchman, 16 December 1914, MRA 151 and Thomas Evans to Buchman, March 27, 1915, MRA 151.
11. Day to Buchman, [1921 or 1922?], MRA 24.
12. Day to Buchman, November 9, 1920, MRA 24.
13. Day to Buchman, November 23, 1923, MRA 24.
14. Hill, "Buchman and Buchmanism," 142.
15. Buchman to Shoemaker, January 12, 1921, MRA 83.
16. Frederick Lawrence to Buchman, [1927?], MRA 54.
17. See records in MRA 25.
18. Buchman to Pete Nicely, March 14, 1923, MRA 66.
19. Buchman to Shoemaker, March 20, 1923, MRA 83.
20. Buchman to Charles Haines, November 7, 1923, MRA 39.
21. Buchman to Mike Hockaday, December 17, 1919, MRA 151.
22. Edward Aspee to Buchman, October 11, 1919, MRA 151.
23. Milton Knowles to Buchman, December 13, 1919, MRA 151.
24. S.M. Shoemaker, Jr., "The Philadelphian Society Report of the General Secretary to Board of Directors," February 25, 1920, SCA 11. (Emphasis in original.)
25. Shoemaker, "Report," 1920.
26. Buchman to Day, January 5, 1922, MRA 24.
27. Buchman to Shoemaker, April 4, 1923, MRA 83.

28. Shoemaker, "Report," 1920.
29. Howard Carson Blake, conversation with the author, Princeton, NJ, June 4, 1994.
30. Buchman to Mackenzie, May 20, 1921, MRA 139.
31. Day to R.G. Bell, undated, MRA 240.
32. Begbie, *More Twice-Born Men*, 92.
33. Day to "friends," November 1, 1920, MRA 24.
34. Buchman to Douglas Mackenzie, May 20, 1921, MRA 139.
35. Shoemaker to Buchman, January 11, 1923, MRA 83.
36. Benson, *The Eight Points of the Oxford Group*, xiv.
37. Buchman to Melancthon Jacobus, February 10, 1922, MRA 49.
38. Buchman to Charles Haines, January 25, 1922, MRA 39.
39. Buchman to Henry Van Dusen, March 17, 1922, MRA 96.
40. Buchman to Shoemaker, October 23, 1923, MRA 83.
41. Buchman to Charles Haines, March 31, 1924, MRA 39.
42. "Student Conference in Millbrook," MRA 140.
43. W.P. Fraser, "House Parties With a Purpose," undated, MRA 154.
44. "After Baltimore Conference, May 1923," MRA 140.
45. Peggy Hess to Day, undated, MRA 240.
46. "After Baltimore, 1923," MRA 140. (Emphasis in original.)
47. Edith Glowermeir to Sherwood Day, June 13 [no year], MRA 240. (Emphasis in original.)
48. Buchman to Melancthon Jacobus, October 27, 1920, MRA 49. In later years Buchman's British supporters would portray this Cambridge visit as the beginning of the movement, but Buchman had already started his work on American university campuses.
49. Buchman to Douglas Mackenzie, July 16, 1921, FB 27/349.
50. A.J. Russell, *For Sinners Only* (London: Hodder and Stoughton, 1932), 19.
51. Marjorie Harrison, *Saints Run Mad: A Criticism of the "Oxford" Group Movement* (London: John Lane, The Bodley Head, 1934), 21.
52. R.A. Knox, "A Roman Catholic's Comment," in F.A.M. Spencer, ed., *The Meaning of The Groups* (London: Methuen, 1934), 80–81.
53. Unless otherwise indicated, the quotations in this section come from Harold Begbie, *More Twice-Born Men*.
54. Speer, *The Principles of Jesus Applied to Some Questions of To-Day* (New York: Fleming H. Revell, 1902), 34–35.
55. Day to Buchman, September 17, 1919, MRA 24.
56. Lean, *Buchman*, 79; Clark, "The Oxford Group," 110.
57. Guldseth, *Streams*, 104–105.
58. Report, Erdman Harris to Philadelphian Society Directors, November 24, 1922, MRA 260.
59. Ray Purdy [?], "A New Call to Christian Evangelism," undated, MRA 151. (Emphasis in original.)
60. Ray Purdy, "Annual Report of the General Secretary of the Philadelphian Society to the Board of Directors," September 1, 1925, SCA 1.
61. Ray Purdy, "R. Purdy '20 Denounces Mediocrity on Campus," *Daily Princetonian,* November 26, 1924, 1.
62. Purdy to H. Alexander Smith, September 3, 1926, MRA 214.
63. Thomas C. Roberts, telephone conversation with the author, September 21, 1994. But Roberts states that he liked Shoemaker; "his religion didn't bother me," because he was more tolerant than Buchman.
64. Shoemaker, *I Stand by the Door*, 62.
65. Buchman to Shoemaker, December 22, 1923, MRA 83.
66. Report of the General Secretary, October 20, 1920, Minutes of the Board of Directors, Scrapbook 7, SCA.
67. Buchman to Shoemaker, March 29, 1921, MRA 83.

68. The student was Edward Steese; the quotations are from a planned but unpublished anti-Buchman newspaper, *The Cannonade*. Edward Steese Papers, Box 30, Department of Rare Books and Special Collections, Princeton University.
69. Lean, *Buchman,* 103.
70. Shoemaker to Buchman, May 4, 1922, MRA 83.
71. Ernest W. Mandeville, "Buchman Method of Evangelization," *The Churchman,* October 16, 1924, 13–15.
72. "Personal Work," *Time,* October 18, 1926, 26.
73. "This Evening," *Daily Princetonian,* October 21, 1926, 2. (Emphasis in original.) Unfortunately, no one ever recorded these facts and knowledge, so they remain largely rumor.
74. "Philadelphian Society Subject of Open Forum," *Daily Princetonian,* October 20, 1926, 1.
75. "Princeton Inquires Into 'Buchmanism,'" *New York Sun,* October 23, 1926.
76. C.G. Poore, "Students Roused By 'Buchmanism,'" *New York Times,* November 7, 1926, 6.
77. For more detail on the Princeton controversy, see my dissertation, "Disastrous Disturbances: Buchmanism and Student Religious Life at Princeton, 1919–1935" (Ph.D. dissertation, Princeton University, 1995).
78. Henry P. Van Dusen, "Apostle to the Twentieth Century," *Atlantic Monthly* 154:1 (July 1934), 5.

Three   Possessing and Reproducing
a Quality of Life

1. "Buchman Religion Explained to 1,000," *New York Times,* May 27, 1931.
2. Purdy to Buchman, undated [Spring 1926?], MRA 71.
3. Day to Buchman, December 7, 1927, MRA 25.
4. Unknown sender to Purdy, January 25, 1928, MRA 71.
5. Purdy notes, March 7, 1929, MRA 231.
6. Datebook, 1925–1926. Papers of Samuel Shoemaker, Box 1, Collection 269. Archives of the Billy Graham Center, Wheaton, IL.
7. Shoemaker to James Vermillon, September 9, 1936, SMS RG101-5-46.
8. Elsa Purdy to Helen Dominick Smith, February 18, 1928, MRA 71.
9. Howard Blake to Buchman, [1928?], MRA 13.
10. Blake to Buchman, May 25, 1928, MRA 13.
11. Purdy to Buchman, May 26, 1928, MRA 71.
12. Driberg, *The Mystery of Moral Re-Armament,* 197–198.
13. Blake to Buchman, November 6, 1928, MRA 13.
14. Helen Smith to Buchman, [1929?], MRA 83.
15. Purdy to Buchman, May 26, 1928, MRA 71.
16. Buchman to Ritter Shumway, February 7, 1930, MRA 231.
17. For instance, Eugene Blake to Buchman, August 20, 1927, MRA 13; John Roots to Buchman, October 12, 1928, MRA 76; Charles Haines to Buchman, October 11, 1929, MRA 39; Helen Smith to FB, undated, 1929, MRA 83; Ritter Shumway to Buchman, March 30, 1929, MRA 83.
18. Buchman to H. Alexander Smith, April 1, 1927, MRA 84.
19. Purdy to Buchman, September 15, 1926, MRA 151.
20. Spoerri, *Dynamic Out of Silence,* 70.
21. Buchman to Shoemaker, January 1923 [?], MRA 83.
22. Buchman to Pete Nicely, June 5, 1924, MRA 66.

23. Open Letter, October 15, 1925, MRA 24.
24. Samuel Shoemaker, "A Personal Worker," *The Messenger*, October 1925.
25. Shoemaker to Purdy, January 20, 1925, MRA 213.
26. Day to Margaret Tjader, March 3, 1927, MRA 154.
27. Purdy to Buchman, November 7, 1929, MRA 137.
28. Buchman to Day, May 28, 1927, MRA 25.
29. "Men, Masters, and Messiahs," *Time*, April 20, 1936, 37.
30. "Traveling Team," *Time*, March 26, 1934, 40.
31. "Where Does the Money Come From?", MRA 336.
32. Buchman to Charles Haines, December 8, 1921, MRA 39.
33. Buchman to George F. Seiberling, November 10, 1921, MRA 82.
34. Buchman to Shoemaker, December 13, 1921, MRA 83.
35. Shoemaker to Buchman, March 15, 1923, MRA 83.
36. Buchman to Susan Duncan, March 22, 1921, MRA 137.
37. Buchman to Charles Haines, December 10, 1926, MRA 39.
38. Shoemaker, undated manuscript, MRA 265.
39. Buchman to Purdy, May 24, 1928, MRA 231.
40. Day to Buchman, April 5, 1922, MRA 24.
41. "Noted Tokeneke Resident Dies," *Norwalk (CT) Hour*, February 18, 1952.
42. Buchman to Tjader, May 26, 1917, MRA 90.
43. Buchman to Tjader, December 2, 1922, MRA 90.
44. Tjader to Day, June 1924, MRA 90.
45. Purdy to Buchman, November 7, 1929, MRA 137.
46. Tjader to Buchman, July 30, 1925, MRA 90.
47. Day to Buchman, August 31, 1924, MRA 24.
48. Day to Buchman, July 15, 1927, MRA 25. (Emphasis in original.)
49. Frederick Lawrence to Buchman, January 6, [1927?], MRA 54.
50. Shoemaker to Purdy, November 30, 1924, MRA 213.
51. S.M. Shoemaker, Jr., *Twice-Born Ministers* (New York: Fleming H. Revell, 1929), 10.
52. Shoemaker, *I Stand by the Door*, 60.
53. Samuel M. Shoemaker, *Calvary Church Yesterday and Today: A Centennial History* (New York: Fleming H. Revell, 1936), 276.
54. Samuel Shoemaker, "Thursday Evening at Calvary," undated, MRA 290.
55. Edith Day Robinson, "The Weather Vane," unknown New York paper, MRA 290.
56. Shoemaker, *Children of the Second Birth*, 14.
57. Shoemaker, *Twice-Born Ministers*, 11, 52.
58. Shoemaker, *Children of the Second Birth*, 104.
59. Shoemaker, *Twice Born Ministers*, 174.
60. Shoemaker, *Children of the Second Birth*, 132.
61. Shoemaker, *Children of the Second Birth*, 6, 65, 72, 138.
62. Cited in Harris, *The Breeze of the Spirit*, 37.
63. Harris, *Breeze of the Spirit*, 13.
64. Shoemaker, *Children of the Second Birth*, 116, 6.
65. H. Kenaston Twitchell to Buchman, [1928?], MRA 93.
66. Twitchell to Buchman, undated, MRA 93.
67. MRA 140.
68. Twitchell to Buchman, December 17, 1929, MRA 93.
69. Twitchell to Buchman, June 30, 1929, MRA 93.
70. Twitchell to Buchman, April 19, 1929, MRA 93.
71. Twitchell to Buchman, July 11, 1928, MRA 93.
72. Buchman to "Housepartyites," August 11, 1924, MRA 140.
73. Buchman to Purdy, June 11, 1928, MRA 231.

74. Buchman to Blake, March 6, 1928, MRA 13.
75. Rosamond Thomas to Buchman, [1924?], MRA 90. (Emphasis in original.)
76. Loudon Hamilton to Buchman, July 16, [1926?], MRA 40.
77. "News Bulletin #4 from South Africa," August 28, 1929, MRA 152.
78. "Extract from Report of the Acting Principal of the Diocesan College Rondebosch at the Annual Prizegiving on Wednesday December 11th, 1929," MRA 152.
79. [John Roots?], May 8, 1929, MRA 152.
80. Letter, September 29, 1929, MRA 152. (Emphasis in original.)
81. Loudon Hamilton to Buchman, March 27, 1929, MRA 307.
82. Telegram to Buchman, October 7, 1928, MRA 152; "News Bulletin #4 from South Africa," August 28, 1929, MRA 152.
83. "Jack" to Buchman, July 24, 1928, MRA 152.
84. "News Bulletin #4 from South Africa," August 28, 1929, MRA 152.
85. Report from unknown leader, August 30, 1929, MRA 154.
86. "News Bulletin #4 from South Africa," August 28, 1929, MRA 152.
87. Professor Brooks, Report of Bloemfontein Houseparty, October 6, 1929, MRA 152.
88. Lean, *Frank Buchman*, 138.
89. Hadley Cantril, *The Psychology of Social Movements* (New York: [Chapman and Hall, 1941] John Wiley and Sons, 1963), 146.
90. Harrison, *Saints Run Mad*, 21.
91. R.H.S. Crossman, "Some Conclusions," in Crossman, *Oxford and the Groups* (Oxford: Basil Blackwell, 1934), 114.
92. Purdy to Buchman, October 1, 1928, MRA 71.
93. Twitchell to Buchman, December 26, 1929, MRA 93.
94. Kaplan, "The Oxford Group," 68.
95. Wayne Parrish, "Buchman Uses Church Here to Direct 'Groups,'" *New York Herald Tribune*, December 2, 1931.
96. Harris, *Breeze of the Spirit,* 47.
97. Shoemaker, *I Stand by the Door,* 81.
98. Harris, *Breeze of the Spirit,* 24.
99. Newsletter, March 22, 1935, MRA 300.
100. "Dave" to Purdy, November 7, 1930, MRA 234.
101. Buchman to Dorothy and Russell Firestone, June 15, 1932, MRA 32.
102. Buchman to Russell Firestone, January 12, 1933, MRA 32.
103. Team Letter from Shoemaker for April 22–May 2 House Party at Briarcliff [no year], MRA 154.
104. Shoemaker to H. Alexander Smith, February 26, 1932, HAS 41.
105. House Party Invitation, April 1928, MRA 154.
106. House Party Invitation, February 1932, MRA 254.
107. House Party Invitation, February 1933, MRA 334.
108. Note, May 17, 1929, MRA 153.
109. Mary Reynolds, "Briarcliff Is On!", undated, MRA 154.
110. MRA 240.
111. MRA 234.
112. "Asheville list," MRA 254.
113. Note, MRA 234.
114. Announcement of House Party at Minnewaska, September 9–15, 1927, MRA 240.
115. Day to Mr. Lathrop, April 27, 1927, MRA 247.
116. Buchman to Day, April 29, 1927, MRA 25. Buchman and his colleagues were regular guests at the Sanitarium, evidently recovering from overwork. "They say it's only a matter of rest before I am O.K.," Day told Buchman in 1928. "Physically I am in good shape—but the nervous system has had too much work." Day to Buchman, May 17, 1928, MRA 25.

Buchman himself spent a month at Battle Creek over Christmas 1926. MRA 120. In 1939 he told Kellogg that there were "fourteen of us actually staying in the Sanitarium now. I value all of your help in making this place a demonstration spot for people from all corners of the world to realize what a true aristocracy of health can mean for the future of civilization." Buchman to John Harvey Kellogg, March 23, 1939, MRA 51.

117. "Daily Schedule," MRA 241.
118. "What is a Houseparty? A Journalist's Impression," [1929?], MRA 334.
119. "Suggestions for Study," MRA 247.
120. Helen Smith to Buchman, June 25, 1929, MRA 83.
121. Blake to Buchman, January 6, 1928, MRA 13.
122. Helen Smith to Buchman, June 25, 1929, MRA 83.
123. Eleanor Forde to Buchman, January 3, 1928, MRA 65.
124. "Notes on Sin," MRA 256.
125. "The Cross," November 4, 1930, MRA 256. (Emphasis in original.)
126. Note from "A Guest at the Houseparty," [Summer 1928?], MRA 247.
127. Cleveland Hicks to Buchman, December 1, 1928, MRA 44.
128. Logan Roots's remarks at Minnewaska house party, summer 1927, MRA 76.
129. Blake to Buchman, January 6, 1928, MRA 13.
130. "Facts about the Briarcliff III House-Party," January 1930, MRA 234.
131. "Says 'Buchmanism' Broke Up Beer Club," *New York Times*, January 5, 1933.
132. Ted Shultz to Day, August 21, 1927, MRA 247.
133. J.S. Coleman, Jr., "Unique Appeal of 'The Groups' Stirs Religious Life of Asheville," *Asheville Citizen-Times*, March 29, 1931, B6.
134. Bertha Goldston, "They Came to Weaver College," MRA 234.
135. Mildred Carter to Purdy, April 15, 1931, MRA 234. (Emphasis in original.)
136. Unknown to Buchman, April 30, 1931, MRA 256.
137. [David Sweets], "Things Old and New," reprint of editorial from the *Christian Observer*, MRA 256.
138. Purdy to Buchman, April 30, 1931, MRA 231.
139. Purdy to Buchman, April 18, 1931, MRA 231.
140. "Newsletter," March 22, 1935, MRA 300.
141. "Class at 11 West 53rd Street, 26 January 1928," MRA 240.
142. Purdy to Buchman, November 7, 1929, MRA 137.
143. Shoemaker to Purdy, February 27, 1934 SMS RG101-3-6.
144. Blake to Buchman, November 14, 1929, MRA 13.
145. Blake to Buchman, May 22, 1930, MRA 13.
146. Charles Haines to Buchman, May 3, 1928, MRA 39.
147. William and Marjorie Hart, September 26, 1932, MRA 42.
148. Purdy to Buchman, December 16, 1927, MRA 71.
149. Haines to Buchman, August 13, 1928, MRA 39.
150. Russell Firestone to Buchman, October 25, 1932, MRA 32.
151. Harold Martin to Irving Harris, March 8, 1937, MRA 334.
152. Dave to Purdy, February 4, 1931, MRA 234.
153. Howard Augustine to Buchman, 21 July 1933, MRA 333; Howard Augustine to Buchman, July 17, 1933, MRA 333.
154. Blake to Ritter Shumway (?), 11 January 1932, SMS RG101-2-1.
155. Lean, *Buchman*, 98. The imputation is mine, not Lean's.
156. James D. Newton, *Uncommon Friends: Life With Thomas Edison, Henry Ford, Harvey Firestone, Alexis Carrel, & Charles Lindbergh* (San Diego, CA: Harcourt Brace Jovanovich, 1987), 84.
157. Cleve Hicks to Frank Buchman, December 1, 1928, MRA 44.
158. Shoemaker, *Calvary Church*, 247.
159. Shoemaker, *I Stand by the Door*, 82.

160. *Alcoholics Anonymous Comes of Age: A Brief History of A.A.* (New York: Alcoholics Anonymous Publishing, 1957), 58–59, 63.
161. Joseph Kessel, *The Road Back: A Report on Alcoholics Anonymous* (New York: Alfred A. Knopf, 1962), 99.
162. *Alcoholics Anonymous Comes of Age*, 67–70. (Emphasis in original.)
163. John F. Woolverton, "Evangelical Protestantism and Alcoholism 1933–1962: Episcopalian Samuel Shoemaker, the Oxford Group, and Alcoholics Anonymous," *Historical Magazine of the Protestant Episcopal Church* 52:1 (March 1983), 61.
164. *Alcoholics Anonymous Comes of Age*, 20.
165. Woolverton, "Evangelical Protestantism," 61.
166. Ernest Kurtz, *Not-God: A History of Alcoholics Anonymous* (Center City, MN: Hazelden Educational Services, 1979), 45.
167. "Foreword to Second Edition," *Alcoholics Anonymous: The Story of How Many Thousands of Men and Women Have Recovered From Alcoholism* (New York: Alcoholics Anonymous World Services, 1976), xvi.
168. Woolverton, "Evangelical Protestantism," 63.
169. *Alcoholics Anonymous Comes of Age*, 39.
170. See, for instance, the voluminous work of amateur historian "Dick B.," including *New Light on Alcoholism: God, Sam Shoemaker, and A.A.* (Kihei, HI: Paradise Research Publications, 1994). From a different angle, John H. Peterson, Jr., "The International Origins of Alcoholics Anonymous," *Contemporary Drug Problems* 19:1 (Spring 1992), 53–74.

Four   Rising Tide

1. "Canada's Greatest Conquest," *The (Montreal) Witness* (Oxford Group Supplement), June 15, 1935, 1.
2. Samuel M. Shoemaker, Jr., "House-Parties across the Continent," *The Christian Century* 50:34 (August 23, 1933), 1057–1059.
3. "Oxford Group Letter," August 5, 1933, MRA 336.
4. "The Challenge of Youth," *The North American House Party*, June 10, 1934, MRA 336.
5. "Storm Troops Mobilized for Aggressive Action," *The North American House Party*, June 8, 1934, MRA 336.
6. "Concerning Strikes," *The North American House Party*, June 8, 1934, MRA 336.
7. Chester S. Williams, "Buchmanism 'Settles' the Coast Strike," *Christian Century*, July 25, 1934, 969–967.
8. Twitchell to John [Roots?], November 8, 1934, MRA 256.
9. Form letter from Scoville Wishard, December 1, 1934, MRA 215.
10. Form letter from Wishard, November 18, 1934, MRA 256.
11. Form letter from Wishard, December 1, 1934, MRA 215.
12. "Oxford 1936," MRA 335.
13. "Dr. Buchman Offers World-Saving Plan," *New York Times*, April 26, 1932, 22.
14. "The God-Controlled Nation," February 17, 1937, MRA 335.
15. "Spiritual Hunger March in Cambridge," Cambridge (England) *News*, February 20, 1934.
16. Kaplan, "The Oxford Group," 161.
17. Samuel M. Shoemaker, *National Awakening* (New York: Harper and Brothers, 1936), 75.
18. "Statement by John U. Sturdevant, Associate Editor of the *American Weekly*, New York," September 1938, MRA 335.
19. "Dr. Buchman Asks a Divine Platform," *New York Times*, June 21, 1936, 28.
20. Buchman, June 19, 1936 broadcast, cited in "What Dr. Frank N.D. Buchman Said about Democracy and Dictatorship in 1936," MRA 306.

21. John O'Donnell, "Cult Storms Landon Train, Chants Praise," *New York Daily News*, September 15, 1936, 7.
22. "Three Weeks with the Oxford Group in Geneva and Berne," September 25, 1935, MRA 303.
23. Garth Lean to Margaret Williams, November 27, [no year], MRA 303.
24. Unknown to Lean and Morris Martin, December 23, 1936, MRA 256.
25. "Oxford 1936," MRA 335.
26. "America, Diagnosis and Cure," undated, MRA 328.
27. "The Oxford Group in America," MRA 328.
28. "Bids Women Lead to New World Order," *New York Times*, October 19, 1935, 9.
29. Cantril, *The Psychology of Social Movements*, 152, quoted in Clark, "The Oxford Group," 115.
30. "America, Diagnosis and Cure," undated, MRA 328.
31. "The Oxford Group in America," MRA 328.
32. Cited in Purdy to Shoemaker, December 20, 1934, SMS RG101-3-6. Concerning *Gabriel Over the White House,* Jonathan Alter, *The Defining Moment: FDR's Hundred Days and the Triumph of Hope* (New York: Simon and Schuster, 2006), 185.
33. "Phil B." to Shoemaker, September 24, 1933, SMS RG101-1-38. It is possible that the author is Philip Marshall Brown, who had taught international relations at Princeton and was part of a Group cell in Williamstown, MA.
34. Hallen Viney, "An impression of the Nazi rally at Nuremberg 1934," MRA 256.
35. Samuel Duker, "God and Dr. Buchman," *The Nation*, August 7, 1937, 151.
36. Kaplan, "The Oxford Group," 169.
37. Memorandum on "The Moral Re-Armament Movement," October 17, 1946, United States Department of Justice.
38. Stanley G. Payne, *A History of Fascism, 1914–1945* (Madison: University of Wisconsin Press, 1995), 7–14.
39. Layman With a Notebook, *What Is the Oxford Group?* (Oxford: Oxford University Press, 1933), 13.
40. "Bids Women Lead to New World Order," *New York Times*, October 19, 1935, 9.
41. Buchman, August 9, 1936 broadcast, cited in "What Dr. Frank N.D. Buchman Said about Democracy and Dictatorship in 1936," MRA 306.
42. D.A. Davis to Irving Harris, December 7, 1933, MRA 334.
43. William A.H. Birnie, "Hitler or Any Fascist Leader Controlled by God Could Cure All Ills of World, Buchman Believes," *New York World-Telegram*, August 26, 1936.
44. "What Dr. Frank N.D. Buchman Said About Democracy and Dictatorship in 1936," MRA 306.
45. "Translation of a Secret Instruction to the Districts of the Secret Police of the S S," March 4, 1938, MRA 306. It is impossible to judge the validity of this document.
46. "Christianity in Germany," *Times* of London, December 29, 1945, cited in "What Dr. Frank N.D. Buchman Said about Democracy and Dictatorship in 1936," MRA 306. Members regularly identified the Group as the "pacemaker" in evangelism or other activities.
47. Margot Appleyard and Sydney Cook, "Public Inspiration," October 2, 1936, MRA 303.
48. Buchman to Lean and Martin, November 26, 1936, MRA 346.
49. Margot Appleyard and Sydney Cook, "Public Inspiration," October 2, 1936, MRA 303.
50. Lean to Williams, November 27, [1938?], MRA 303.
51. Marjorie Evans to Buchman, May 10, 1935, MRA 149.
52. Team letter, February 11, 1936, MRA 236.
53. "What of Buchmanism?", *The Churchman*, December 15, 1928, 9.
54. Buchman to Purdy, July 20, 1928, MRA 231.
55. Buchman or Twitchell to Hanford Twitchell, June 15, 1931, MRA 256.
56. For the term, see for instance, "Playing on Astroturf," *The National Journal*, April 19, 1986.
57. Form letter from Dubois Morris and Peg Williams, March 10, 1937, MRA 303.

58. Shoemaker to Purdy, August 24, 1935, MRA 215.
59. "God Controlled Press Is Objective Put Forward," *The North American House Party*, 8 June 1934.
60. A.J. Russell, *One Thing I Know* (London: Hodder and Stoughton, 1933), 56.
61. Garth Lean and Reginald Hume, "Positive News Articles in Nordic Press Make Journalistic History," *Berkshire Eagle*, October 20, 1937, MRA 333.
62. F.E. Dougall, "Editor's Comment," *The Witness*, Oxford Group Weekly Supplement, June 15, 1935, 1.
63. Irving Harris [?] to A.R. Kessinger, June 28, 1937, MRA 334.
64. Buchman or Twitchell to Hanford Twitchell, June 15, 1931, MRA 256.
65. Shoemaker to Bishop Tucker, December 30, 1938, MRA 154.
66. Buchman to Garth Lean, November 26, 1936, MRA 346.
67. "News Letter," October 18, 1932, MRA 346.
68. Letter to Buchman, January 12, 1934, MRA 149; John Beck or Marjorie Evans to Buchman, March 10, 1934, MRA 149.
69. Mass mailing from Dubois Morris and Margaret Williams to American leaders, April 9, 1937, MRA 335.
70. Garrett Stearly to Buchman, November 23, 1937, MRA 234.
71. *Rising Tide*, December 1937, MRA 467; quotations at 11 and 23.
72. *Rising Tide*, December 1937, MRA 467; quotations at 33 and 45.
73. *Rising Tide* publicity letter, December 8, 1937, MRA 342.
74. *Rising Tide* publicity letter, November 18, 1937, MRA 342.
75. *Rising Tide* publicity letter, December 1, 1937, MRA 342.
76. Mr. Rochford to Mr. Johnson, December 10, 1937, MRA 342.
77. *Rising Tide* publicity letter, November 11, 1937, MRA 342.
78. *Rising Tide* publicity letter, December 9, 1937, MRA 342.
79. *Bridgebuilders*, 1936, MRA 300.
80. Flyer for *Youth Marches On*, MRA 329.
81. FB 27/349.
82. Guy Bolton, P.G. Wodehouse, Howard Lindsay & Russel Crouse, *Anything Goes*, 1934, Act 2, Scene, 3.
83. Rachel Crothers, *Susan and God* (New York: Random House, 1938), quotation at 19. (Emphasis in original.)
84. Cited in Van Dusen, "Apostle to the Twentieth Century," 13; origin unknown, emphasis in original.
85. Hallen Viney, "An impression of the Nazi rally at Nuremberg 1934," MRA 256.
86. "Active Summer Season," ca. 1934, MRA 335.
87. "An Oxford House Party: A Report Based on 2 Years' Experience," [1932?], MRA 149.
88. "Ten Thousand Christian Revolutionaries," August 6, 1935, MRA 303.
89. James Butterfield, "Youth on the March," House party newspaper, July 21, 1934, MRA 334.
90. Beverly Baxter, "What I Think of the Oxford Group," *Maclean's Magazine*, September 1, 1937, 10.
91. T. Willard, Hunter, *Busdrivers Never Get Anywhere: A Rendezvous with the Twentieth Century* (Claremont, CA: Regina Books, 2002), 151.
92. Ruth Bennett to "Californian Family," Easter 1936, MRA 300.
93. *Bridgebuilders*, 1936, MRA 300.
94. Ruth Bennett to "Californian Family," Easter 1936, MRA 300.
95. *Bridgebuilders*, 1936, MRA 300.
96. "As Seen By An Outsider," *Newsweek*, June 6, 1936, reprinted in *The New Witness*, June 16, 1936, MRA 154; "British Leader Explains Birth of Buchmanism," *New York World-Telegram*, June 1, 1936.

97. "Confessions Urged by Oxford Leaders," *New York Times*, May 30, 1936, 32.

98. "Press Release—June 6th, 1936—Oxford Group Afternoon Meeting," MRA 335.

99. Memorial Day program, May 30, 1936, MRA 335.

100. Dubois Morris and Margaret Williams to "Julie," March 10, 1937, MRA 303.

101. Marie Clarkson, "Houseparty Diary," June 4, 1938, MRA 346.

102. "A Summons to Enlist," MRA 335.

103. "Youth Marches On," MRA 335.

104. "Oxford Group Youth Camp, A Summary," December 26, 1938–January 2, 1939, MRA 335.

105. Sven Stolpe, "God's Dictatorship Rescues the World," MRA 333.

106. "Oxford Group 'New Enlistment' Youth Camp," March 25–28, 1937, MRA 335.

107. "Oxford Group Youth Camp, A Summary," December 26, 1938–January 2, 1939, MRA 335.

108. "News Bulletin," January 11, 1937, MRA 303.

109. "Oxford Group Camp—Rorøs, Norway," July 30–August 9, [1937], MRA 333.

110. "Oxford Group Youth Camp Bulletin," August 9, 1937, MRA 333.

111. "Oxford Group Youth Camp, A Summary," December 26, 1938–January 2, 1939, MRA 335.

112. "New Enlistment Sends Out Patriots Tomorrow," June 25, 1938, MRA 335.

113. Buchman, meeting notes, March 16, 1939, MRA 307.

114. H.W. (Bunny) Austin, *Moral Re-Armament: The Battle for Peace* (London: William Heinemann, 1938), 62–63.

115. "Heralds of the New World Order," March 23, 1939, MRA 346.

116. Austin, *Moral Re-Armament*, 6.

117. Garrett Stearly to National Team, February 7, 1939, MRA 335; Form letter from British team (Bill Jaeger and Geoffrey Gain), December 19, 1938, MRA 316; "Latest News of British National Welcome to MRA," undated, MRA 335; Team letter, February 3, 1939, MRA 346.

118. Form letter from Day, James Newton, and Dubois Morris, March 17, 1939, MRA 335.

119. Letter to National Team from Day, Dubois Morris, and Sciff Wishard, March 8, 1939, MRA 335.

120. "Latest News of British National Welcome to MRA," undated, MRA 335.

121. Form letter from Day, James Newton, and Dubois Morris, March 17, 1939, MRA 335.

122. Form letter from Jaquelin Smith, Day, and Dubois Morris, March 23, 1939, MRA 335.

123. Garrett Stearly to National Team, February 7, 1939, MRA 335.

124. Purdy to Franklin Roosevelt, December 29, 1938, MRA 231.

125. Emily Hammond to Franklin Roosevelt, April 16, 1939, MRA 342.

126. John Roots, meeting notes, March 16, 1939, MRA 307.

127. Oxford Group press release, March 4, 1939, MRA 344.

128. "Moral Re-Armament through Sport," May 1939, MRA 154.

129. "People," *Time*, August 28, 1939, 51.

130. "12,000 at Garden in Buchman Rally," *New York Times*, May 15, 1939, 1.

131. Reprint from *New York Herald-Tribune*, May 15, 1939, MRA 329.

132. Reginald Holmes to Harry Saylor, June 1, 1939, MRA 334.

133. "MRA in Washington," *Time*, June 12, 1939, 54.

134. "Statement by a group of secretaries…," June 4, 1939, MRA 401.

135. Statement, May 26, 1939, MRA 401.

136. Hunter, *Busdrivers*, 136–137.

137. James Waldo Fawcett, "First Anniversary Finds Moral Re-Armament World Force," (Washington) *Sunday Star*, June 4, 1939, C6.

138. "The National Meeting on Moral Re-Armament," June 4, 1939, MRA 401.

139. MRA 389.

140. Text of "A Call to the Nations," Hollywood Bowl, July 19, 1939, MRA 389.
141. Press release from Garrett Stearly, July 1939, MRA 154.
142. "MRA: A Call to the Nations," July 19, 1939, MRA 154.
143. Invitation, Second World Assembly for Moral Re-Armament, July 21–31, 1939, MRA 154.
144. Buchman, "A World War Against Selfishness: Guidance or Guns?", July 22, 1939, MRA 154.
145. Statements from Del Monte Assembly, July 1939, MRA 389.
146. Buchman speech at "Second National Assembly for Moral Re-Armament," July 30, 1939, MRA 389.
147. "Moratorium on Hate, Fear Advocated," Portsmouth (VA) *Star*, October 30, 1939, 4.
148. "Heralds of the New World Order," December 8, 1939, MRA 346.
149. "Heralds of the New World Order," September 28, 1939, MRA 346.
150. Notes from Muriel Roberts, 1939, MRA 389.
151. Shoemaker, "House-Parties Across the Continent," 1058.
152. Samuel Shoemaker, "The Decision of 1941," January 10, 1942, SMS RG101-6-6.
153. Shoemaker, "The Decision of 1941."
154. Shoemaker, "The Decision of 1941."
155. Lean, *Buchman*, 304–305.
156. Shoemaker, "The Decision of 1941."
157. Lean, *Buchman*, 312–314.

Five Change! Unite! Fight!

1. "National Unity through Moral Re-Armament," 1940, MRA 328.
2. "A Soldier's View of Labor's Task," undated [1942], MRA 142.
3. Newton, *Uncommon Friends*, 217.
4. "Oxford Group News," April 10, 1940, MRA 347.
5. "National Unity through Moral Re-Armament," 1940, MRA 328.
6. "How to Spread a New Spirit," undated, MRA 328. (Emphasis in original.)
7. "Oxford Group News," September 26, 1940, MRA 347.
8. "Oxford Group News," May 18, 1940, MRA 347.
9. Buchman to John Roots, July 20, 1940, MRA 76.
10. Howard Blake, "The Growth of MRA in America," April 27, 1950, MRA 284.
11. Purdy to Shoemaker, August 7, 1940, MRA 216.
12. "News of a New World," November 20, 1940, MRA 347. (Emphasis in original.)
13. Newton, *Uncommon Friends*, 230–231.
14. "News of a New World," November 20, 1940, MRA 347.
15. Purdy to Harry Truman, August 21, 1940, MRA 268.
16. "News of a New World," November 20, 1940, MRA 347.
17. "Cowboy Scene," undated [1940], MRA 361.
18. "Finale," undated [1940], MRA 361. (Emphasis in original.)
19. "You Can Defend America," Words by John M. Morrison, music by Richard M. Hadden, 1940, MRA 361.
20. Buchman to Irving Harris, September 19, 1940, MRA 42.
21. "'You Can Defend America': National Training Center for Total Victory—Mackinac Island, 1942," MRA 392.
22. "News of Labor Advance in Detroit," undated [ca. 1942], MRA 142.
23. "American Labor and Moral Re-Armament," undated [ca. 1945], MRA 249.
24. Lee Ellmaker, "Morale," *Philadelphia Daily News*, November 29, 1943, 2.

25. George Green, "Patriot Revue Doesn't Convince But Entertains," Columbia (SC) *State*, March 4, 1942.

26. *You Can Defend America* (Washington, DC: Judd & Detweiler, 1941).

27. Purdy to Truman, December 2, 1940, MRA 268.

28. Team letter, May 30, 1941, MRA 249.

29. Purdy to Truman, December 2, 1940, MRA 268; Statement by Richard Byrd, March 1941, MRA 16; Statement by Mary McLeod Bethune, MRA 361; Newton, *Uncommon Friends*, 230–231.

30. "Your Part in Winning the War," undated [1942], MRA 242.

31. "What I Have Learned about My Part in Winning the War," undated [1942], MRA 44.

32. "Your Part in Winning the War," undated [1942], MRA 44.

33. "You Can Defend America; What Others Are Doing about It," undated [1942], MRA 361.

34. "To Have Morale Means," undated, MRA 361.

35. "School for Home Defense, Tallwood, Maine," 1941, MRA 153.

36. "Curriculum for Weekend School for Home Defense," 1941, MRA 153.

37. General Schedule, September 27–28, 1941, MRA 153.

38. Announcement, School of Home Defense, September 27–28, 1941, MRA 153.

39. Open letter from Blakes and Wishard, November 11, 1941, MRA 347.

40. Nan Hall, "Tallwood," undated [1941], MRA 361.

41. "Onward Buchman Soldiers," *Time*, May 25, 1942, 59.

42. MRA 291.

43. George Fraser, "Victory Starts in the Home," 1944, MRA 361.

44. Program for *You Can Defend Barbados!*, MRA 44.

45. Press release, MRA 244.

46. George Fraser, "Let's Get Together," MRA 361. Capitalization in the original.

47. Twitchell to Buchman, 14 October 1943, MRA 94.

48. Invitation to "The North American Assembly for Moral Re-Armament," December 27-January 7, 1947–1948 [?], MRA 94.

49. Buchman to Clara Ford, December 7, 1944, MRA 32.

50. Roots to Buchman, October 10, 1944, MRA 342.

51. Roots to "Birch and Clarice," September 5, 1945, MRA 342.

52. Buchman to Truman, April 2, 1941, MRA 93.

53. Buchman to Colonel Langston, April 1, 1942, MRA 76.

54. Undated and unsigned memorandum, MRA 298.

55. Unknown to Roots, June 19, 1942, MRA 76.

56. Tom O'Connor, "The Case of Dr. Buchman and the Draft Deferments," *PM*, January 6, 1943, 6.

57. *In Fact*, January 18, 1943, MRA 240.

58. "John" to Purdy, February 2, 1943, MRA 268.

59. Purdy et al. to labor leaders, February 2, 1943, MRA 333.

60. H. Birchard Taylor to Paul V. McNutt, February 13, 1943, MRA 76.

61. Clergy statement, undated [1943?], MRA 304.

62. Letter from Purdy et al., April 12, 1943, MRA 304.

63. Austin, *Frank Buchman*, 97–98.

64. "'You Can Defend America': National Training Center for Total Victory—Mackinac Island, 1942," MRA 392.

65. "The Story of Mackinac," ca. 1942, MRA 326.

66. Blake to Buchman, June 19, 1948, MRA 13.

67. Equipment list, 1956, MRA 398.

68. "Welcome to Mackinac," 1957, MRA 398.

69. "Memorandum on the Oxford Group," undated [ca. 1947], MRA 297.

70. Press release, October 1950, MRA 324.

71. "Caux—A New World Center," *Neue Zuricher Zeitung*, September 28, 1946, MRA 379.
72. "Memorandum on the Club House," February 22, 1948, MRA 254.
73. Twitchell to Buchman, February 9, 1948, MRA 94.
74. Unknown to "John," February 26, 1948, MRA 297.
75. "Where Does the Money Come From?", MRA 336.
76. "Treasurer's Report," February 20, 1952, MRA 297.
77. "Where Will the Money Come From?", undated [ca. 1948], MRA 298.
78. Schedule of contributions, December 31, 1941, MRA 297.
79. Financial Report, December 31, 1961, MRA 274.
80. Treasurer's reports, MRA 297.
81. "Financial Resume of the Work of Moral Re-Armament," 1958, MRA 297.
82. "Establishing Sound Unionism in the Liberated Countries," ca. 1942, MRA 142.
83. Duncan Corcoran, "Cable from Caux-sur-Montreux, Switzerland," September 21, 1946, MRA 379.
84. Roots to Buchman, March 11, 1949, MRA 342.
85. "Settlement of Strike," February 1952, MRA 304.
86. Testimony of John Riffe and Rose Riffe, June 21, 1954, MRA 353.
87. Frank Buchman, *For All Men Everywhere* (London: Moral Re-Armament, 1954), MRA 151.
88. Unknown to Buchman, March 18, 1953, MRA 304.
89. John Riffe to George Meany, March 1956, MRA 329.
90. John Hayward to Nelson Rockefeller, June 12, 1959, MRA 75.
91. William Grogan, *John Riffe of the Steelworkers: American Labor Statesman* (New York: Coward-McCann, 1959).
92. "World Program of Moral Re-Armament: Some Recent Achievements," February 27, 1952, MRA 328.
93. Carnegie proposal, 1958, 22, MRA 296.
94. Roots to Buchman, June 8, 1952, MRA 76.
95. "Ruhr Gives Answer to Communism as Youth March in Berlin," World Labor Information Service, May 28, 1950, MRA 324.
96. "Moral Re-Armament to Offer German Miner's Play Tonight," *New York Times*, June 17, 1960, 38.
97. Newton, *Uncommon Friends*, 299.
98. Larry Shapiro to David Behnke, September 11, 1950, MRA 324.
99. Twitchell to Buchman, March 31, 1951, MRA 94.
100. "Bruce" to Twitchell, June 12, 1953, MRA 304.
101. Twitchell to Buchman, April 16, 1951, MRA 94.
102. James Peneff, "Behncke Links Row to Moral Re-Armament," *Chicago Sun-Times*, July 14, 1951.
103. Eric Bramley, "MRA: Can It Solve Airline-Labor Problems?", *American Aviation*, 6 August 1951, 41.
104. "How 'Right' Settled a Strike," *Pathfinder*, January 24, 1951, 24.
105. June 4, 1952, MRA 249.
106. Twitchell to Buchman, April 26, 1951, MRA 94.
107. Pan American World Airways memorandum, August 13, 1951, MRA 149.
108. Roots to Buchman, February 19, 1951, MRA 76.
109. Report on youth mission, undated, MRA 335.
110. Vincent Vercuski to Paul Seeds, March 29, 1949, MRA 324.
111. Press Release, October 1950, MRA 324.
112. "Report to the Officers and Executive Council of the American Federation of Labor," February 6, 1953, MRA 249.
113. Resolution, undated [August 1945?], MRA 244.

114. Robert Perrin, "Moral Re-Armament Blasted," *Detroit Free Press*, July 26, 1953, MRA 249.
115. George Meany to George Johns, May 17, 1961 MRA 249.
116. Colin Ward, "Moral Re-Armament Exposed," unnamed publication, MRA 153.
117. Newton, *Uncommon Friends*, 93.
118. Gertrude Seiberling to Buchman, August 31, 1942, MRA 82. (Emphasis in original.)

Six   Ideological Warfare

1. MRA 326.
2. Speech by Douglas Cornell, July 25, 1959, MRA 296.
3. R.A.E. Holme, "An Open Letter to Company F," undated, MRA 268.
4. Hanford Twitchell, "Conflict of Ideologies," September 8, 1952, MRA 268.
5. Undated document, MRA 249.
6. "How to Live Your Ideology," undated [1948?], MRA 313.
7. For instance, Roots to Buchman, September 30, 1947, MRA 76.
8. Statement by Howard Reynolds, March 16, 1954, MRA 313.
9. Draft letter from Purdy [?] to "Mr. Timberlake," undated [1961?], MRA 268.
10. MRA 312.
11. Lean, *Buchman*, 321.
12. "Ideological Training: The World Today: The War of Ideas," September 27, 1948, MRA 312.
13. Team letter, August 26, 1943, MRA 347.
14. Bill Jaeger, "The Full Dimension of Change," June 24, 1949, MRA 312.
15. Nancy Dole, August 25, 1948, MRA 312.
16. "Ideological Training: World Communism," August 25, 1948, MRA 312.
17. Team letter, August 26, 1943, MRA 347.
18. "Training Center for Total Victory," August 15, 1942, MRA 392.
19. "Ideological Training Course," MRA 313.
20. "Training Center for Total Victory," August 15, 1942, MRA 392.
21. "Ideological Training: Families Can Be Fun," September 30, 1948, MRA 312.
22. "Outline for 3-Day Ideological Course," undated [1950?], MRA 312.
23. "Ideological Training: What Makes a Statesman," May 10, 1948, MRA 313.
24. H. Kenaston Twitchell, Jr., "Psychological Warfare," undated [1953?], MRA 268.
25. "The Significance of Frank Buchman," undated, MRA 312.
26. Twitchell to Buchman, June 21, 1944, MRA 94.
27. Press release, October 1950, MRA 324.
28. "Christ the Cure," July 28, 1946, MRA 379.
29. Geoffrey Williamson, *Inside Buchmanism: An Independent Inquiry into the Oxford Group Movement and Moral Re-Armament* (London: Watts and Company, 1954), 167.
30. "Pageant of Nations with Inspired Ideology," October 2, 1946, MRA 379.
31. Unknown to Garrett Stearly, August 19, 1952, MRA 303.
32. Telegram to Buchman, December 7, 1957, MRA 143.
33. Syllabus for "A Series of Informal Meetings," Fall 1949, MRA 401.
34. Reginald Hale to "the Vets," June 14, 1947, MRA 254.
35. "Report of Instructors, Training Course for Danish Officers," March 1947, MRA 300.
36. H.K. Twitchell, Jr., "Psychological Warfare," undated [1953?], MRA 268.
37. John Roots, "Our World Task," in "Ideological Training Course," MRA 313.
38. *New World News*, 3 (May/June 1947): 11–13.
39. "To Change the World," *Time*, June 14, 1948.
40. Letter from Dick Channer et al., February 1948, MRA 313.

41. Peter Edson, "Dr. Buchman Is Back," *Washington Daily News*, December 14, 1947.
42. Williamson, *Inside Buchmanism*, 60.
43. Brooks Atkinson, "At the Theatre," *New York Times*, February 7, 1951, 47.
44. Undated document, MRA 249. Concerning Sokolsky, "The Man in the Middle," *Time*, May 24, 1954.
45. Twitchell to Buchman, February 9, 1951, MRA 94.
46. Louis Calta, "Horton to Return in Comedy Revival," *New York Times*, February 17, 1951, 21.
47. "Report on Moral Re-Armament World Assembly," MRA 398.
48. "Play From Ghana Presented Here," *New York Times*, August 4, 1957, 38.
49. Buchman to President and Madame Chiang Kai-shek, September 1, 1957, MRA 19.
50. Buchman to Queen Helen of Roumania, December 30, 1959, MRA 77.
51. Peter Howard, *Pickle Hill* (London: Blandford Press, 1960).
52. A valuable analysis of the plays as theatre is Richard H. Palmer, "Moral Re-Armament Drama: Right Wing Theatre in America," *Theatre Journal* 31:2 (May 1979), 172–185.
53. "Confessions at Caux," *Time*, January 27, 1947, 69.
54. Twitchell to Buchman, March 30, 1948, MRA 94.
55. "Actions of MRA in America, November 1, 1959–October 31, 1960," MRA 298.
56. Unknown to various congressmen, March 21, 1957, MRA 268.
57. Buchman to Penfield Sieberling, June 30, 1958, MRA 82.
58. John Hayward to Nelson Rockefeller, June 12, 1959, MRA 75.
59. Garrett Stearly and Gilbert Harris, financial/strategy memorandum, ca. 1953, MRA 298.
60. "Moral Re-Armament," undated, MRA 254.
61. Draft letter from Purdy [?] to "Mr. Timberlake," ca. 1961, MRA 268.
62. Grant proposal, 1959, MRA 296.
63. "Washington Team Meeting," October 10, 1947, MRA 353.
64. Peter Howard to Buchman, February 28, 1960, MRA 47.
65. Quoted in Roots to Buchman, November 16, 1945, MRA 76.
66. H. Kenaston Twitchell, *Regeneration in the Ruhr: The Unknown Story of a Decisive Answer to Communism in Postwar Europe* (Princeton: Princeton University Press, 1981), 76–81. (Emphasis in original.)
67. Loudon Hamilton to FB, March 27, 1952, MRA 40.
68. Loudon Hamilton to FB, February 19, 1952, MRA 40. MRA was quite proud of its links to Konrad Adenauer, chancellor of West Germany from 1949 to 1963. He did not attend meetings at Caux or Mackinac, but he regularly sent warm greetings to the assemblies, which pleased Buchman deeply. The evangelist told the chancellor that he was "the man of the hour," and then reported that the Germans at Mackinac celebrated Buchman's birthday and saw MRA as the world's answer. Buchman to Konrad Adenauer, June 6, 1959, MRA 6. Despite his apparent praise of Moral Re-Armament, however, neither Adenauer's memoirs nor his biographers mention the movement. Konrad Adenauer, *Memoirs 1945–1953* (Chicago: Henry Regnery, 1965).
69. Paul Campbell to Buchman, March 24, 1948, MRA 18.
70. "Full Employment Pioneered in Denmark Through MRA," July 1, 1958, MRA 300.
71. Kensuke Horinouchi, June 11, 1948, MRA 401.
72. "Japanese Ideological Mission to the World Assembly for Moral Re-Armament and the Western Democracies," June–August 1950, MRA 94.
73. Twitchell to Buchman, July 26, 1950, MRA 94; Roots to Buchman, July 25, 1950, MRA 76.
74. Garrett Stearly and Gilbert Harris, financial/strategy memorandum, ca. 1953, MRA 298.
75. Roots to Buchman, July 29, 1950, MRA 76.
76. "Cable from Caux-sur-Montreux, Switzerland," September 18, 1946, MRA 379.
77. Twitchell to Buchman, January 8, 1949, MRA 342.

78. [John Roots?], "U.S. Policy in China," undated [1949?], MRA 342.

79. Roots to Buchman, February 10, 1949, MRA 342.

80. "Gordon, Chris, Joe" to Buchman, December 30, 1957, MRA 304.

81. "Some Background Facts on the South-East Asian Assembly for Moral Re-Armament," undated [1957?], MRA 379.

82. "Asian Assembly for Moral Re-Armament," March 28 to April 8, 1957, MRA 379.

83. "Philippine, Korean Cabinet Ministers Moved by Japanese Apology," April 2, 1957, MRA 379.

84. "Baguio Assembly Creates Force for Asian Unity," March 26, 1958, MRA 379. Buchman's biographer suggests that the evangelist was a regular correspondent of Mohandas Gandhi, although the Indian's biographers do not mention Buchman. Lean, *Buchman*, 408. The son of Gandhi's youngest son Devadas, Rajmohan, spoke at many MRA gatherings, implicitly linking the movement to his famous family. He focused particular attention on Asia, where he worked to persuade leaders to send their citizens to Caux. He told Buchman in 1959 that he was acting on "your theme verse for Asia: 'Clean up your nation from bottom to top, start with the President and then don't stop.'" Rajmohan Gandhi et al. to Buchman, April 14, 1959, MRA 34.

85. K.D. Belden, *Meeting Moral Re-Armament* (London: Grosvenor Books, 1979), 60.

86. "South-East Asian Conference for Moral Re-Armament," December 31, 1953–1954 January 1954, MRA 279.

87. "Muslims, Christians United on MRA Platform," September 15, 1959, MRA 294.

88. James Coltart et al. to Gamal Nasser, undated, MRA 76.

89. "Shah of Iran Honors Dr. Buchman With Highest Award," July 18, 1959, MRA 316.

90. Frank Buchman, *For All Men Everywhere* (London: Oxford Group, 1954), MRA 151.

91. Corporate report, 1955, MRA 254

92. Corporate report, 1956, MRA 254.

93. Paul Campbell to Buchman, March 24, 1948, MRA 18.

94. Adolphus Staton, "Ideology that Will Win," undated [ca. 1959], MRA 333.

95. MRA 254.

96. Arbatov, "Buchmanism Is an Ideological Weapon of Warmongers," November 21, 1952, MRA 153.

97. Jorma Simpura, "What Is MRA?", (Helsinki) *The Communist*, March 1956. Excerpted in MRA 153.

98. One historian of the Cold War claims that MRA was a front for the American government's Psychological Strategy Board. Frances Stonor Saunders, *The Cultural Cold War: The CIA and the World of Arts and Letters* (New York: New Press, 1999), 151.

99. *Moral Re-Armament: A Study of the Movement Prepared by the Social and Industrial Council of the Church Assembly* (London: Church Information Board, 1955).

100. For a compilation, see the chapter on "Buchmanism" in William C. Irvine, *Heresies Exposed* (Neptune, NJ: Loizeaux Brothers, 1983).

101. H. Wallace Bird, "What the Oxford Group Has Given the Churches," *The Record*, August 23, 1946, 484. (Excerpted in MRA 151.)

102. William J. Whalen, "A New Attitude Toward Moral Re-Armament?", *U.S. Catholic*, April 1966, 32–36.

103. Gabriel Marcel, "Et In Spiritum Sanctum," August 30, 1956, MRA 292.

104. William J. Whalen, "A New Attitude Toward Moral Re-Armament?", *U.S. Catholic*, April 1966, 32–36.

105. Alex Bennett to Loudon Hamilton, October 26, 1950, MRA 40. (Emphasis in original.)

106. "Moral Re-Armament and the Participation of Catholics," MRA 292.

107. Bernardus Kaelin, "Four Mighty Pillars," September 20, 1960, MRA 292.

108. "Some Activities of MRA, 1960–1962," MRA 254.

109. Howard to Buchman, January 17, 1960, MRA 47.

110. Twitchell to Buchman, April 15, 1958, MRA 94.
111. Madeline (?) to Purdy, December 14, 1941, MRA 216.
112. Twitchell to Buchman, September 22, 1945, MRA 94.

Seven   Tomorrow's American

1. Clarence W. Hall, "Sing Out, America!", *Reader's Digest*, May 1967. (Emphasis in original.)
2. Unknown to Basil [Entwisle?], February 28, 1948, MRA 295.
3. *The College of the Good Road* (Washington, DC: College of the Good Road, 1950), 9.
4. "A Training Course in Inspired Democracy," 1948, MRA 312.
5. "Concerning Some Aspects of Organization of the College of the Good Road," undated [1949?], MRA 295.
6. "Sub Committee Report on Possible Curriculum of American College of the Good Road," November 9, 1949, MRA 295.
7. "Concerning Some Aspects of Organization of the College of the Good Road," undated [1949?], MRA 295.
8. Caux: Report of the World Assembly for Moral Re-Armament (Caux-sur-Montreux, Switzerland: Editions de Caux, 1949), 182.
9. *The College of the Good Road* (Washington, DC: College of the Good Road, 1950), 11–12.
10. Roger Hicks, *The College of the Good Road* (Caux-sur-Montreaux: College of the Good Road, 1949). (Emphasis in original.)
11. Unknown to Basil Entwisle, February 28, 1949, MRA 295.
12. *The College of the Good Road* (Washington, DC: College of the Good Road, 1950), 17, 10.
13. Roger Hicks, *The College of the Good Road* (Caux-sur-Montreaux: College of the Good Road, 1949).
14. "Draft of Statement on Finance of the College of the Good Road," undated, MRA 298.
15. Roger Hicks, "The College of the Good Road," ca. 1949, MRA 295.
16. "A German Student's Monthly Report," excepted in Roger Hicks, *The College of the Good Road* (Caux-sur-Montreaux: College of the Good Road, 1949).
17. *The College of the Good Road* (Washington, DC: College of the Good Road, 1950), 13.
18. Roger Hicks, *The College of the Good Road* (Caux-sur-Montreaux: College of the Good Road, 1949).
19. Minutes of the Board of Trustees, College of the Good Road, May 31, 1950, MRA 296.
20. Lean, *Buchman*, 483, 503, 522.
21. Morris Martin, *Always a Little Further: Four Lives of a Luckie Felowe* (Tucson, AZ: Elm Street Press, 2001), 171–172.
22. Ken Twitchell Jr. and Bruce F. Currie, "Memorandum to the Board of Directors," 1963, MRA 254.
23. Peter Howard, *Design for Dedication: Selections from a Series of Addresses* (Chicago: Regnery, 1964), 87.
24. "MRA and Mr. K," *Miami News*, May 7, 1963, 9A.
25. Howard, *Design for Dedication*, 82, 60.
26. Martin, *Always a Little Further*, 178.
27. Howard, *Design for Dedication*, 92–93, 74.
28. "Notes on conversation with Miss Irons," February 26, 1965, MRA 284.
29. "Moral Re-Armament, Inc., Annual Report 1965," MRA 297.
30. "'Dare' Group or 'Dead' Group, Who Will Run the Show?", *Tomorrow's American*, January 18, 1965, MRA 467.
31. "Hundreds Gather for Big MRA Rally," *Los Angeles Herald-Examiner*, June 25, 1964, E-8.

32. John P. Collins, "From the Island," 1965, MRA 292.
33. Open letter from Reginald Owen, undated, MRA 326.
34. "MRA Youth Plan to Build New World," *Los Angeles California Eagle*, August 6, 1964.
35. Press release, June 19, 1964, MRA 398.
36. "Moral Re-Armament, Inc., Annual Report 1965," MRA 297.
37. Peter Howard, "Which Way America?", *Tomorrow's American*, July 24, 1964, MRA 467.
38. "Moral Re-Armament, Inc., Annual Report 1965," MRA 297.
39. Peter Howard, "Which Way America?"
40. Charles Wilkinson, "'It's a World Revolution,'" *Hamilton (Ontario) Spectator*, August 29, 1964, 12.
41. Peter Howard, "Which Way America?"
42. Paul Campbell, "Health and Sex," *Tomorrow's American*, June 30, 1964, MRA 467.
43. Press Release, June 19, 1964, MRA 398.
44. Karin Everson, "Students Seek Answers in Seminars," *Tomorrow's American*, June 22, 1965, MRA 467.
45. Welcome letter, MRA 398.
46. [Pauline Sterling], "Most Pay Their Own Way," *Detroit Free Press*, July 12, 1964, 6D.
47. *Tomorrow's American*, June 26, 1964, MRA 467.
48. *Tomorrow's American*, July 20, 1964, MRA 467.
49. John Engstrom, "Compromise...the Mortal Enemy of Freedom," *Tomorrow's American*, July 22, 1964, MRA 467.
50. John Engstrom, *Tomorrow's American*, July 4, 1964, MRA 467.
51. "Delegates Wire Johnson Alternative to Race Crisis," *Tomorrow's American*, August 12, 1964, MRA 467.
52. Steve Cornell, "Speak Up!", *Tomorrow's American*, October 19, 1964, MRA 467.
53. "Blanton Belk Sees Youth Learning 'Giant Purpose,'" *Tomorrow's American*, August 5, 1964, MRA 467.
54. "Northwest Setting Fast Pace, Led by Student Heads, Indians," *Tomorrow's American*, September 21, 1964, MRA 467.
55. Frank McGee, *A Song for the World: The Amazing Story of the Colwell Brothers and Herb Allen: Musical Diplomats* (Santa Barbara, CA: Many Roads, 2007), 47f, 96f.
56. *Tomorrow's American*, August 7, 1964, MRA 467.
57. McGee, *Song for the World*, 125.
58. McGee, *Song for the World*, 126–127.
59. Suzanne Clark, "Colwell Hour Bows in Studio Debut," *Tomorrow's American*, June 19, 1965, MRA 467.
60. "Colwell's Sing-In: People, People, People," *Tomorrow's American*, June 27, 1965, MRA 467.
61. "'Sing-Out' Flies to East Coast," *Tomorrow's American*, August 7, 1965, MRA 467.
62. "Youth Forces Launch from Mackinac Hit West Virginia, Captivate Cape Cod," *Tomorrow's American*, August 15, 1965, MRA 467.
63. Press release, August 1965, MRA 350.
64. Stephen Wilberding, "Staging Area for U.S. Policies," *Tomorrow's American*, August 30, 1965, MRA 467.
65. *Tomorrow's American*, November 1, 1965, MRA 467.
66. "Moral Re-Armament, Inc., Annual Report 1965," MRA 297.
67. Fred Small to Thomas Gleason, November 1965, MRA 330.
68. Program for *Sing-Out '66*, MRA 330.
69. David Allen, *Born to Upturn the World* (Los Angeles: Moral Re-Armament, 1967), 10, 6.
70. Stephen Wilberding, "'Sing-Out '65' to Invade East Coast," *Tomorrow's American*, July 20, 1965, MRA 467.
71. Calvin Trillin, "U.S. Letter: Chicago," *The New Yorker*, December 16, 1967, 128f.
72. McGee, *Song for the World*, 129.

73. "100 Youths Surprise W. 25th St. with Song Fest," *New York Times*, August 17, 1967, 33.
74. Howard Crook, "'Sing-Out' Movement Called Revolution of Youth," *Norfolk (Virginia) Journal and Guide*, May 13, 1967.
75. Program for *Sing-Out '66*, MRA 330.
76. "A Different Welcome," *Tomorrow's American*, April 17, 1967, MRA 468.
77. Clarence W. Hall, "Sing Out, America!", *Reader's Digest*, May 1967.
78. Program for *Sing-Out '65*, 1965, MRA 350.
79. Geoffrey Frost, "What's Up With People," *Tomorrow's American*, December 12, 1966, MRA 468.
80. "Sing-Out Experience Is Up-To-Date Education," *Tomorrow's American*, November 14, 1966, MRA 468.
81. Charlotte Hale Smith, "Teens Tell World about America," *Atlanta Journal-Constitution Magazine*, February 18, 1968.
82. *Texas Magazine*, October 15, 1967, 26.
83. Program for *Up With People*, MRA 351.
84. Smith, "Teens Tell World about America."
85. "Will It Last?", *Tomorrow's American*, June 19, 1967, MRA 468.
86. *Tomorrow's American News*, October 7, 1968, MRA 602.
87. "Moral Re-Armament Annual Report, 1966," MRA 297.
88. Inaugural Program for Mackinac College, October 1, 1966, MRA 326.
89. Jesse Helms, "WRAL-TV Viewpoint," March 22, 1966, MRA 350.
90. Virginia Gilmore to MRA, July 5, 1966, MRA 350. (Emphasis in original.)
91. "Moral Re-Armament, Inc., Annual Report 1965," MRA 297.
92. Gen. Ralph E. Haines, Jr. to Eric Millar, July 20, 1966, MRA 350.
93. Don Morton et al. to Sing-Out '65 Cast, 1965, MRA 350.
94. *Tomorrow's American*, January 17, 1966, MRA 468.
95. McGee, *Song for the World*, 129.
96. Program for *Sing-Out Australia*, February 27, 1966, MRA 350.
97. McGee, *Song for the World*, 128.
98. Linda Salmonson, "'Sing-Outs' Become the Vogue," *Tomorrow's American*, December 20, 1965, MRA 467.
99. Betsy McCully, "'Mobilizing America' Conference in Conn." *Tomorrow's American*, October 17, 1966, MRA 468.
100. Francea Flanders, "Youth Confer in Palm Springs," *Tomorrow's American*, February 27, 1962, MRA 468.
101. "Action Now Demonstration Opens," *Tomorrow's American*, June 13, 1966, MRA 468.
102. Brochure, "Action Now," 1966, MRA 350.
103. J. Blanton Belk Jr., "Will You Tackle What Needs To Be Done?", June 5, 1966, MRA 284.
104. Brochure for music teachers, MRA 426.
105. Jarvis Harriman to William Dickerson, August 10, 1966, MRA 350.
106. "Moral Re-Armament, Inc., Annual Report, 1967," MRA 297.
107. "Moral Re-Armament Annual Report, 1966," MRA 297.
108. "Why Study?", *Tomorrow's American*, May 1, 1967, MRA 468.
109. "Moral Re-Armament, Inc., Annual Report, 1967," MRA 297.
110. Program for *Sing Out '65*, 1965, MRA 350.
111. Martin, *Always a Little Further*, 203–204.
112. "Mackinac College Trustees Meet, Appoint Dr. Cornell First President," *Tomorrow's American*, November 29, 1965, MRA 467.
113. "Newly-Chartered Mackinac College Opens Next Fall," *Tomorrow's American*, November 29, 1965, MRA 467.
114. "New College Seeks Incorporation," *Tomorrow's American*, July 16, 1965, MRA 467.

115. J. Blanton Belk Jr., "Will You Tackle What Needs To Be Done?", June 5, 1966, MRA 284.
116. "Moral Re-Armament, Inc., Annual Report 1965," MRA 297.
117. S. Douglas Cornell, "Mackinac College to Herald a New Age in Education," *Tomorrow's American*, July 16, 1966, MRA 467.
118. Martin, *Always a Little Further*, 209.
119. "More Than a College," undated [1965?], MRA 326.
120. William Henry, telephone conversation with author, August 28, 2008.
121. Michael Redman, email message to author, August 25, 2008.
122. Martin, *Always a Little Further*, 206.
123. Jeff Jurmu, "Mackinac College Goal High," *Tomorrow's American*, February 6, 1967, MRA 468.
124. Belk, "Will You Tackle What Needs To Be Done?"
125. *Tomorrow's American News*, October 21, 1968, MRA 602.
126. "Why Study?", *Tomorrow's American*, May 1, 1967, MRA 468.
127. Katherine Minton, telephone conversation with author, August 12, 2008.
128. Ellen Hodges, "Mackinac College: New, Different," *Tomorrow's American*, April 3, 1967, MRA 468.
129. Brian Marshall, telephone conversation with author, September 11, 2008.
130. Redman, e-mail message.
131. "More Than a College," undated [1965], MRA 326.
132. "Mackinac Ends Its First Year," *Tomorrow's American*, June 5, 1967, MRA 468.
133. Jeff Jurmu, "Mackinac College Goal High," *Tomorrow's American*, February 6, 1967, MRA 468.
134. "Why Study?", *Tomorrow's American*, May 1, 1967, MRA 468.
135. Ellen Hodges, "Mackinac College: New, Different," *Tomorrow's American*, April 3, 1967, MRA 468.
136. Cameron McGregor, telephone conversation with author, October 24, 2008.
137. Martin, *Always a Little Further*, 209.
138. "Moral Re-Armament, Inc., Annual Report, 1967," MRA 297.
139. *Tomorrow's American News*, January 13, 1968, MRA 603.
140. Martin, *Always a Little Further*, 218–219.
141. Donald Janson, "Moral Re-Armament Cuts U.S. Operations," *New York Times*, August 10, 1970, 30.
142. J. Blanton Belk, Jr. "Man's Gotta Go Somewhere," December 26, 1968, MRA 284.
143. Martin, *Always a Little Further*, 218–219.
144. "Moral Re-Armament, Inc., Annual Report, 1968," MRA 297.
145. Program for "Up With People," December 12, 1969, MRA 351.
146. *Tomorrow's American News*, November 17, 1969, MRA 603.
147. *Tomorrow's American News*, January 13, 1969, MRA 603.
148. *Tomorrow's American News*, April 7, 1969, MRA 603.
149. *Tomorrow's American News*, July 14, 1969, MRA 603.
150. McGee, *Song for the World*, 142, 156, 166, 137.
151. John Wenzel, "A New Up With People," *Denver Post*, February 11, 2007.
152. Martin, *Always a Little Further*, 211.
153. Janson, "Moral Re-Armament Cuts U.S. Operations."
154. Martin, *Always a Little Further*, 208–209.
155. Minton, telephone conversation.
156. Martin, *Always a Little Further*, 213–214.
157. "Moral Re-Armament, Inc., Annual Report, 1968," MRA 297.
158. H. Kenaston Twitchell Jr., letter to author, August 30, 2008.
159. Janson, "Moral Re-Armament Cuts U.S. Operations."

Epilogue   Remaking the World

1. Lean, *Buchman*, 93.
2. Trevor Beeson, "When the White Begins to Fade," *Christian Century*, June 28, 1972, 704.
3. "USA homepage, Initiatives of Change USA," http://www.us.iofc.org/home, accessed November 26, 2008.
4. A useful scholarly investigation of these movements is Robert Wuthnow, *Sharing the Journey: Support Groups and America's New Quest for Community* (New York: Free Press, 1994).
5. Rustum Roy, telephone conversation with the author, April 23, 2006.
6. See Nicky Gumbel, *Searching Issues* (London: Kingsway, 2001).
7. "Oxford Group 'Doesn't Exist' Judge's Ruling," *Toronto (Canada) Daily Star*, March 9, 1939.

INDEX

CPI Antony Rowe

Chippenham, UK

2017-03-01 22:05